New Approaches to Theodor Fontane

This collection of essays offers eight incisive perspectives on the novels and essays of Theodor Fontane (1819–1898). While Fontane scholarship has primarily focused on the "objective" portrayal of nineteenth-century German/Prussian culture and on the authenticity with which his work supposedly mirrors social reality, this collection investigates rhetorical and communicative patterns in his works that call this mirroring effect into question, emphasizing the difficulty — and ultimate impossibility — of "realist" representation.

Here nineteenth-century German realism is re-evaluated as a set of normative conventions — one which, at crucial points in Fontane's narratives, breaks down. But it is precisely at these points of breakdown where some of the most repressed and excluded aspects of Fontane's culture can be uncovered. Each of the essays reads the textual unconscious in a different way: as patterns of cultural disturbance, as the unmasking of male hysteria, as essayistic gaps, as gender prejudice. The authors present readings of Fontane that attempt to give an account of the multi-layered interplay of cultural codes and rhetorical conventions present in Fontane's time with reference to some of the most recent advances in literary, psychoanalytical, and media theory.

Marion Doebeling is an independent scholar, writer, and translator. She received her Ph.D. in German literature from the University of California, Davis.

Studies in German Literature, Linguistics, and Culture

Edited by James Hardin
(*South Carolina*)

NEW APPROACHES TO THEODOR FONTANE

CULTURAL CODES IN FLUX

Edited by
Marion Doebeling

CAMDEN HOUSE

First published 2000
Camden House
Drawer 2025
Columbia, SC 29202–2025 USA

Camden House is an imprint of Boydell & Brewer Inc.
PO Box 41026, Rochester, NY 14604–4126 USA
and of Boydell & Brewer Limited
PO Box 9, Woodbridge, Suffolk IP12 3DF, UK

ISBN: 1–57113–143–4

Library of Congress Cataloging-in-Publication Data

New approaches to Theodor Fontane: cultural codes in flux / edited by
   Marion Doebeling.
      p.   cm. – (Studies in German literature, linguistics, and culture)
      Includes bibliographical references and index.
      ISBN 1–57113–143–4 (alk. paper)
      1. Fontane, Theodor, 1819–1898—Criticism and interpretation.
   2. Realism in literature. I. Doebeling, Marion, 1961–   .
   II. Series: Studies in German literature, linguistics, and culture
   (Unnumbered)
   PT1863.Z7C85   1999
   833'.8—dc21   98–33269
                                                                      CIP

A catalogue record for this title is available from the British Library.

This publication is printed on acid-free paper.
Printed in the United States of America

*I would like to dedicate this volume
to my dissertation advisor,
Clifford Albrecht Bernd,
at the University of California at Davis*

Contents

Acknowledgments

I WOULD LIKE TO EXPRESS my sincere appreciation to the following colleagues for their helpful comments and suggestions throughout the various stages of development this book has undergone: Clifford Albrecht Bernd, Mary Kay Flavell, and Willi Goetschel. I would also like to thank my former students Stefan Siegel and Andrew Jainchill for their help in formatting various stages of this book. My sincere gratitude also goes to Cathy D'Ambrosia of Reed College.

Reed College provided me with two generous financial awards, in the fall of 1995 and in the summer of 1996, which allowed me to enlist Eric Schwab to translate several of the articles in this volume.

I would also like to thank the Consul General of the Federal Republic of Germany in Seattle, Dr. Birmelin, for his generous support, which helped make the publication of this volume possible.

M. D.
December 1999

MARION DOEBELING

Introduction:
Breaking the Mimetic Chain —
Patterns of Cultural Unground

THEODOR FONTANE (1819–1898) is well known as a master in the description of details and the portrayal of *causerie*. For many decades his novelistic work has been regarded as a highlight of nineteenth-century German realism. Fontane's novels, begun after his sixtieth year, have largely been read as exemplary representations, and even historical documents, of nineteenth-century German, or, more specifically, Prussian culture. Scholars of German literature in the former German Democratic Republic, viewing Fontane from a Marxist perspective, considered his portrayal of the aristocracy's decay and the gradual empowerment of the bourgeoisie to be exemplary, even though not revolutionary. West German and post-unification German as well as Anglo-American scholarship have mostly focused on the problem of realism in Fontane's writings as simply one of representation, while mostly denying ideological orientations in their investigations. Both of these traditions, however, view Fontane's works as more or less objective portrayals of the Prussian culture of the time, a view which extends into the circle of historians.

When I was finishing my dissertation on Fontane in the fall of 1989, I met a German historian in the stacks of Doe library at Berkeley. As we were both in the Fontane section, I inquired about her interest in Fontane as a historian. She told me that she had received more valuable insights about nineteenth-century Prussian culture from Fontane's novels than from any historical book on the period. Her dissatisfaction with the existing "realistic" representations of nineteenth-century Prussian culture in the documents of her discipline implied that the fiction from this period can provide something more significant, or more "truthful," about Prussian culture than historical scholarship inspired by positivism and empiricism. Fontane himself stressed the importance of literary sources in historical research when he wrote to H. Wichmann in 1881:

> und ich glaube fast noch weniger dran, daß man aus Archiven das Material zur Geschichtsschreibung holen muß. Dies vornehme historische Herunterblicken auf alles, was nicht in Akten und Staatspapieren steht, ist in meinen Augen lächerlich — die wahre Kenntnis einer Epoche und ihrer Menschen entnimmt man aus ganz anderen Dingen. In sechs altfritzischen Anekdoten steckt *mehr* vom alten Fritz als in den Staatspapieren seiner Zeit.[1]

In Fontane's view, archives are not the only sources that should be used in writing history. He suggests that anecdotes, essays, memoirs and other literary vignettes are equally valid sources. Today, New Historicism, poststructuralism, psychoanalysis, gender studies, cultural studies, and post-colonial studies have made us keenly aware of the importance that literary sources play in historical research. On the other end of the spectrum, namely in the field of German studies or Germanistik, Fontane's novels are still predominantly considered truthful representations of Prussian history and culture. This is reflected in the terminology assigned to his novels; they are referred to as *Zeitromane* (novels representing a particular time period) and *Gesellschaftsromane* (novels representing a particular society). Fontane's *Gesellschaftsromane* are said to primarily portray the interactions between the dying aristocracy and the upcoming bourgeoisie.

The emergence of the proletariat, however, is missing from Fontane's work. His novels are seen as illuminating a variety of domestic constellations from a psychological and therefore individualistic perspective, rather than from one based on analysis of social class. However, both traditions, the one critical of Fontane's individualistic psychologisms and the other, which has mostly celebrated Fontane as the master of nineteenth-century German realism, do agree on the fact that his narratives contain almost obsessively detailed descriptive passages. Moreover, as recent Fontane scholarship in the United States has shown, these narratives intrigue the reader over and over again due to their disturbing omissions and exclusions. Although these omissions do not rule out the possibility of a historical interpretation, they indicate that within the structure of Fontane's texts "realism" has become a highly problematic category of representation. When such omissions are considered, Fontane's work appears as anything but a realistic and objective account of nineteenth-century German society. Thus, as Walter Müller-Seidel has pointed out, realism appears both realistic and highly unrealistic since it incessantly oscillates between layers of authenticity and inauthenticity depending upon the ideological framework of both author and narrator.[2] Fontane as narrator thus methodically destabilizes various eighteenth-century aesthetic ideals, such as those of beauty and harmony, which were still upheld by the better part of the cultural milieu the author lived in and portrays.

This collection of essays provides arguments and perspectives for the understanding of literature as history and of history as literature. Fontane's novels present themselves as *interpretations* of culture and history. They can therefore be read as both fiction and history, precisely because the one never exists entirely without the other.[3] Interpretation, as Rainer Nägele asserts in the introduction to his collection of essays on Walter Benjamin, is an "extensive activity," a "stasis of time as well as ek-stasis out of it." Nägele elaborates:

> As in any true ek-stasis, there is a radical turn, a kind of vertiginous switch, in which "history" appears again at the horizon. At the moment when the touch with temporal extension threatens to get lost in intensive interpretation, the artifacts that were introduced as *geschichtslos* (without history) open up now in the act of interpretation a specific historicity (*spezifische Geschichtlichkeit*) — not history, but historicity, that is, they still do not have a history, but they are marked by historical relations.[4]

In this sense Fontane's realist texts are certainly not history *pure*, but rather markers of historical *relations* that are offered up to the literary critic or historian for interpretation. The reader or literary scholar of the late twentieth century approaches the figures in Fontane's novels to a certain extent as temporal characters, as lives of a time gone by. Hence, both literary critics and historians, each group with their different strategies of interpretation, can derive various layers of historical significance from Fontane's literary texts.

While Fontane scholarship has primarily focused on his so-called objective cultural portrayal — the authenticity with which his works "mirror" social reality — this collection of essays investigates rhetorical and communicative structures within the novels themselves that call this mirroring effect into question. Emphasis is therefore placed on the difficulty and ultimate impossibility of constructing a congruent relationship between stimuli that are perceived as the world of objects but are inseparable from the representational medium that seeks to portray them. Questions such as the following are investigated in this volume: To what extent do Fontane's novels veil the notion of truthful or objective representation precisely by being so objectively realistic and detail-oriented? In what sense does such realist detail paradoxically reveal only what it conceals? What are the underlying aesthetic, epistemological, and ideological implications and consequences of these representational gestures? How do Fontane's novels, through their relentless description of details, in fact deflect and estrange any vision of the totality of nineteenth-century culture by revealing the fallibility of the established network of signifiers that mirror that culture? Details in Fontane's works, as we will learn, are often nothing but marginalia of everyday life, residues lacking any structural connection to the course of events in the narrative. But interestingly enough, it is this very selection of details that arouses suspicion in the contemporary reader. In the end, as Roland Barthes has pointed out in his essay "L'effet de réel," they hardly say anything more than "nous sommes lá" (We are here).

But what precisely is veiled within Fontane's "realistic" details? His personal fascination with the art of still life suggests that a comparison of this genre with his texts may be illuminating. Like a still life that lacks any visible human presence — which is what meaning in the history of the visual arts has always been derived from — Fontane's realism seeks to gently veil any lack of meaning by gestures of displacement. His narratives often provide *Oberflächen*, surfaces, objects, vacuous conversational patterns, rather than *Tiefenstrukturen*, or structures of contextual, even metaphysical meaning. What is absent from Fontane's novels and novellas are expressions and representations of human desire and passion. Indicative of his time, the narrator opts for various displacement strategies, and many times these are responsible for the tragic fates of his central female characters. Human desire and passion, which had once been literally representable, especially in the French novels of the eighteenth century, have now become impossible to portray directly. Therefore, the nineteenth-century German realists, especially Fontane, began to hide the repertoire of human desire behind carefully selected objects of the daily lives of the Prussian gentry, or grande bourgeoisie.

Just as a still life only alludes to the human presence from which it seeks to reconstruct meaning *ex negativo*, the central, propelling stimuli of Fontane's characters, such as gender differences, desire, sexuality, and cultural prejudice, are hidden behind strict patterns of representational and behavioral norms and conventions, as recent Fontane scholarship has begun to demonstrate. This book begins to unravel such networks by exposing how such descriptive details represent more than the objects they refer to, precisely because they often become the locus to which human passion and sexual desire are displaced, as authors such as Hermann Rapaport have recently shown. Such narratological displacement strategies produce a surface structure of the *real* that is not only realistic and detail-oriented but also provides responses to a variety of nineteenth-century cultural displacements that were produced by the materialization of culture and human life brought on by the Industrial Revolution. Realist literary details as well as the "art of literature" thus began to gradually lose their symbolist and metaphysical value. Realist details therefore lose both their symbolist and metaphysical meaning by simply appearing as tokens of materiality. They have thus undergone a metamorphosis. They themselves are now reminders of an absence of metaphysical truth.[5]

Robert Holub, in his book *Reflections of Realism*, has pointed to the importance of omissions and elliptic constructions in German realism.[6] By focusing our attention on these gaps and exclusions we become aware of the highly paradoxical enterprise of Fontane's texts. The essays in this book examine the manner in which these texts conceal reality as much as they illuminate it. As Holub suggests, Fontane's texts "call their own foundations into question by revealing aporias at the basis of realism itself." The "realistic" surface obscures ideological fields "in which a moral code of both repression and renunciation" can be observed.[7]

The readings presented here reflect the multi-layered interplay of cultural codes and rhetorical conventions present in Fontane's time. The authors in this collection provide a variety of contemporary readings supporting the notion that nineteenth-century German realism broke away from any kind of visionary totality, from what Lukács called a "transcendental roof." Realism emerges as a paradoxical enterprise that continually calls its own foundations and powers of representation into question.

The reader's understanding of and response to Fontane's canonical nineteenth-century novels has undergone slow but remarkable change with the emergence of more recent approaches to literature such as post-structuralism, Lacanian psychoanalysis, and feminist theory. Although the primary texts are still the same, the reader's hermeneutical horizon has changed. Germanists today find themselves in an intriguing position. The epistemological models of hermeneutical understanding and interpretation, though not entirely obsolete, have become relativized by other reading strategies. Reflective gaps have been inserted into notions such as "truthful" and "objective" representation, since the agencies from which such concepts originate have been dismantled by Foucault and his followers as ideological tools in the service of power: the power of a ruling class, a segment of society, an interest group, a government, the media, and so on.

Jean-François Lyotard has argued that the evolution of the tradition of realism has been determined by the standards and prejudices of particular cultures and their normative epistemological conventions.[8] The way in which nineteenth-century culture regarded the representation of objects as realistic therefore differed greatly from the conceptions of realism in the Middle Ages, the Renaissance, and other epochs. Nineteenth-century German Realism is thus reevaluated as a set of normative conventions which, at crucial points within the narratives, breaks down. This breakdown unveils an ideological ground that is difficult or nearly impossible to access with the representational conventions available to German Realism itself.[9] It is this very ground that we need to investigate now. It is here where some of the most crucial, repressed, and excluded aspects of Fontane's culture can be uncovered. This ground can be understood as the textual unconscious, which reveals new insights into the phenomenon of German Realism. The repression underlying German Realism furthermore reveals a dimension of silence amidst a lively *trompe l'oeuil* assemblage of details. But how can we compel this background of silence to speak to us today? Each of the essays presented in this volume reads the many variants of the textual unconscious in a different way. It thus resonates back to us as patterns of disorder, of appearance and validation, or as patterns of communica-

tive disturbance, essayistic gaps, even male hysteria, and racial as well
as gender prejudice.

Despite the legacy of the deconstruction of meaning ever since
post-structuralism and post-modernism, we, as literary scholars and
critics of late twentieth-century Western culture, are still responsible
for communication. We need to maintain some form of successful
communication despite the eradication of the direct link between
signifier and signified. In a global context of decisive political
changes that demand the attention of the intelligentsia, many invalu-
able and profound approaches and insights to literature are available
to demonstrate that any text may, and in fact *should*, produce different readings. But we also need to remember that such readings are
not accidental and relativistic, but are instead always influenced by
the surrounding intellectual and ideological climate of the subject or
group who is producing such readings. Access to the *Bedeutung-
sschichten*, the many layers of meaning, will necessarily vary in different cultural contexts and historical periods. A reading that is aware
of its own historicity should not be content to understand itself as a
project of endless approximation and *Aufschub* (postponement) but
rather as a contribution to knowledge understood as an ever-
expanding network of communicative attempts.

However temporally situated meaning may be, it can still serve as
evidence of the historicity of the interpretation it was produced
from. If we want to be taken seriously as literary critics today, we
must not only investigate our patterns of culture, but also rewrite
traditional patterns of thought and signification, so that new, culturally sensitive and specific epistemologies may emerge. This new dynamic epistemology will not rely on dogmatic and crystallized forms
of knowledge and meaning, but on the continuous project of rethinking and rewriting our cultural pasts and presents. In this sense,
we, as literary scholars and critics, need to come to some moment of
a crystallization, however transient, in the process of rethinking the
meaning and construction of cultural icons, such as Fontane's literary works. The following essays employ various contemporary approaches to literature and literary theory, thus providing incisive
readings of Fontane's texts and the representational malaise inherent
in nineteenth-century German realism.

Horst Turk's article, "The Order of Appearance and Validation.
On Perennial Classicism in Fontane's Society Novel *Schach von*

Wuthenow," presents an interpretation of Fontane's first *Gesell-schaftsroman*. The framework of Turk's investigation is theme and subject oriented in order to give a historically grounded definition of nineteenth-century realism. Critically evaluating the paradigmatic realist theories of Auerbach, Sterne, Goodman, and Blumenberg, Turk seeks to capture a definition of realism from the angle of representability. In his investigation, Turk considers both the classical and romantic variables of representation. The classical variant is accounted for in terms of *appearance* and *representation*, while the romanticist variant is constructed in terms of *action* and *acting*. The subjectivist and contextualist variants of realism are also integrated into his discussion according to the order of experience and judgment for the subjectivist perspective, and according to language and writing for the contextualist one. Turk analyzes these variants and constituents of realism by focusing his discussion on the structure of conflict in Fontane's *Schach von Wuthenow*. He examines the *Ausweglosigkeit*, or aporia, into which conflict is diverted through the superficialities of conversational codes in the tradition of the *ancien régime*. Turk investigates conversation as a gesture of exteriority, the repression rather than expression of a person's "real" concerns and desires. The narrative of conversation must then preclude objective or truthful and thus "realistic" representations of the characters' desires and thoughts. The conflict in *Schach von Wuthenow* is suspended by relegating it to the realm of exteriority, of salon conversation and causerie. This is done, as Turk argues, in the name of classicism, which permeates Fontane's novels, especially his early historical ones.

From this classicist assessment of one of Fontane's early novels we move toward the opposite component in his applied aesthetics: to the anticipation of modernism. Interestingly enough, traces of modernism are especially prevalent in his essayistic work. Fontane's choice to adopt the genre of the essay illuminates the other side of his work, which has not yet received sufficient attention in scholarship. By exploring the essayistic interlude in Fontane's work, which followed his early poetry and first novels, Fontane's œuvre will emerge as one that leaves narrow definitions of nineteenth-century German realism behind. My article "On the Theory of the Essay and Fontane's England Essays as Modernist Signature," illuminates this period of Fontane's work written when he both visited and lived in

London for more than four years during the middle of the nine-teenth-century. As the investigation into the modernist tradition of the essay and the notion of experience ranging from Michel de Montaigne in the sixteenth century to Fontane in the nineteenth century shows, Fontane's England essays reveal a completely differ-ent moment of consciousness than do his earlier poetry and ballads, which were largely inspired by English Romanticism. This essayistic period in Fontane's life casts light on his later realist novels, which fall somewhere between "classicism" and "realism." Fontane thus emerges as a cultural critic of nineteenth-century England as well as Prussia, who contemplates and employs various elements of mod-ernist narrative structures. A shift in epistemological models can be observed in Fontane's work when he decides to illustrate a fragment of the London experience in the form of an essay that defies system-atic structures of representation, epistemology, and cultural knowl-edge.

After exploring Fontane's essayistic interlude, which demon-strates the range of his aesthetic practice, we once again turn to his novels. Ernst Hannemann, in his article "Body and Nobility: The Interrelationship between Social Position and Bodily Condition in *Stine*," analyzes the narrative structures in this still understudied novel, demonstrating subversive energies within the historical body of Waldemar, the central male character. Although Waldemar re-mained a member of the Prussian aristocratic power elite during the second part of the nineteenth century, his character represents, ac-cording to the French theorist Gilles Deleuze, a plurality of irreduci-bly dominated and dominating forces which make it difficult to arrive at a clearly delineated position characteristic of "realist" repre-sentation. The conflict for Fontane's "realism" arises when words are applied to actions, to be represented in a system of order that can no longer be integrated into the genealogical narrative. The body of nobility under investigation as an "obvious site of social control" demystifies the aura of aristocratic power on the verge of an epoch increasingly dominated by competition and the division of labor. The body of Waldemar thus emerges as a "blind monumentality"[10] which has lost its referential powers and become a static icon on the stage being prepared for the upcoming event of modernity. This loss marks the break away from congruent notions of "realistic" repre-sentation, for it presents a *body* which can no longer *embody* holistic and dialectically sound conceptions. This shift in power relations seems to call for a shift in the representability of culture during the late nineteenth century, while simultaneously summoning us, the readers, to re-evaluate the very foundations of our interpretive acts.

Sara Shostak's contribution, "The Trauma of Separation: Public and Private Realms in *Effi Briest*," approaches the traumatic divisions both within and between individuals, created by the demands and constraints of modern society. Shostak argues that the social construction of oppositional categories such as "male" and "female," "public" and "private," have long served to obfuscate the politics that occur in familial relationships. A critical analysis and redefinition of these categories of identity and experience allows for a re-examination of the workings of power and the influence of society in the "private" realm of the family. Drawing from Fontane's representation of an aristocratic family in his novel *Effi Briest*, Shostak examines the ways in which the role of the family as a socializing institution both structures and strains relationships between parents and children, husbands and wives. Shostak also examines the process of socialization itself as a mechanism that insures the continuance of this socio-moral hegemony. In particular, she focuses on the process of "internalization" which, as she demonstrates, severely inhibits an individual's potential to interpret the pains and difficulties of her or his life. In the tradition of liberalism, people are taught that the locus of blame or change always lies in themselves. The "correctness" of society's fundamental tenets are protected by dividing individuals within themselves and against one another. Shostak concludes that in order to heal the trauma of separation, the ways in which self and society are defined must be reexamined. But for now it is the very trauma of separation upon which structures of identity and existence are based and perpetuated. Shostak utilizes both nineteenth-century theories of self and society as well as recent feminist criticism in her essay.

Tilman Lang's article, "*Cécile:* Reading a Fatal Interpretation" focuses his reading on the significance of media-technical formations and transformations in Fontane's non-canonical novel *Cécile*. Given the recent focus of literary studies on the way in which the transmission of cultural knowledge and customs are a result of changes in the network or mode of transmission of information,[11] Lang's contribution is both timely and urgent.[12] Lang studies *Cécile* as a text staging

a variety of models of the real, or *Wirklichkeitsmodelle*, which belong
to different historical discourse formations. These discursive formations, however, only produce meaning in relation to contemporary
nineteenth-century media-technological developments. Lang explores the logic of the novel's unfolding in relation to these "newly
produced realities." He presents the argument that the central conflict in *Cécile* can be understood as a competition for achieving the
"correct" reading of the real. The various readings of the real introduced by the most central characters in the narrative are in fact, as
Lang elaborates, an effect of new and contemporary media-
technological developments. In other words, Lang addresses the
question of how and to what extent media-technological developments influence and produce those cultural orders which are then
accepted as the real. From this perspective, a reading of the work is
produced that, surprisingly, accounts for male hysteria vis-á-vis a
world that is revealed as an unstable universe where the most crucial
impossibility of the creation of meaning resides in the process of
reading and being read, as well as in the impossibility to transmit
such readings.

Randall Holt's article, "History as Trauma: The Absent Ground
of Meaning in Fontane's *Irrungen, Wirrungen*" exposes realism's
inability to come to terms with a self-conscious historical and social
positioning of its subjects. In Fontane's much read and discussed
novel *Irrungen, Wirrungen* (*Delusions, Confusions*) Holt relocates
the former romantic positioning of the cultural and political unconscious as being displaced into the structures of daily life as they
emerge around the bucolic, lower-class environment of Lene
Nimptsch. If the German Romantics treated the uncanny as a way to
explore and explain the modern condition as primarily characterized
by anxiety and fear, then realists, such as the narrator in *Delusions,
Confusions*, repress the outspokenly uncanny by re-inventing
strangely anachronistic, bucolic scenes, which, in their own narratological construction, are already doomed to collapse. Insisting
upon the dimly illuminated layers of consciousness of the fragile
lower-classes on the outskirts of Berlin, the narrator invests their
language, which is highly fragmentary and symbolic, ontologically
pre-analytical and therefore pre-historical, with a dubious power. On
the one hand this language in good Berlin dialect reflects the latently
simple and idyllic lifestyle of a pre-industrial era, despite the smoke-

stacks on the horizon, which are rendered by the narrator only in passing. On the other hand, this language also bespeaks the historical unground of an entire class of people who are drifting between the poetic and largely unilluminated regions of Romanticism in language and the realities of a society that is silently but forcefully changed toward a modernistically administered, early industrial one, where bourgeois money and modern science have bypassed the exclusive power of birth and tradition — and, strangely enough, also the Romantic uncanny.

Willi Goetschel's contribution, "Causerie: On the Function of Dialogue in Fontane's *Der Stechlin*," analyzes the function of conversation in Fontane's last novel *Der Stechlin*, generally considered to be a novel on the art of conversation. Deviating from the many conventional stylistic analyses of *Der Stechlin*, Goetschel critically evaluates the role and social function of the conversationalists in the novel. His thesis suggests that *Der Stechlin* does not portray genuine dialogues in the sense of Martin Buber. The novel, on the contrary, introduces patterns of causerie and representations of "Vergegnungen" or controversies, rather than "Begegnungen" or encounters. In order to secure this point, Goetschel traces the underlying skepticism in Fontane's notion of conversation back to the essayistic tradition of Montaigne. Moving from Montaigne to Simmel and Horkheimer in his assessment of the relationship between essayism and causerie, Goetschel unravels the crucial nexus between the skeptical and essayistic moments of consciousness as testimony to an essential resistance to change within the authoritarian structures of our societies. As Horkheimer suggests, the person who attacks ideology without a representation of its basis, only delivers poor or, for that matter, no criticism at all. And even *esprit* will not change this fact. This holds true, as Goetschel argues, for Fontane's conversations and causeries. Conversation can thus be understood as a function of political *Geselligkeit* and not as an expression of individuality as described in traditional scholarship on *Der Stechlin*. Conversation or causerie is rather the expression of its own socialization. Causerie understood as a process of socialization manifests itself as inauthentic individuality within the confinements of Prussian culture.

Sabine Cramer's article "Grete Minde: Structures of Societal Disturbance" points out the significance of secondary figures in Fontane's early prose and defines the role they play in these works, one which presages the decisive function he would later assign his secondary figures. Not only are they well defined individually, but they also reflect and represent the social, political, and historical forces at work in the society of their day. Through the circumstances and events of their own personal lives and their interaction with the main characters, the secondary figures have a significant impact upon the events that propel the narrative to its dramatic conclusion. In *Grete Minde,* a work representative of the author's early novels, these figures affect and alter the intentions of the primary characters and propel them toward their ultimate fates.

Future Fontane scholarship will need to place more emphasis on his culturally and historically problematic representations of female characters. It will also have to reassess the various layers of the linguistic and historical unground that the essays in this volume address, but now in relation to other Fontane texts that could not be taken into consideration in this volume.

Notes

[1] Theodor Fontane, Letter to H. Wichmann, dated June 2, 1881, in: *Theodor Fontane, Briefe in zwei Bänden,* 2 (Munich: Nymphenburger Verlagshandlung 1981), 51. English translation: " . . . and I believe even less that one has to obtain the material for writing history from archives. This elegantly prejudiced historical looking down on everything that cannot be found in official files and state documents is, in my opinion, ridiculous — true knowledge of a period and its people needs to be taken from very different things. In six anecdotes about Old Fritz [Frederick the Great] there is *more* of the old Fritz than in the state documents of his time."

[2] Walter Müller-Seidel, *Theodor Fontane: Soziale Romankunst in Deutschland* (Stuttgart: J. B. Metzeler, 1975).

[3] The crucial insight that history writing is also an interpretive enterprise has been introduced to history as an academic discipline by contemporary cultural historians and the New Historicists.

[4] Rainer Nägele, ed. *Benjamin's Ground: New Readings of Walter Benjamin* (Detroit: Wayne State UP, 1988), 17.

[5] The telegraph was a crucial means of modern communication in the late nineteenth century. Paradoxically, it leads to the impossibility of the transmission of timely information in Fontane's novel *Cécile.*

[6] Robert C. Holub, *Reflections of Realism: Paradox, Norm, and Ideology in Nineteenth-Century German Prose* (Detroit: Wayne State UP, 1991).

[7] Holub, 152.

[8] Jean François Lyotard, *The Postmodern Condition: A Report on Knowledge*, trans. Geoff Bennington and Brian Massumi (Minneapolis: U of Minnesota P, 1984), 73–80.

[9] French Realism, like Gustave Flaubert's *Madame Bovary* for example, was already in the 1850s able to represent human desire and sexuality much more directly and forcefully than German Realism was able to in the 1880s and 1890s. Repression, therefore, did not surface for French culture to the traumatic extent it did for the German.

[10] The expression *blinde Monumentalität* or "blind monumentality" is borrowed from Horst Turk's article, "Realismus in Fontanes Gesellschafts-roman. Zur Romantheorie und zur epischen Integration," *Jahrbuch der Wittheit zu Bremen* 9 (1965): 407–456.

[11] An important study in the area of media and its interconnection with German literary studies is Friedrich Kittler's book entitled *Aufschreibe-systeme*, translated as *Discourse Networks 1800/1900*, by Michael Metteer and Chris Cullens (Stanford: Stanford UP, 1990).

[12] See also Norbert Bolz, *Theorie der neuen Medien* (Munich: Raaben Verlag, 1990). In this work Bolz comes to terms with the abyss between book culture and telematics. In order to bridge this gap he explores the linkage between these two cultures from Nietzsche to contemporary media theory and media culture.

HORST TURK
University of Göttingen

The Order of Appearance and Validation: On Perennial Classicism in Fontane's Society Novel *Schach von Wuthenow*

IN FONTANE'S NOVEL *SCHACH VON WUTHENOW* (1887; 1982)[1] a statement by Victoire succinctly introduces the constellation of problems to be addressed. "Society is sovereign," she declares — rationalizing her forthrightness in accepting the Prince's invitation — and then adds: "Besides, the whole situation here is exceptional. The Prince is the Prince" [i.e. he is above society], "Frau von Carayon is a widow" [i.e. she is beyond any suspicion], "and I . . . am myself" [i.e. Victoire is free because of her role as outsider]. What, then, does the initial statement intend, that "Society is sovereign?"

It can be interpreted in at least two ways: psychologically and politically. Victoire herself provides an initial explanation — and one that is particularly suited to Schach — when she adds, "What society validates is valid, what it objects to is objectionable" (615).[2] Von Alvensleben also interprets Schach as being of a "peculiar nature, which, whatever fault one may find with him, does at least pose some psychological questions" (571). These questions seem to be based only partially on the person Schach; they are also based in part on his social position. As a character, Schach possesses the advantages and weaknesses of a handsome man. Von Alvensleben continues: "I have never met a man, for instance, about whom everything could be traced back so exclusively to aesthetic issues . . ." — yet in the second half of the sentence he indicates that this aesthetic disposition is less an artistic than a societal distinction, "which may perhaps bear a certain relation to his having extravagant ideas about the intactness of marriage" (571). The statement "Society is sovereign" here would seem to mean simply that society, not the individual, is "sovereign." But shortly afterward, von Alvensleben remarks that Schach is "morbidly dependent, dependent to a point of weakness on the judgment of others, especially those of his social standing" (571). What, then, does this story stand for?

Victoire reduces this question with almost terminological precision to a social category.[3] Her concluding judgment of Schach is that he was "by his very nature set upon the representation and validation of a certain *grandezza*" (682). This basic feature of behavioral culture in the royal court, however, seems to come into conflict with the military duty of obedience when the monarch intervenes — but the conflict is also encouraged, in this case, by a process of political opinion-formation that has fallen into the hands of a military which sees itself as the representative of good society. "Our gentlemen officers," von Bülow explains at one point, "are suddenly indulging in an oppositional fervor that is just as naïve as it is dangerous" (559). Von Bülow himself is introduced by the narrator as the supposed "head of those military *frondeures*... who at the time determined — or terrorized — political opinion in the capitol" (555). But even this latter perspective is valid only from the viewpoint of his opponents and their — in his opinion — false loyalty. Von Bülow himself wonders: "Why do those gentlemen, who every day claim to be smarter than the King and his ministers, why do they carry on with such language? Why are they talking politics? Whether a battallion should be allowed to politicize is another issue, but *if* it does politicize, it should at least politicize correctly" (559). Thus we encounter the second, political interpretation of the sentence, "Society is sovereign." It is "sovereign" in the sense that the sovereignty of the state is repressed by the sovereignty of society.

Granted that this interpretation also gives our question a historical dimension.[4] It becomes all the more surprising that Fontane brings to bear a standard of humane, if not moral, values upon the person who represents that dimension. The reason for this — how could it be otherwise? — is Schach's stubborn adherence to the behavioral codex of the *ancien régime*. It is according to such a standard that von Alvensleben defends him against von Bülow: "'And yet you underestimate Schach. He is regardless one of our best.' 'So much the worse.' 'One of our best, I say, and *really* a good man. He doesn't just act so chivalrous, he really *is*, too. In his own way, of course'" (572). Yet how are we supposed to imagine that Schach is "*really* a good man?" The thesis would imply that someone who never was "himself" is precisely therein "himself." Von Nostitz agrees with von Alvensleben: "Alvensleben is right. . . . I don't care much for him, but it's true, everything about him is genuine, even his stiff superiority, as boring and as insulting as I consider it to be. And *therein* lies his difference from us. He is always himself . . . " (572). Fontane's realism seems inordinately dependent on the subject here. However, the opposite conclusion is also conceivable: that Fontane, supported by his "subject," is setting forth a different tradition or "form" of realism. Indeed his narrative approach can be connected as much to humanistic classicism[5] as to realism[6] — not to mention that the very *concept* of realism cannot be grasped independently from the underlying historical shape or concept of reality at that time.[7]

In the following remarks I will address this question in more detail, first of all by taking a closer look at the "basic impulse of the Homeric style" that Erich Auerbach traces through Western literature.[8] Connecting this impulse to a concept of reality based on the criterion of "instantaneous evidence" (Blumenberg),[9] I will show how the question of such concepts of reality becomes pertinent to our initial line of inquiry. Auerbach emphasizes, namely, that a decisive concern in the Western tradition is "to represent phenomena in a fully externalized form, visible and palpable in all their parts, and completely fixed in their spatial and temporal relations." The same principle, he adds, is valid for "psychological processes": "here too nothing must remain hidden and unexpressed. With the utmost fullness, with an orderliness that even passion does not disturb, Homer's personages vent their inmost hearts in speech."[10] Anyone familiar with Fontane listens closely at this point. Almost effortlessly, it seems, both the positive and the negative determinations apply, and do so even though Fontane is the furthest thing from epic in a Homeric sense — or in any familiar sense of the term.[11] Auerbach stipulates that a certain "perspective" goes missing here, which in turn is represented by another, hardly less antique impulse: the opening-out of the present moment into the "depths of the past"[12] and onto the "claim to absolute authority" of a "structure of universal history";[13] the "'background' quality, multiplicity of meanings and the need for interpretation" of events and situations;[14] the element of the "developing and having developed" in individuals;[15] in short: it is the "politico-religious," "historicity," and the "social activity."[16] Just as an "uninterrupted connection"[17] of relations can be found in Homer, this other impulse distinguishes the Old-Testament narrative of the sacrifice of Isaac. One could also say: the Biblical constitution of reality stands within the order of fate and action, whereas the Homeric stands within the order of appearance and validation; or likewise, where the Bible defines reality as "that which the subject does not control,"[18] in Homer it is produced through momentary evidence.

The decisive point, however, comes in Auerbach's reference to the model of feudal authority.[19] Precisely under the altered conditions of the nineteenth century, such a reference allows us to anchor his arguments in the subject currently under consideration. Like other authors in the epoch of realism, Fontane avails himself of a repertoire of historically determined conceptions of reality. He chooses among them by following the particular givenness of his subject. This explains how in a "novel of 'good society'" he can perpetuate aesthetically *and* sociologically rigid categories[20] and yet, in contrast to the authentic "basic impulse of the Homeric style," manage to problematize this categorical framework in such a way as to reveal its historical contingency. Fontane seizes upon the impulse not in its authentic, original shape — this distinguishes him in the history of Classicism from that of both the German eighteenth and the French nineteenth centuries — but rather in the derivative modern shape that it assumes under the conditions of the *ancien régime* and which persisted (along with it) in nineteenth-century Prussia. One could also view Fontane's distinctness and well-roundedness, his seamlessness and articulateness from the perspective of *clarté*; in that case, however, within both the aesthetic and the social realm the order of appearance and validation would no longer be grasped as inherently justified.

Narrative beginnings such as this one — in the "Salon of the Frau von Carayon and her daughter Victoire, residing on Behrenstrasse," where "several friends were gathered for their usual evening visit, . . . but admittedly only a few, since the great warmth that day had lured even the most loyal members of that circle outdoors" (555) — not only sketch out, right from the first sentence, the place, time and circumstances of the story, that is Berlin, on the *jour fixe* in the salon of a lady of nobility, with friends of the house but also, even before the action has been set in motion, immediately make known a certain lack.[21] Restricting himself at first to the visible and the audible, the narrator seems to approach the event from outside, as if respecting its familiarity and intimacy: "Of all the officers of the *Regiments Gendarmes* who seldom were missed on these evenings, only one had appeared, Herr von Alvensleben, who had taken a seat next to the beautiful lady of the house while simultaneously expressing his regret, jokingly, that precisely *he* who truly deserved that seat was missing" (555). It is by no means incidental that the narrator has von Alvensleben take a seat next to the lady of the house first, before turning attention to the other guests seated across from them, "on the side of the table facing the center of the room" (555). Like the compliment von Alvensleben pays as he takes his seat, this arrangement fits unnoticeably into the order of appearance and validation. There are rules not only for the spatial arrangement in the field of appearances, but also for the social arrangement in the field of value: the other two guests present are "gentlemen in civilian clothes" ("Herren in Zivil," i.e. not in military uniform). This circumstance accrues a certain weight because — if for no other reason — the narrator does not name one of them, von Bülow, until after the introduction. It also provides the occasion to segue from the social to the temporal arrangement: "Across from them, on the side of the table facing the center of the room, sat two men in civilian clothes, who, although they had been familiar with this circle for only a few weeks, had already managed nonetheless to earn themselves a dominant position within it." For the arrangement in time, information about preceding events is required, along with indications about present function: "This was particularly true for the somewhat younger gentleman of the two, a former corps lieutenant, who, having returned to his home country following an adventurous life in England and in the United States, was generally regarded as the head of those military *frondeures* who at that time determined — or terrorized — political opinion in the capitol" (555). All this information is offered without an introduction by name. And when the name finally is mentioned *en passant*, it serves merely to exemplify a familiar maxim: "His name was von Bülow. Nonchalance was a key part of his ingenuity . . ." — whereby the narrative flow has already segued to an arrangement in the field of behavior.

Beginning with this maxim, a scene is staged that easily makes its point about extravagant individualism: "and thus with both feet stretched wide in front of him and his left hand in his trouser pocket," the narrator continues, "he jabbed and fenced about with his right hand, lively gesticulations giving emphasis to his pulpit speech. He could only speak, as his friends said, by giving speeches, and — he spoke virtually all the time." Hence it is no wonder that the third and for the moment last guest, von Bülow's publisher Sander, is introduced by way of a contrast — like the "gentlemen in civilian clothes" previously, but this time with a different purpose. Sander is bourgeois; as such, he is placed at the end of the series of introductions. He maintains a commercial rather than a socially determined connection to von Bülow. Yet this, certainly, does not determine the construction of the narrative sequence. Rather the narrator selects the contrast in external appearances because it poses a direct reversal of their social position:

> Der starke Herr neben ihm war der Verleger seiner Schriften, Herr Daniel Sander, im übrigen aber sein vollkommener Widerpart, wenigstens in allem, was die Erscheinung anging. Ein schwarzer Vollbart umrahmte sein Gesicht, das ebensoviel Behagen wie Sarkasmus ausdrückte, während ihm der in der Taille knapp anschließende Rock von niederländischem Tuche sein Embonpoint zusammenschnürte. Was den Gegensatz vollendete, war die feinste weiße Wäsche, worin Bülow keineswegs exzellierte. (555)[22]

From the positioning in the field of appearances and in the field of society, to the positioning in the field of history and in the field of behavior, then back to the field of appearances, the narrative follows a clearly arranged and articulated scheme of construction. In hierarchical progression the general is placed before the particular, the rule before the application, the order of representation before what is represented. If one considers then that Frau von Carayon has hardly been mentioned, and her daughter only by name, then precisely in this, in the form of an exclusion, a motif for the story begins to emerge. For the question arises: what precondition, through "the conversation that was just being conducted" (556), must have already been established in order for Victoire — or the late-arriving Schach, for that matter — to be drawn into the narrative proceeding? In Fontane, not only the art of exposition as the art of exact description, but also the art of involvement as the art of distinguished conversation, finds its master. The viewpoint that binds these strains of mastery is the art of exclusion, and this is tied, furthermore, to the choice of an external motivation.

The order followed is questionable from the beginning: first, because of the *absence* of one representative figure, whose existence is justified expressly as a representative of representation itself; second, because of the *presence* of one represented figure, Victoire, who, as we shall see, is not presentable as far as outward appearances are concerned; and third, finally, because of the latent co-presence of a situation that — albeit in another, though comparable, sense — requires a representation of the unpresentable. The protagonist in this latter situation is von Bülow, who is hardly one to glorify the Prussian state and is instead its critic. Where the narrator shows him conversing with the ladies, the reader is given the opportunity to identify the date of the story's beginning through references to the military-political situation in the year 1806. This also serves as an introduction to Fontane's craft of entrusting the motivating substance of his stories to salon conversations: "The conversation that was just being conducted seemed to revolve around the recently concluded Haugwitz mission, which in Bülow's opinion had not only restored a desirable understanding between Prussia and France, but also had brought along for us the occupation of Hannover as a 'dowry'" (556). Along with the historical content in a narrower sense, here everything that makes up the action itself also comes as motivating substance. For Frau von Carayon proves from the beginning to be a woman of guts and spirit, one who is just as practiced in the amenities of conversation as in the refined tact of confronting what she disapproves of. Concerning the "dowry," she notes adversely that "one cannot very well give away what one does not have . . ." (556) — a comment that is revealing not only about the occupation of Hannover, which was previously an English territory, but also about the capacity of the speaker herself to bring matters to a point. It says something, moreover, about the speaker's skill at conversational indirection. Her using the expression "what one does not have" instead of the more expected "what does not belong to one" gives the narrator the opportunity to bring Victoire into the picture momentarily. Even then, she is not really seen; as the narrator continues: "whereupon, hearing this word, the daughter Victoire, who until then had busied herself unnoticed at the tea table,

cast an affectionate glance at her mother. . . ." Not until a few min-
utes later will Victoire leave her seat beyond the light of the lamp,
and we see then why she glanced affectionately at her mother, and
understand under what consideration, and with what and whom in
mind, Frau von Carayon used that gentle change of phrase. One
hears immediately, moreover, the particular attitude that Victoire has
managed to assume in her (subtly comparable) situation. That flash
of a "*beauté qui inspire seule du vrai sentiment*" in the "*beauté du diable*," around which a later conversation will revolve, has its prelude
here. Similarly preluded is the indifference towards those natural appearances which are so vital to someone like Schach, as the representative of "propriety," yet not to von Bülow, who represents
unsparing renewal: "Victoire, who had abandoned her place at the
tea table the moment the conversation touched upon Poland, now
looked across at the speaker menacingly and said: 'You must know,
Herr von Bülow, that I love the Poles, indeed *de tout mon coeur*.'
And saying this, she leaned forward out of the shadows into the light
of the lamp, in whose shine all could now clearly recognize her profile, which once must have equaled her mother's, but through numerous pox-scars had lost its previous beauty. Every one had to see
it," the narrator says to emphasize the moment, "and the only one
who *didn't* see it, or if he did see it regarded it with utter indifference, was von Bülow" (557).

As far as plot is concerned, the conflict at the center of *Schach von
Wuthenow* is virtually unsurpassed in its triviality and cold-
bloodedness. It also represents a procedure whereby political and social problems are displaced into matters of psychology and morality,
so that these in turn can provide a model of confirmation to legitimate the very order that is called into question. Such a strategy has
always been part of that repertoire of representational modes with
which Classicism — confronted, unlike antiquity, with the problem
of historical change — sought either to impose its cherished order
against the old, or if not, at least to uphold it, as the order of appearance and validation, against the new. In Fontane this strategy
undergoes one last sublimation, but it also achieves a certain sort of
ultimate self-transparency. The conversations commenting on events
in the story are particularly illuminating in this regard.

"Just as many a marriage plan miscarries due to an unpresentable
mother," von Alvensleben remarks in assessing Schach's relationship

to Frau von Carayon, "so here it would miscarry due to an unpresentable daughter. Her lack of beauty actually embarrasses him, and he is petrified by the thought of seeing his normality, if I may put it thus, connected in any way with her abnormality" (571). Still the deciding point is that Schach, as much as Victoire, is motivated here from the outside, but only in accordance with his own standards. Victoire, without intending anything in particular for her own sake, attempts to provoke the words that need to be spoken between Schach and her mother by placing herself in the middle. She believes her role as an outsider gives her this right, as long as, for instance, the ambiguity that arises from the invitation to the country outing is kept within the boundaries of a proper tone distinguished by a certain *esprit*. But having a reason to hesitate is itself no protection from misfortune, and indeed such reservations can even bring misfortune about, unpredictably, if one is conscious that they are unjustified. Victoire steps out of her role as outsider with a certain ingenuousness. The passage reads:

> Victoire hatte sich mittlerweile bereits an den Schreibtisch gesetzt, und ihre Feder kritzelte: "Herzlichst akzeptiert, trotzdem die Ziele vorläufig im Dunkeln bleiben. Aber ist der Entscheidungsmoment erst da, so wird er uns auch die richtige wählen lassen." Frau von Carayon las über Victoires Schulter fort. "Es klingt so vieldeutig," sagte sie. "So will ich ein bloßes Ja schreiben, und du kontrasignierst." "Nein, laß es nur." Und Victoire schloß das Blatt und gab es dem draußen wartenden Groom. Als sie von dem Flur in das Zimmer zurückkehrte, fand sie die Mama nachdenklich. "Ich liebe solche Pikanterien nicht, und am wenigsten Rätselsätze." "Du dürftest sie auch nicht schreiben. Aber ich? Ich darf alles [. . .]" (576–77)[23]

The social-colloquial tone permits much, but carries the danger that nothing is taken as intended, especially when principles come into play.

Even though we learn nothing here about Schach's reaction to the note, later on we witness his being manipulated, which allows us to adduce a particular susceptibility to innuendo. And we see how Victoire becomes irritated by her companion's faux pas during the country outing. Schach also endures an irritation based on a faux pas, this time by the Prince. As a bearer of the St. Andrew's Cross he is compelled in some degree to prove himself, and thus he consents to a compromise that he cannot possibly desire. The Prince, within whose circle von Bülow also circulates, takes sides with von Bülow in

his estimation of the *good* Czar Alexander, a provocation that is repeated in the discussion about genuine and false honors in respect to
the failed *demarches* for Iffland. His agreement with Schach about
the value of the Haugwitz mission falls by the wayside, however, to
Schach's frustration. Thus Schach, in his capacity as the representative of propriety, feels himself suddenly thrice affronted when the
discussion reverts again to the Czar's five categories of beauty. Inspired by the account of Victoire's musical performance, the idea has
the same requisite attractiveness for Schach as for the rest of those
present, and thus he wanders into the Prince's trap. "I ask you, what
is beauty?" demands the Prince, reverting to the still-unexhausted
subject.

> Einer der allervaguesten Begriffe. Muß ich sie an die fünf Kategorien
> erinnern, die wir in erster Reihe Seiner Majestät dem Kaiser Alexander
> und in zweiter unsrem Freunde Bülow verdanken? *Alles ist schön* und
> *nichts.* Ich persönlich würde der Beauté du diable jederzeit den Vor-
> zug geben, will also sagen einer Erscheinungsform, die sich mit der
> des ci-devant schönen Fräuleins von Carayon einigermaßen decken
> würde. (607)[24]

Von Nostitz objects, out of respect for Victoire's honor; but the
Prince explains that such *beauté du diable* also must include that
witty-elegaic variety which has been through the "purgatory fires":
"'This [type of beauty] has something universal about it, which
reaches far beyond mere questions of race or complexion. Just like
the Catholic church. The one like the other is based on an inwardness, and that inwardness, which is decisive for *our* question, is called
energie, fire, passion.' Nostitz and Sander smiled and nodded" (607–
8). As nonsensical as such bluster may be, it nonetheless accom-
plishes its unintentional effect. When von Nostitz and Sander acknowledge such *"energie"* — which in *"our"* question," that is in
respect to Morgarten and Sempach, is under discussion — with a
smile, they thereby imply some secondary meaning relating to
Schach. When the Prince subsequently equates erotic defeats or vic-
tories with military ones, he once again aligns himself with Schach's
opponents. When he suggests the universal standard for the erotic to
be a "beautiful wife" and a "non-beautiful lover," the story's further
developments are set on a fatal course. What is demanded, in each
case, is that Schach prove he has good heart, a heart with the *energie*
to seize the moment. Schach considers himself put to the test by the

Prince, although the latter is unaware of it. He must prove a state-ment that contradicts his very "nature" and his social position most of all: that "behind apparent ugliness is hidden a higher form of beauty" (609) — prove it, if not in the military, then in the erotic realm. Crucial impetus meanwhile comes from the moral argument. The Prince escalates his argument to the point of demonstrating a humane world-order: "Believe me, gentlemen, the heart decides, *only* the heart. Whoever loves, whoever has the power of love, is also worthy of love, and it would be horrifying if this were otherwise" (608). In this way, during the dinner with the Prince, immediately before the seduction of Victoire, Schach is motivated by the conver-sation to make himself into the interpreter of the Prince's wishes (609). The seduction is occasioned by Schach's coming to commu-nicate the Prince's invitation to the Carayon ladies to visit his social circle. Couldn't Schach's *faux pas* with Victoire during the country outing be explained similarly, along the lines of an unintentional al-though not insubstantial external motivation? The conversational form allows Fontane not only to spin a web of uncontrolled, opin-ion-shaping themes, but also a web of uncontrolled, emotion-eliciting motivations.

In fact, however, the really intricate aspect of the conflict lies not with Schach but with Victoire. In her case, not only does the argu-ment become the motive, but also the means becomes an end. For what drives Victoire to deceive her mother with Schach on the night of the great military parade? The answer is that Schach confronts her with an inimitable bluntness, to some degree obligating her mor-ally — as a form of self-defense — to fall in love. Victoire cannot maintain her sovereignty in respect to society from within society. "Now listen to me," she had declared by way of justifying her deci-sion to answer Schach's earlier invitation. "Something has got to happen, Mama. People are talking so much, even to me, and since Schach continues to keep his silence and since you are not *allowed* to speak, I have to do it instead of you two and marry you off" (576). She does however allow that this will be an inversion of the way of the world — "In other cases mothers marry off their daughters, here it is different, . . . I'm marrying you off" — and Frau von Carayon does admit that she "finally . . . and really only" (577) loves her daughter. Still it seems to accord with both the subject and its criti-cal illumination that the attempt is made. A fate like Victoire's cannot be kept for too long outside of the established reality; at some point there has to come a moment of trial and confirmation, at least when, like Schach, one grants credence to the conviction that the *beauté qui inspire seule du vrai sentiment* is the only one that counts. "The only thing that is valid," he explains immediately before the seduction, "is the one eternal truth, that the soul creates the body, or rather illuminates and transfigures it . . . . I implore you to get hold of yourself and to believe again that you have a right to life and to love" (616–17). The precondition for this is that Victoire, like Schach himself, lets herself be lured out of her position of safety. This occurs, as with Schach, as a result of external motivations; only here it is Schach himself, through an unkindness that she cannot comprehend, who calls the respectability of their relationship into question. Already the Prince's bluster has left Schach, with his in-stinct for equilibrium, feeling obligated to an unnoticably elevated personal attachment. He does not suspect that this, just like the blithe self-denial in the name of *esprit*, could land him on a false footing. That he failed to strike the proper tone during the country outing, when he offered Victoire his arm while strolling back from the church — this much was forgivable, as was Victoire's rejoinder countering his defense of the Order of Knights Templar with a cri-tique of Philipp le Bel and all "other historical personages who carry the epithet 'the Beautiful'" (588). The conversation began, after all, with a forgotten local hero, Achim von Haake, who, referring to a song-book verse, "Thou shalt respect the dead and do no injury to his countenance," had insisted upon erecting his completed grave-stone while he was still living. When Victoire, with reference to Lessing's *Nathan*, casts doubt on the depiction of Haake's costume, Schach, without realizing it, agrees with her just a tad too warmly: "'*Always* right, my dear Victoire.' And the tone of these words struck her heart and trembled there, although Schach was not aware of it" (587). Victoire, for her part, makes the comment about the Order to which Haake supposedly belonged more out of sheer *jeu d'esprit* than against Schach, yet it also comes "out of some obscure intuition": "But beauty, one must admit, makes for selfishness, and he who is selfish is ungrateful and disloyal." (588) Following this *tête à tête* it must strike Victoire as a direct affront when Schach leaves her side for her mother's before they've even reached the village gate: "Victoire watched them move ahead, crestfallen, and wondered about the switch [in companions] which Schach had made without a single word of apology. 'What was that?' And she blushed as, with a sudden burst of mistrust, she answered her own question" (589).

In order to be sure of herself, Victoire writes to her friend Lisette; pursuing her own wish, she appeals precisely to that quality Schach failed to demonstrate to her:

> Es ist ein Satz, daß Männer nicht eitel sein dürfen, weil Eitelkeit lächerlich mache. Mir scheint dies übertrieben. Ist aber der Satz dennoch richtig, so bedeutet Schach eine Ausnahme. Ich hasse das Wort 'ritterlich' und habe doch kein anderes für ihn. *Eines* ist er vielleicht noch mehr, diskret imponierend, oder doch voll natürlichen Ansehns, und sollte sich mir *das* erfüllen, was ich um der Mama und auch um meinetwillen wünsche, so würd es mir nicht schwer werden, mich in eine Respektsstellung zu ihm hineinzufinden. (592)[25]

And it is precisely in regard to such respect that Schach has wounded *her* in this case, and in a way that — if her reaction is not based entirely on overwrought sensitivity — hardly attests to any "natural eminence." Lisette von Perbandt rightly points out the contradiction in Victoire's behavior here and indicates the danger involved in regarding the whole world with unchecked mistrust. It is not only for Schach but also, more importantly, for Victoire herself to decide. In this situation, that means Victoire must admit she is in love with Schach:

> Ich finde, je mehr ich den Fall überlege, daß Du ganz einfach vor einer Alternative stehst und entweder Deine gute Meinung über S. oder aber Dein Mißtrauen *gegen* ihn fallen lassen mußt. Er sei Kavalier, schreibst Du mir, "ja das Ritterliche," fügst Du hinzu, "sei so recht eigentlich seine Natur," und im selben Augenblicke, wo Du dies schreibst, bezichtigt ihn Dein Argwohn einer Handlungsweise, die, träfe sie zu, das Unritterlichste von der Welt sein würde. Solche Widersprüche gibt es nicht. (613)[26]

One sees that Victoire too is motivated from outside, by another's judgment. It is her friend, moreover, despite her otherwise shrewd view of matters, who makes faulty judgment the basis for events to come: that is, that such contradictions do not exist, that the "mirror" is lying to Victoire, that it "doesn't matter" how "we women . . . win a man's heart" (613). Victoire in turn falls in love with Schach for reasons of self-respect, in order to be able to remain in agreement with herself. Is it not true in her case, as it is (in a different way) for Lisette von Perbandt, that she is operating under an illusion and thus is out of touch with reality? Could Victoire realistically expect that society itself would create for her a freedom outside of society?

The intricacy of these plot complications consists in no small part in the fact that both Schach and Victoire only become what they are by taking on a certain role at a certain time: Schach becomes a fully-fledged representative of "propriety"; Victoire becomes, in the fullest sense, free. Victoire becomes what she is insofar as, in her case, the means becomes the end. From the moment she decides to intervene personally for her mother's sake, and through her anguish over the "tone of his words," to her finally disregarding society's judgment altogether, Victoire operates always from her role as an outsider who has resolved "not to pass blindly by whatever good we have bartered," and instead to rejoice in her "freedom" (615). But what sort of a freedom would this be that would always include the necessity, at the most decisive moments, for Victoire to understand herself only as the means, never as the end of her actions? If not for Schach falling in love with her instead of her mother, this freedom would have remained illusory. But then, Schach does not really fall in love with her, he simply yields to a social impulse, but this still does not mean that feelings and moral values are not involved. For him, the whole matter appears as though, to a certain degree — except of course as far as she is concerned — he has managed to leap over his own shadow. Not only does he represent propriety, now he is also able to assert his solidarity with it. Precisely this has been at the root of what was so tedious and in some ways insulting about his aloof demeanor, that he was so insistent *merely* "upon the representation and validation of a certain *grandezza*" (682). Concerning this manner of fulfilling his representative duty, one could say that he stands not so much *for* "good society" as rather *in its stead*. One could also say that since representation suffices for him, as a person he necessarily remains incomprehensible. This consequence becomes significant in the political context, where he comes off as the "embodiment of that Prussian narrowness" whose worldview does not reach beyond the "three articles of belief" of the army of Frederick the Great (572). Schach *becomes* a full-fledged representative of the old society only in relation to Victoire, just as she becomes fully free only in relation to him. But the difference here is that, in view of both the initial conditions and the accomplished goal, Victoire can also regard herself as personally beyond all that has occurred. This possibility is lacking for Schach because his situation poses a different problem. Precisely as a "good" man he remains a representative of the old, "good" society, only now one who is in conflict with himself. A certain honesty towards himself may also come into play here, especially in his incapacity to endure the humor and scorn ("Spott und Witz," 635) of his comrades in the regiment and in the sense of justice ("Rechtsgefühl," 633) which, rather than some "mysterious attraction" (634) of the heart or a misguided enthusiasm for "purification processes" (634), he believes guided his actions. For in fact these latter interpretations, some of which are suggested earlier, some later, do not withstand scrutiny. On the other hand, it is also impossible to bring the actual motive to light. This explains why Schach is paralyzed by such disconcerting indecisiveness that Frau von Carayon must finally compel him to agree to the engagement.

Matters never reach this point, however, because of the anonymous attack. The affair of Schach and Victoire gets played up as a political issue, just as previously Zaccharias Werner's drama was imputed to be a traduction of Luther. Schach had also refused to play the part of Luther during the scandalous "sleigh ride" (625). But certain rivalries within the Prince's circle can likewise be held responsible for the retribution taken against Schach's unpopularity the moment he reveals a weakness. "He could not be less popular," we read in the letter from Sander; "he who plays the loner never really is." In any case, Sander continues, the attack was "cleverly calculated" and really only regrettable as far as the Carayons are concerned (639). One sees how Fontane leaves no loose strands in the web he has spun. For even from the aspect of politics we see how the prerogative of a sovereign state, having fallen into the hands of a social scene that considers itself to be "sovereign," also contributes its part to Victoire's and Schach's fate. Where justice and injustice finally become inextricably bound, the narrator even shows a certain sympathy for Schach. He comments: "What always happens, happened this time too: the Carayons heard nothing about it even though half the city knew . . . . This was certainly fortunate for both mother and daughter; . . . but for the third party involved, for Schach, it was just as certainly a misfortune" (651–52). It is understood: because under these circumstances Frau von Carayon sets in

motion the machinery of social sanction against Schach. Had she
known about the series of defamatory caricatures, she "still would
not have desisted in her demands upon him," but also would have
"allowed him to delay somewhat and granted him some sympathy
and reassurance" (652). But instead she agitates against him more
and more, finally reaching a point of comparing Prussian aristocratic
pride, which spreads its peacock tail in a chicken yard (654), to its
French counterpart, which commands "real palaces" (655) and fell,
moreover, under the guillotine beside the Girondists. Seizing upon
this difference, she musters herself as she had already for the silent
engagement, according to the *really* old way of things, and an-
nounces to Schach that she is taking "different, entirely self-reliant
action" (656) — which indeed she does.

The whole matter is brought before a court that in a certain sense
is the most competent, but also in a certain sense the most incom-
petent: the monarch himself. He, supported by the Queen, has only
one standard for judging such affairs. For Frederick Wilhelm III, the
otherwise relatively sublime estimation of society is reduced to a
military matter.[27] He comments frankly that he treats the case as a
question de raison, while the Queen treats it on a similar level as a
question d'amour. Were it not for the assurance of a trust-fund for
the "Fräulein-Daughter (pardon, my dear Schach)" based upon her
"old family" (666), one could hardly imagine an outlook and comments less suitable than those of Frederick Wilhelm III. "Called
upon you, my dear Schach," the King begins the audience. "The
Carayons: awkward matter. Don't like to play the moralist and the
hairsplitter; loathe it; have strayed myself. But not to get stuck
astray; to make amends. Anyway can't rightly comprehend. Lovely
woman, the mother, *really* liked her; clever woman" (665). For the
sake of "*honnêteté*," which is what matters to him, he requires the
marriage with Fräulein von Carayon or else Schach must "quit the
service." Through his posture and demeanor Schach indicates that
"this would be the most painful thing for him." Thus the King continues: "Okay, so then stay . . . But a *remedeur* must be found, and
soon, and right away" (665–66).

The Queen's moving appeal to regard the situation not as a
question of duty according to the standard of *honnêteté* but rather as
a question of love from the perspective of "two hearts" who "seem
destined for one another" (667) is hardly any help either. There can

be no objection to duty for a military officer. Yet to allow that it was a mysterious attraction of the heart that caused him thus to err would be an affront to his own honesty, something he does not owe the Queen but does owe himself. The Queen is more precise: "For you will not, I hope, deny that it was a mysterious attraction that drew you to this dear, and once so lovely, child" (667). We realize that von Bülow is not so off the mark when he finds the "Schach case" to be of "most serious" interest, "on account of its symptomatic significance." "It is really a phenomenon of our times," he states in a September 1806 letter to Sander:

> Er ist durchaus Zeiterscheinung, aber wohlerstanden mit lokaler Begrenzung, ein in seinen Ursachen ganz abnormer Fall, der sich in dieser Art und Weise nur in seiner königlichen Majestät von Preußen Haupt- und Residenzstadt, oder, wenn über diese hinaus, immer nur in den Reihen unserer nachgeborenen friderizianischen Armee zutragen konnte [. . .].[28]

Even up to the pinnacle of society, the order of appearance and validation remains based upon "self-conceit" and on functioning like "clockwork" (678). Even if Schach could have been judged differently, the conclusion would still be that he had to some degree behaved correctly in falsehood, had followed his own unique moral honesty, and thus arrived at the unavoidable consequence, which he executed in representative fashion.

Thus we have arrived at the point where both a literary *and* political evaluation of *Schach* can be considered. The novel, which Fontane subtitled "Story from the Time of the *Regiment Gendarmes*," derives from an incident from the period immediately following the Wars of Liberation, and ends with both a prognostication and a reminiscence. The prognostication — based, of course, on the premise of the story's immanent chronology — comes from the hand of von Bülow. In September 1806, on the eve of the battles of Jena and Auerstädt, he recalls:

> Schach tadelte mich damals als unpatriotisch. Unpatriotisch! Die Warner sind noch immer bei diesem Namen genannt worden. Und nun! Was ich damals als etwas bloß Wahrscheinliches vor Augen hatte, jetzt ist es *tatsächlich* da. Der Krieg ist erklärt. Und was das bedeutet, steht in aller Deutlichkeit vor meiner Seele. [Preußen werde] an derselben Welt des Scheins zugrundegehen, an der Schach zugrunde gegangen ist. (680)[29]

But *how* does Schach come to ruin? According to his friend and regiment comrade's judgment, it is for being "*really* a good man, . . . in his own way of course" (572). This "way" is precisely the problem here, particularly considering that it is integrated into the narrative with a certain amount of perspective. And this perspective leads in turn to a sort of hindsight that oversteps the story's local framework. Indeed it would be rewarding to investigate the intercultural distribution of the personages Fontane selects for his works. Already the comparison of French and German aristocracy made by an *aigrierte* Frau von Carayon has caught our attention. What are the advantages Fontane derives from drawing a wider, pan-European perspective? The question pertains to the way of life of European aristocracy, first of all, and secondly to certain nuances in the practicalities of patriotism. There is hardly any basis for assuming that Fontane, like von Bülow, is taking the side of Bonapartism, yet he also holds out little prospect for the party of Legitimism represented in the person of Schach. The only one in the "Story from the Time of the *Regiment Gendarmes*" who really comes away unscathed is Frau von Carayon, with her "entirely self-reliant action."[30] But if her degree of foreignness equips her with different points of reference and thus serves as an alleviating condition, the way she comports herself within society enters into tragicomic collaboration with Schach's exclusively "local" conditions.

In the end Schach can find only "*one* way" (668) to escape the situation with honor: a bullet in the head while riding home in the coach after the wedding. A direct *order* from his supreme commander had to be followed, while the other's appeal to the heart of the delinquent ran counter to his *nature*. Factoring in this difference reveals in Schach a remarkable resistance to the intervention of the two Majesties: he is "stunned" but by no means "converted" (668). This remark is illuminating: the applicable principles that oblige him in this case either have never been at his disposal personally — on this point the conflict resembles Kleist's "Prince of Homburg," only with a different outcome — or else they are, as in the case of the Queen's outflanking maneuver, simply false. It is not simply a matter of duty conflicting with inclination, nor a conflict between rival duties, nor in the least some sort of conflict between individual and society. Rather it involves the peculiar grace of "good society's" system of appearance and validation coming into conflict with the system of commands and obedience on the side of the state. This conflict between state and society, involving the widest conceivable reduction and/or exclusion of the individual or the person, pervades Fontane's narrative. And precisely therein lies the confirmation of Fontane's perennial classicism as well: it makes possible this ongoing alterity of perspectives.[31] About Schach's inner conflict the narrator comments:

> Die gnädigen Worte beider Majestäten hatten eines Eindrucks auf ihn nicht verfehlt; trotzdem war er nur betroffen, in nichts aber umgestimmt worden. Er wußte, was er dem König schuldig sei: *Gehorsam!* Aber sein Herz widerstritt, und so galt es dann für ihn, etwas ausfindig zu machen, als Gehorsam und Ungehorsam in sich vereinigte, was dem Befehl des Königs und dem Befehl seiner Natur gleichmäßig entsprach. Und dafür es nur *einen* Weg. (668)[32]

Opposed to this is the behavior of Frau von Carayon. Although Fontane does not explicitly contrast it with its Prussian variant, he does make his point implicitly nonetheless, and with a certain idealtypical succinctness.

Double-bind situations have long been regarded as the preferred stylistic device for transforming political or social problematics into moral ones. In this regard the conflict management demonstrated by Frau von Carayon on the occasion of the "silent engagement" is strictly classical. She understands — as does Victoire and to a certain degree Schach as well — how to reach unavoidable decisions in a way that is both true to principle and free of illusions. The fact that she does this so soberly, without particular enthusiasm, demonstrates her timely realism. But the model itself (that of a latent collision of duties, or also in the sense of a conflict between duty and inclination) that places "the defense or advocacy for *Josephine* von Carayon" in the competency of her antagonist but also, just as decisively, allows her to remain the "advocate of *Frau* von Carayon, . . . of her house and her good name" (631 — italics added), — this model is not an invention of the epoch of realism. Rather — stated emphatically — it is an invention of classicism. Through this means Fontane examines the onset of European absolutism, whose successful beginnings were due, among other reasons, to an enormous enthusiasm for decisiveness on the part of its protagonists. But for Josephine as a descendent of the nineteenth century — and not just as one who is Prussian-born — this enthusiasm has lost its force. What endures is the capacity for decisiveness. "My dear Schach," she begins her response, "I am not so foolish as to make a scene or to preach to you about morality; one of the things I hate most of all is such virtuous babble. From my youth onward I have lived in this world, I know this world and have had my own experiences of the heart" (631). But she is just as unwilling to witness a "comedy of generosity" on her daughter's part; she is too weak for this because of her love for Victoire. "I belong to this society" — so begins her advocacy for the "Frau von Carayon" — "whose conditions I fulfill and whose laws I follow. This I was raised to do" (632). On both sides, to Schach and to Victoire, she defends the integrity of her identity: that *to* which she owes her place in society, but also that *for* which the society she belongs to itself exists. She too must strive to remain in agreement with herself; but unlike Schach, this is not because she regards defensively the judgment of others whose uncritical principles she does not share. Taking instead an offensive approach, she subjects herself directly to the judgment of others, in order to test her ability to uphold her principles regardless of the outcome. This procedure resembles a strategy of persuasion, and compared with the approach of the two Majesties, it becomes clear that the way to aim for an obligatory effect on Schach is to insure that the requisite conditions for his wishes are either yielded or withheld. The deciding passage during the discourse of Frau von Carayon reads:

> Sie sehen, ich gebe mich Ihrem Urteil preis. Aber wenn ich mich auch bedingungslos einer jeden Verteidigung oder Anwaltschaft für Josephine von Carayon enthalte, für *Josephine* (Verzeihung, Sie haben eben selbst den alten Namen wieder heraufbeschworen), so darf ich doch nicht darauf verzichten, der Anwalt der *Frau* von Carayon zu sein, ihres Hauses und ihres Namens. (631)[33]

Schach gives his answer once he has "had a chance . . . to pull himself together again." The deciding sentence of his rejoinder reads: "If *that* which he knows now had been made known to him earlier he would've taken the very steps of his own free will that Frau von Carayon is now requiring of him" (632). One recognizes that a certain moral culture, be it merely a latent one, is presupposed whenever the sovereignty of society is to be established, or re-established. For the same is true for the sovereignty of society as for the sovereignty of the state: it must be based on the sovereignty of its members.

Considering when the story was written, relative to the time of the actual event and to its fictive date, the materials and their execution seem to suggest that Fontane undertook an experiment, by no means unrealistic per se, of confronting the nationalistically defined patriotism of the Wars of Liberation as seen from the perspective of the 1870s with its predecessor, the republican-bourgeois patriotism of both the *ancien régime* and the Revolution. While this may be only *one* aspect of the functional history of perennial Classicism, it is in any case an aspect of that phase in which Fontane's *Schach von Wuthenow* was written. Yet as far as I am aware, a functional history of Classicism relating not only to Fontane's storytelling but also, beyond that, to the history of architecture and art, has yet to be written. Meanwhile, in terms of the history of style, such perennial Classicism certainly counts, along with perennial Romanticism and Realism, as one of the most significant stabilizing elements within the already elaborated "alterity-horizon" of European culture. For in the field of a simultaneity of the unsimultaneous, this horizon has developed more on the basis of alternating, competing constellations than on the basis of discrete, competing national histories. Perhaps the analysis of representational modes and their accompanying conceptualizations within the comparative European context should no longer be bound so exclusively to a perspectivization based upon national literatures, and should instead, here as elsewhere, direct its attention more emphatically to the representation of the "other" within the "proper."

Translated by Eric Schwab

Notes

[1] An English version, translated by E. M. Valk, has been published under a different title, "A Man of Honor." Cf. *Theodor Fontane, Short Novels and Other Writings*, The German Library Vol. 48, ed. Peter Demetz (New York: Continuum, 1982). For stylistic and terminological reasons, however, all translations of Fontane in this article are original, given by Eric Schwab.

[2] Theodor Fontane, *Schach von Wuthenow. Sämtliche Werke*, vol. 2, pt. 1, ed. W. Keitel (Munich: Hanser, 1962). Here and in subsequent quotations Fontane is cited from this edition by page number in brackets.

[3] On these categories, see Jürgen Habermas, *Strukturwandel der Öffentlichkeit* (Darmstadt und Neuwied: Luchterhand, 1986). For their application to *Schach von Wuthenow*, cf. Manfred Dutschke, "Geselliger Spießrutenlauf," *Text & Kritik. Sonderband für Theodor Fontane*, ed. H. L. Arnold (Munich: Text & Kritik, 1989), 107–108.

[4] Cf. W. Müller-Seidel, *Theodor Fontane: Soziale Romankunst in Deutschland* (Stuttgart: Metzler, 1975).

[5] See for example Peter Demetz, *Formen des Realismus: Theodor Fontane* (Munich: C. Hanser, 1964), 119. However, in his formulation of "classical humanism" Demetz places the accent on the humanism rather than the classicism.

[6] One could name here: P. Sterne, *Über literarischen Realismus* (Munich: Beck, 1983), who makes the connection to Erich Auerbach, *Mimesis: Dargestellte Wirklichkeit in der europäischen Literatur* (Bern/Munich: Francke, 1946); in translation, E. Auerbach, *The Representation of Reality in Western Literature*, trans. Willard Trask (New York: Anchor Books, 1957 — all quotations and page citations from this edition). Another viewpoint would be Georg Lukács, "Ästhetik Teil 1. Die Eigenart des Ästhetischen," *Werke*, vol. 11, pt. 1 (Darmstadt/Neuwied: Luchterhand, no year). On the terms of discussion, cf. Wolfgang Preisendanz, *Wege des Realismus* (Munich: Fink, 1977); W. Preisendanz, ed., *Theodor Fontane* (Darmstadt: Wiss. Buchgesellschaft, 1985); Richard Brinkman, ed., *Begriffsbestimmung des literarischen Realismus* (Darmstadt: Wiss. Buchgesellschaft, 1974); Klaus Detlef Müller, ed., *Bürgerlicher Realismus: Grundlagen und Interpretationen* (Königstein/Ts.: Äthenäum, 1981).

[7] This is the type of argument made by Hans Blumenberg, "Wirklichkeitsbegriff und Möglichkeit des Romans," *Nachahmung und Illusion: Poetik und Hermeneutik*, vol. 1, ed. H. R. Jauss (Munich: Fink, 1969). On

the concept of realism and its problems: Nelson Goodman, *Languages of Art: An Approach to a Theory of Symbols* (Brighton/Sussex, 1981); cf. also Horst Turk, "Mimesis Praxeos. Der Realismus aus der Perspektive einiger neuerer Theorieansätze," *Jahrbuch der Raabe-Gesellschaft* 1983, 136–171.

[8] Auerbach, *Mimesis*, 4. Auerbach speaks in another passage of four "basic types" (19). The peculiarity of his approach is that he explicates a conception of reality on the basis of the modes of its representation (10).

[9] Blumenberg, "Wirklichkeitsbegriff," 10. Blumenberg distinguishes, in total, four historical versions of the concept of reality: the "reality of instantaneous evidence," "guaranteed reality," reality as the "realization of a self-cohesive context," and reality as "that which the subject does not control" ("Wirklichkeitsbegriff," 13).

[10] Auerbach, *Mimesis*, 4.

[11] This has been attempted, however, by F. Th. Vischer, *Ästhetik* (Reutlingen: Mächen, 1846–58) — as Demetz rightly notes (*Formen des Realismus*, 123). Cf. also the reference to Chr. Lugowski, *Die Form der Individualität im Roman* (Frankfurt, 1976) in H. Schlaffer, "Das Schicksalsmodell in Fontanes Romanwerk. Konstanz und Auflösung," *Germanisch-Romanisch Monatsschrift*, NF 16 (1966): 392–409; and Andreas Poltermann, "'Frau Jenny Treibel' oder die Profanierung der hohen Poesie," *Text & Kritik. Sonderband: Theodor Fontane* (1989): 131–147.

[12] Auerbach, *Mimesis*, 5.

[13] Ibid., 12.

[14] Ibid., 19.

[15] Ibid., 14.

[16] Ibid., 18.

[17] Ibid., 19.

[18] Blumenberg, "Wirklichkeitsbegriff," 13. On the applicability of Blumenberg's categories, cf. Horst Turk, "Die Schrift als Ordnungsform des Erlebens. Diskursanalytische Überlegungen zu Aldabert Stifter," in J. Fohrmann/H. Müller, eds., *Diskurstheorien und Literaturwissenschaft* (Frankfurt am Main: Suhrkamp, 1988), 400–418.

[19] Auerbach, *Mimesis*, 18.

[20] For a contrary view cf. Demetz, *Formen des Realismus*, 122–23. Demetz considers "good society" to be a "mobile aesthetic category" merely masked by "sociological elements."

[21] On this and the following remarks cf. U. Johnson, *Jahrestage 4* (Frankfurt am Main: Suhrkamp, 1983), 1694–1707.

[22] The English translation by Eric Schwab is given without reference to page numbers, since only the passages relevant to this article were translated. "The strong gentleman next to him was the publisher of his writings, Herr Daniel Sander, but otherwise his utter counterpart, at least as pertains to appearance. A full black beard framed a face that carried an expression of equal parts contentment and sarcasm, while his coat of Dutch fabric, fitted tight at the waist, snugly enclosed his *embonpoint*. What completed the contrast was the finest white linen, of a quality that von Bülow's by no means exceeded." (555)

[23] English translation: "Victoire meanwhile had already sat down at her writing desk and scribbled away with her quill: 'Heartfully accepted, even though we are still in the dark about the destinations [or "objectives," *Ziele*]. But once the moment of decision is reached, we know it will be the right one.' Frau von Carayon read this over Victoire's shoulder. 'It sounds so suggestive,' she said. 'Then I will write a simple yes, and you sign it too.' 'No, leave it as it is.' And Victoire folded up the sheet and gave it to the groom waiting outside. As she came back from the hallway into the room, she found her mother looking thoughtful. 'I'm not fond of such titillations, least of all sentences that are riddles.' 'Well you also couldn't have gotten away with writing it. But me? I'm allowed to do anything' . . . " (576–77).

[24] English translation: "One of our most vague concepts. Must I remind you of those five categories, for which we have in the first place His Majesty Kaiser Alexander and in the second our friend Bülow to thank? *Everything* is beautiful and *nothing*. I personally would always prefer the *beauté du diable* — a form of appearances, that is, which would correspond, in some degree, to the *ci-devant* beautiful young Lady von Carayon." (607)

[25] English translation: "There is a saying that men are not allowed to be vain, because vanity makes one look foolish. To me this is an exaggeration. Yet if the saying is indeed true, then Schach constitutes an exception. I hate the word 'chivalrous' but I can't think of any other for him. Perhaps *one* thing more than that: discreetly imposing, or even just full of natural eminence; but if all *that* should come true that I wish for Mama and also for myself, I know I would have no trouble finding a way to regard him with respect." (592)

[26] English translation: "The more I consider the case, I think you are faced quite simply with an alternative: you have to give up either your high opinion of S. or else your mistrust of him. You tell me he is a cavalier, 'indeed chivalry,' you write, 'is part of his very nature,' and at the very same time your mistrust charges him with behavior that, if true, would be the

most unchivalrous thing in the world. These kind of contradictions don't exist." (613)

[27] This view of a military schematism of orders and obedience as the basic schema for Prussian society in *Schach von Wuthenow* is also pointed out by Dutschke, "Geselliger Spießrutenlauf," 106; for a more detailed account cf. K. Büsch, "Die Militärisierung von Staat und Gesellschaft im alten Preußen," in M. Schlenke, ed., *Ausstellung Preußen: Versuch einer Bilanz*, vol. 2 (Reinbek: Rowohlt, 1981).

[28] English translation: " . . . although of course with regional limitations; a case whose causes are quite abnormal, and which could take place in this way and shape only in His Royal Majesty of Prussia's capitol and residential city, or, beyond that, still only within the ranks of our late-born army of Frederick the Great. . . . "

[29] English translation: "Schach chastised me at the time as unpatriotic. Unpatriotic! Those who do the warning have always been called this name. And now! What once appeared to me as just a probability has now become *fact*. War is declared. And what that means stands before my soul in utter clarity [Prussia will] come to ruin by following the same world of appearances that ruined Schach."

[30] A completely different appraisal of Frau von Carayon is arrived at by Jürgen Manthey, who sees her as the figure who finally "brings down" ("zur Strecke bringt") Schach. Cf. Jürgen Manthey, "Die zwei Geschichten in einer. Über eine Lesart der Erzählung 'Schach von Wuthenow,'" *Text & Kritik*, 117–18.

[31] For more specifics cf. Horst Turk, "Alienität und Alterität," in *Jahrbuch für Internationale Germanistik* 22, vol. 1 (Bern, New York: P. Lang, 1990), 8–31.

[32] English translation: "The gracious words of both Majesties had not failed to make an impression on him; nonetheless he was only stunned, but by no means converted. He knew what he owed the King: *Obedience!* But his heart resisted, and thus he felt his only valid course was to find a way that would unite obedience and disobedience, that would accord equally with both the King's orders and those of his own nature. And there was only *one* way to do this." (668)

[33] English translation: "As you see, I am surrendering myself to your judgment. Yet even if I refrain unconditionally from any defense or advocacy for Josephine von Carayon, for *Josephine* (forgive me, but you yourself summoned up this old name again), still, I cannot allow myself to be excused from being the advocate of *Frau* von Carayon, of her house and her name.'" (631)

MARION DOEBELING

On the Theory of the Essay and Fontane's England Essays as Modernist Signature

THIS ESSAY IS CONCERNED WITH A PART OF Fontane's work that has so far attracted only little critical attention: his essayistic work written in the years between 1844 and 1859. The year 1844 marks Fontane's first visit to the nineteenth-century metropolis par excellence, London, and the time-frame of 1855–58 circumscribes the four-year period during which Fontane resided there as visitor, journalist, writer, and essayist. But even contemporary Fontane research has almost paradigmatically excluded this essayistic interlude from scholarly attention.[1] In this article I will analyze some of Fontane's England essays while simultaneously providing a partial re-evaluation of his novelistic œuvre from the vantage point of the cultural-critical tradition of the essay.

Research in the field of German literature has demonstrated that many German-speaking nineteenth-century literary realists such as Keller, Stifter, Raabe, Storm, and even Fontane predominantly subscribed to the notion of *Verklärung* (transfiguration or mystification) in their artistic representations.[2] However, in nineteenth-century realism, the notion of *Verklärung* implied a phenomenological structure that remained partially hidden from direct observation. Reality thus represented as *Verklärung* automatically pointed to its own representational malaise or insincerity, since the process of camouflage remained its central component. Realists like Keller, Stifter, Raabe, Storm, and Fontane were thus primarily engaging in a literary practice of aesthetic camouflage, partially conscious, partially unconscious, vis-à-vis a culture that was increasingly reshaping its social boundaries because of the emergence of the industrial proletariat, and, in more general terms, because of the gradual emergence of mass culture.

If we follow a nineteenth-century contemporary of Fontane, Otto Ludwig, in his treatise entitled "Poetic Realism," we will soon discover that, according to Ludwig, poetic realism seeks to present the world's totality (*Weltzusammenhang*) to its readers. A linguistic world is supposedly created in which a necessary totality becomes more clearly observable and thus understandable than any other. Ludwig insists upon realism's desire to construct not a piece of the world, but one that is whole and therefore provides closure. He holds that realism seeks to create a concept of the world of objects that contains all its conditions and questions within itself. Ludwig also describes the human figures or characters of literary realism. Each human figure, according to Ludwig, is constructed in a necessary and tightly woven fashion, mirroring reality itself. But at the same time, these human figures ought to be transparent enough for the reader to perceive the totality of the world of objects they represent.[3] There are two points of emphasis in Ludwig's assessment of nineteenth-century poetic realism. First, he is concerned with whether realism can go beyond a simple mimetic and therefore one-dimensional representational enterprise. Second, he focuses on the central representational telos: the portrayal of a thoroughly secular totality.

However, in Fontane's numerous essays on England, no such totality can be detected. Even the notion of a totality of truth found in the extraordinary, as Andreas Huyssen suggests in relation to Fontane's realism in his book *Bürgerlicher Realismus*,[4] is not applicable to Fontane's essayistic work. The reader of Fontane's England essays who is looking for any kind of narratological or aesthetic totality will be disappointed.

In the context of the England essays, individual experience remains subjective, and is not driven by a desire to create any kind of representational network based on causality, precisely because, according to Fontane, London as paradigm of modernity escapes the nineteenth-century striving for order, control, and domination, as we will see later in this article. What was still representable for poetic realism, even though rendered predominantly in idealist terms, seems to increasingly escape representation in Fontane's England essays. Fontane continuously refers to such representational difficulties throughout his essays on London. In Kantian terms, Fontane's experience of London as paradigm of modernity remains ultimately sublime. It is an experience that literally escapes representation.

Fontane employs the genre of the essay, which had been introduced by his contemporary Hermann Grimm in German-speaking lands earlier in the nineteenth century, as an introduction to further discussions on topics ranging from contemporary politics to philosophy, the arts, and literature. Fontane's cultural-critical essays on London open up a space for a new anti-systematic cultural history, because they trace patterns of cultural history that are open-ended and that lead the reader to further questions, reflections and critiques. But the writing subject, the essayist himself, also deserves further attention in this context. The essayist can now no longer be envisioned as an unproblematic and centered subject in the idealist tradition of thinkers such as Fichte, Hegel, and the early Marx. Here the essayist also reveals a part of his own private self. The essayist is continuously redefining his own perspective and prejudice within the discursive realm of his textual creations. The continuously changing discourse network which the essayist seeks to represent therefore becomes his own mirror, however manneristically refracted it may be. Both essay and essayist witness and represent the challenges and cultural concerns, the turmoils as well as the discontinuities, of the culture they are experiencing.

Ever since the now almost classical works on the genre of the essay by prominent literary critics of the early twentieth century, such as Georg Lukács, Max Bense, and Theodor W. Adorno, the genre has received at least some scholarly attention. More recent works on the essay by contemporary scholars such as Réda Bensmaïa, John McCarthy, and Thomas Harrison investigate particularly the boundaries between traditionally accepted and rejected literary forms. These recently published works, like their predecessors, address some of the most crucial aesthetic, philosophical, cultural, and historical concerns of modernity.[5] They all center on the modernist notion of subjectivity and the various ways in which the essay simultaneously captures and dissiminates this notion of a clearly definable subjectivity that only becomes graspable through the experience of the modern world. In these publications, the subjectivity as well as the tentative, intentional, fragmentary, and ateleological structure of the essay are highlighted. The worldly fragments, or aspects of human perception and experience, which the essay discusses in a predominantly oppositional and reflective fashion, mirror the notion of experience as dynamis, as a textual force that is in constant motion. The telos of the essay as genre as well as that of the essayist must therefore be found in the notion of process itself.

The discursive, experimental field of the essay consists of the discussion of selected topics that stand in a systematic relationship to both the essayist and to his or her cultural tradition while simultaneously referring to other cultural contexts. This is formally emphasized by a more anti-systematic, associative, and acausal representation of ideas and selected topics. However, what paradigmatically distinguishes the essay from other forms of formally prescribed writing, such as philosophical treatises, are not the topics themselves, but the ways in which the essayist treats such topics. In this sense, we can agree with Adorno, who, in his essay on the essay, "Der Essay als Form,"[6] writes that the essay presupposes certain ideas and contexts without stating or summarizing them. In opposition to scientific and academic treatises, the essay defines neither its premises nor its concepts. Therefore, the essay as genre is situated between the realms of academic and creative writing. It requires an educated audience that is willing to go beyond the parameters of pure entertainment literature.

However, the essay is not exclusively representational; it is also a reception-oriented genre. The essayistic process of writing in the tradition of "écriture" that had earlier been established by Michel de Montaigne opens up new ways of writing as well as of perception. It therefore seems more appropriate to position the essay in the field of production aesthetics. It is Max Bense who, in his important essay "Über den Essay und seine Prosa" (On the Essay and its Prose), summarizes the productionist aesthetic effect of the essay, which continuously produces new configurations.

According to Bense, the essayist ponders, questions, and checks his object of investigation from many sides. The essayist collects in his vision what he perceives and puts into words what the subject makes visible within the conditions opened up in the process of writing. The one who "attempts" something is not actually the writing subject. The essayist merely creates textual conditions which put a certain topic into the context of a literary configuration. The telos of this process is therefore no longer perception; rather, to witness how a certain subject behaves in a literary manner; a question is asked and experimentation is performed in reference to a topic.[7] By continuously composing a variety of subjects, the essay produces new configurations, analogous to those produced by a kaleidoscope. These configurations, which only momentarily crystallize into fixed forms, protect the essay from system-theoretical satiation and dogmatic closure. In this context, Fontane offers the following observations on the nineteenth-century essayist Hermann Grimm:

> ... Der Essay ist nie darauf aus, den Gegenstand ein für allemal abzutun, sondern läßt dies und jenes unerörtert, um zu anderem Ort darauf zurückzukommen oder auch *nicht* zurückzukommen. Denn auch ein solches Verzichten im einzelnen muß gestattet sein, wenigstens in unseren Augen. Alle in spanische Reitstiefel Eingeschnürten, alle in Doktrin- und Systemwirtschaft Steckengebliebenen werden für diesen Vorzug freilich keine Würdigung haben, weil ihnen die gerade Linie das Ideal und die bequeme Gliederung die Hauptsache ist. Es sind dies die Leute des Ersten, Zweitens, Drittens. Diese Krücken hat H. Grimm weit von sich geworfen.[8]

In order to capture the genre of the essay as aesthetic signature of modernity more precisely, it is also necessary to investigate the field of experience (*Erlebnis*) more closely. The question of modern experience cannot be addressed without previously recreating an established notion of modernity itself. According to Jürgen Habermas in his book *Der Philosophische Diskurs der Moderne* (The Philosophical Discourse of Modernity), we may safely assume that ever since the end of the eighteenth century the discourse of modernity circled around one central topic, that of the decomposition of religious structures of meaning as a result of increasing strategies of secularization and privatization which resulted in a deficit of traditional patterns of meaning.[9] This in turn produced more abstract and rationalized ontologies and philosophies that were increasingly content in engendering "rational" forms of meaning. This trend toward rationalization brought forth in reaction a variety of irrational, pietistic, and even mystical patterns of thought, as can be observed in Goethe's late novels, especially in *Die Wahlverwandtschaften* (Elective Affinities).

One of the strategies of compensation for the loss of transcendental and mystical values consisted in the almost obsessive belief in the power of reflexive reason, or, expressed differently, in the "mythology of reason"; another consisted of the belief in a rejuvenation of the spiritual qualities in man by means of the creation of a new, mythopoetic art. In the second part of the nineteenth century, Baudelaire, Nietzsche, and Wagner both demanded and created such new types of art. What Hegel had once captured as the implementation of a rational philosophy where the real was the rational and the rational the real, was now transformed from Schlegel to Nietzsche into a critique of reason and the rational linked to an emerging desire for a new mythology. Later, in the early twentieth century, it was of course Heidegger who dissiminated this desire into an ontology of Being (*Sein*), which had already distanced itself from being (*das Seiende*). An incisive re-evaluation of the notion of experience underlies all of these philosophical, aesthetic, and literary approaches to modernity.

The notion of experience (*Erlebnis*) gained increased significance in the nineteenth- and early twentieth-century German intellectual tradition, especially in the cultural-philosophical texts by such diverse thinkers as Wilhelm Dilthey, Georg Simmel, and Walter Benjamin. In their texts, the concept of a more encompassing and all embracing realm of experience (*Erfahrung*) is diametrically opposed to that of the more dissociative and modernist kind: that of *Erlebnis*. *Erfahrung* thus circumscribes a domain of meaning that can be made responsible for the creation of a tradition of meaning without gaps, paradoxes, aporias. *Erfahrung* can be understood in Lukácsian terms as a transcendental roof (*transzendentales Obdach*) in a philosophical sense. Meaning here is still guaranteed by the power of infallible truths, which are generated through the power of concepts that are lined up in causal fashion as though they were both reality and truth at the same time. *Erlebnis* in opposition to *Erfahrung* is characterized by an intentional ephemerality of meaning, by intentionally fragmentary layers of meaning. *Erlebnis* resists integration into culturally predetermined representational contexts. A free space (*Freiraum*) is thus generated that is as ephemeral and momentary as the fleeting "non-essence" of modernity described by Baudelaire in his famous essay "Le Peintre de la Vie Moderne" (The Painter of Modern Life):

> By "modernity" I mean the ephemeral, the fugitive, the contingent, the half of art . . . [10]

Modernist experience (*Erlebnis*) neither derives from nor creates contexts of all-encompassing and noncontradictory forms of meaning. Modernist experience as *Erlebnis* is based upon radical subjectivity and the dissociation of holistic visions and no longer allows for any direct references to contexts of meaning and signification outside of itself. Therefore, the problem of the representability of meaning as anything but radically subjective arises simultaneously. The texts of literary modernism have thus incorporated montage along with the dissociation of any chronological and linear context of meaning in favor of a fragmentary layering that atomizes traditional systems of meaning and signification. The centrality of the role of the human subject ever since the Enlightenment is thus dramatically altered. The essayist as a participant in the tradition that developed into modernity therefore places himself between relics of earlier notions of experience (*Erfahrung*) and dissociative individual and atomistic experiences (*Erlebnis*). The increasing differentiation and atomization of modern society into a multitude of specialty disciplines is paradigmatically reflected in Walter Benjamin's notion of experience. Here, the increase of the influence of the mass media and various technologies which continuously evade and escape the power of structuralization and categorization become visible. In the following I will demonstrate how Fontane's essays as asystematic cultural history become signatures of modernity by accounting for this process of atomization.

Fontane's essay on English painting, entitled "Die öffentlichen Denkmäler" (The Public Monuments), provides one example of the theory of experience (*Erlebnis*) as an ontological grounding of modernity.[11] In it, Fontane emphasizes the fact that contemporary English art is, ironically enough, neither visible nor accessible to the public. The essayist's implicit criticism and rhetorical question therefore reads: how is it possible that in the middle of the nineteenth century, art is created without a public, art that then declares itself its own cultural witness? The essayist's partial answer to this question can be found in the observation that this painterly tradition already escapes the experiences (*Erlebnisse*) of most Londoners. Thus, the atomization of any notion of a holistic culture is implicit from the beginning. Culture as such is now broken up into a variety of smaller cultures (*Kleinkulturen*), which may be so private that they entirely evade the "public" eye. Fontane writes:

> Mit der englischen Kunst ist es wie mit dem Leben überhaupt: die
> Straße, die Öffentlichkeit bietet wenig von beidem. . . . Jeder Fremde,
> der Berlin besucht, . . . wird mehr Eindrücke mit nach Hause bringen
> als ganz London ihm zu bieten vermag.[12]

Any notion of a holistic cultural ideal, such as Georg Simmel would
attempt to restore in the early twentieth century, is already lost in
the view of Fontane's essayistic work.[13]

In another of Fontane's essays, entitled "London" (1844), the
essayist takes back any claim to objectivity and validity by only seeking to portray how the city personally affects him, how he himself
experiences it. Fontane does not want to provide a methodologically
sound and therefore sanctioned insight into the phenomenon of
modernity. Fontane writes: "London has made an indestructible impression on me."[14] In the second paragraph of the essay, he then
moves on to the process of truly experiencing London, only to tell
the reader that this notion of truth in experience consists only of the
understanding of differences or multiple entries in the conception of
truth. Therefore, essayistic truth is no longer a homogeneous structural principle, but a conglomerate of a variety of kaleidoscopic impressions, subjective judgments, even speculations. It circumscribes
contours, rather than the center; it sketches, rather than paints in
clearly distinguishable colors. That which has traditionally been understood as the "entirety," as the "essence" of London can no
longer be represented. Once again we can turn back to Baudelaire
for clarification:

> In this way a struggle is launched between the will to see all and forget
> nothing and the faculty of memory, which has formed the habit of a
> lively absorption of general colour and of silhouette, the arabesque of
> contour.[15]

Fontane's essays are arabesques of contour, sketches that reject
the realist imperative to represent. Arabesques are ornamental ab-
stractions, pure forms, void of representational capacities. Fontane's
essays ultimately portray the impossibilities of representation during
a cultural historical period that demanded presentability and representability as the dogma of modern, rational experience.

If the poetic realists still believed in the essential truth content of
their works, then the essay in contrast points to the impossibility of
constructing such a truth or congruent representability. The newly
emerging masses, which the essayist Fontane captures as "Gewühl

der Menschen" (swarm of people) and which he compares to a "geschäftigen Bienenschwarm" (busy bee-hive) and to "Menschenwogen" (waves of people) in which "der einzelne Tropfen verschwimmt" (the single drop is obscured)[16] are all textual approximations to describe human subjectivity that is no longer representable except in linguistic metaphors borrowed from the realm of nature. Thus individual human subjectivity is entirely evacuated in favor of a metaphoric equation of man and beast as part of the natural universe. Human subjectivity becomes both bestial and sublime, as vast as the ocean, just as Kant once related it in his "Critique of Judgment."

If the poetic realist texts were still able to convey the truth content or essence of a particular conception of the world of objects, however incongruently, then the essay as modernist genre par excellence can only circumscribe the impossibility of such a textual endeavor. For the essayist Fontane, the most central textual gestures become approximations and exclusions. London is only incongruently captured in expressions such as "der Massenbegriff" (the notion of the masses). The essence of London as paradigm of modernity can neither be entirely understood nor represented with abstract nouns, such as "Massenhaftigkeit" (mass culture, or mass ontology), precisely because the singular entity or individuality has ceased to exist in that terminological and cultural landscape. Paradoxically, it is this impossibility of understanding and comprehension that is expressed in Fontane's London essays. Only as a phenomenon that lies beyond detailed and singular description, beyond universal natural phenomena does London as paradigm of modernity take shape. Thus, London can only paradoxically emerge as "a model . . . of an entire world,"[17] which lies beyond the powers of representation.

London becomes perceivable as an annunciation for a world to come, which will no longer be representable with traditional representational means. This paradox of representation surfaces throughout the England essays despite Fontane's continuous attempts to invent new textual constellations in order to describe the phenomenon of modernity. Each textual constellation in his essays is composed in such a way that it may quickly change perspective and tone, so that it may never crystallize in a mere frozen gesture of satiation and closure. "Long phrases," writes Fontane about the London *Times* in his essay "The Times," "now have a bad reputation; sentences appear quickly one after another like revolver shots. . . ."[18] Only in such a manner does Fontane the essayist believe to be able to achieve any textual approximation, however paradoxical, of the phenomenon of modernity. Similarly, Fontane described further aesthetic challenges of modernity in the same essay on "The Times" and its feuilletonistic style. He once again perceives the newspaper's style as characteristic of modernity:

> Der gut geschriebene Times-Leitartikel ist eine Arabeske, die sich graziös um die Frage schlingt, eine Zierart, eine geistreiche Illustration; er ist kokett und will gefallen, fesseln, bezwingen, aber es fällt ihm nicht ein, auf alle Zeit hin überzeugen zu wollen.[19]

Thus, Fontane's England essays circumnavigate the literary-historical divide that marks the end of representational art forms and the onset of literary modernism. The essay as genre in general and Fontane's England essays in particular therefore stage and preserve this moment of consciousness where traditional and more linear forms of representation meet more kaleidoscopic and impressionistic ones. Like arabesques, essayistic texts present impressionistic constellations that stand in close connection to abstract visions of pure form. Thus Fontane's England essays remain intentionally incomplete sketches, akin to Baudelaire's textual sketches on the contemporary artist Constantine Guys in his collection of essays "The Painter of Modern Life."

Notes

[1] Charlotte Jolles, "Fontane als Essayist und Journalist," *Jahrbuch für internationale Germanistik 7* (1975): 98–119.

[2] For the notion of *Verklärung* or mystification in poetic realism, see Fontane's essay "Über lyrische und epische Poesie seit 1848," *Sämtliche Werke*, vol. 21, ed. Kurt Schreinert (Munich: Nymphenburger Verlagshandlung, 1963), 12. This edition of Fontane's works is known as the "Nymphenburger Ausgabe."

[3] Otto Ludwig, "Der poetische Realismus," quoted from *Bürgerlicher Realismus*, ed. Andreas Huyssen (Stuttgart: Reclam, 1974), 45. Translation by the author.

[4] Huyssen, 51.

[5] Réda Bensmaïa, *The Barthes Effect: The Essay as Reflective Text*, Engl. trans. (Minneapolis: U of Minnesota P, 1987); John McCarthy, *Crossing Boundaries: A Theory and History of Essay Writing in Germany 1618–1815* (Philadelphia: U of Pennsylvania P, 1989), Thomas Harrison, *Essayism: Conrad, Musil, Pirandello* (Oxford UP, 1992).

[6] Theodor W. Adorno, "Der Essay als Form," *Noten zur Literatur, Schriften*, 3rd ed. (1974; Frankfurt am Main: Suhrkamp, 1980), 10.

[7] Max Bense, "Über den Essay und seine Prosa," *Merkur 3* (1947): 418.

[8] Fontane, "Hermann Grimm, Goethe," in *Sämtliche Werke*, vol. 21/1 (Munich, 1974), 34. The translations of quotes from Fontane in this article are provided by the author. "The essay never intends to deal with a subject once and for all, rather, the essay leaves this and that untreated, in order to come back to it later or not. For such a denial of certain aspects has to be permitted, at least in our eyes. Anyone who is tied up in Spanish riding boots, everyone who has remained stuck in the labyrinth of doctrines will certainly not have any respect for this trait, because for them the straight line, the ideal and the comfortable structuration remains most important. These are the people who always need to say firstly, secondly, thirdly. Hermann Grimm has thrown such crutches far away."

For further reading on the theory and practice of the essay, see Marion Doebeling, *Theodor Fontane im Gegenlicht: Ein Beitrag zur Theorie des Essays und des Romans* (Würzburg: Königshausen & Neumann, 2000).

[9] Jürgen Habermas, *Der philosophische Diskurs der Moderne*, 3rd ed. (Frankfurt am Main: Suhrkamp, 1986).

[10] Charles Baudelaire, "The Painter of Modern Life," in: *The Painter of Modern Life and Other Essays*, ed. J. Mayne (New York: Phaidon Press, 1964), 13.

[11] Fontane, "Die öffentlichen Denkmäler," *Sämtliche Werke*, vol. 17, 17.

[12] Ibid, 17. "English art is very much like English life: the street, the public displays only little of it. . . . Each foreigner who visits Berlin, . . . will take home more impressions than the entirety of London will offer up to him."

[13] Georg Simmel, *Der Konflikt der modernen Kultur: Ein Vortrag* (Munich and Leipzig: Duncker & Humblot, 1921).

[14] Fontane, "London," *Sämtliche Werke*, vol. 17, 472.

[15] Charles Baudelaire, "The Painter of Modern Life."

[16] Fontane, "London," *Sämtliche Werke*, vol. 17, 473.

[17] "als Modell oder Quintessenz einer ganzen Welt." Fontane, "London" *Sämtliche Werke*, vol. 17, 473.

[18] Fontane, "Die Times" *Sämtliche Werke*, vol. 19, 242. German original: "Lange Perioden sind verpönt; rasch hintereinander, wie Revolverschüsse, folgen die Sätze."

[19] Ibid, 242. "The well-written lead *Times* article is an arabesque which clings gracefully to the question. It is an ornament; it is coquettish and wants to please, captivate, as well as win over, but it certainly is not concerned with the desire to convince once and for all."

ERNST HANNEMANN
Mannheim

Body and Nobility:
The Interrelationship between Social
Position and Bodily Condition in *Stine*

FONTANE'S SHORT NOVEL *STINE* (1890) has always been over-shadowed by his controversial and better known novel *Irrungen, Wirrungen* (1890). Yet *Stine* was certainly a controversial work in its time, and its initial magazine publication caused a furor and delayed the book publication of the work.

In *Stine* as in *Irrungen, Wirrungen*, the conflict between aristocratic and proletarian milieus drives the characters' actions. The narrative style, which reflects the tradition of the German novella of the nineteenth century, unfolds a fairly linear plot that does not branch out to any significant supporting subplots.[1] Paul Heyse described the task of the novella form as poetical transformation of a case "which by virtue of particularity of circumstances and characters, and by its non-universal solution, defies dramatic adaptation."[2] Heyse thus re-fined August Wilhelm Schlegel's earlier concept of the form, which defined the novella as a "story outside of history" recording an event that *could* happen in everyday life.[3] The plot of *Stine* is exactly of that nature: A young and idealistic count with an unlucky past and an unhappy present meets a working-class woman, Stine, at a social gathering where the men are of aristocratic origin and the women of the petit bourgeoisie. Count Waldemar falls in love with Stine and secretly hopes for a future marriage. Both characters consult about their unusual liaison with confidants, Waldemar's uncle and Mrs. Pittelkow respectively, and both receive clear advice against pursuing a conventional relationship because of the insurmountable difficulties presented by their difference in class. Against all odds Waldemar declares his love and intentions to Stine. This pivotal incident results in the collapse of his relationship with her. Having lost all hope for a meaningful life, Waldemar commits suicide.

The figure of Waldemar overshadows the importance of Stine as a dynamic element in the narrative. He tries to change his life, and, as a consequence of his failure to do so, meets a tragic end. The figure of Waldemar, however, is by no means a hero in the traditional sense. Too many factors remain beyond his control: His life appears as a series of haphazard events. Never is he independent, neither in thought nor in decision. He constantly requires the support of his peers.[4] Nonetheless, this figure must be given the central position in the story since his actions and his extended absences are indeed the main driving force of the plot. All activities of the other figures are directly or indirectly aimed at him. At this point one question has to be raised: How can a figure that is as little in control as Waldemar still be the driving force? If one chooses to read Waldemar as a cultural agent invested with reason and intentionality, his endeavors do not make much sense. But that is because the narrator informs the reader about the character's inner life, about his wishes and desires. Without this deeper insight, Waldemar appears to obediently behave along the lines of his class, and in the end, accepts the circumstances he cannot change.

Viewed only from this behaviorist perspective, Waldemar would most likely appear as a reasonable subject. However, this very reasoning makes him passive when it comes to crossing class boundaries. It cannot even be called instrumental, that is, making Waldemar into a opportunist. His futile attempts to find an economical basis for a lasting relationship are rudimentary and dreamlike at best. What we see at work and watch succeed here is the rationality of discipline, the mode of social control in Prussia, a state that adopted ultimate discipline and efficient administration as its ideal. What is customary and appropriate in this social field is that which claims rationality's authority and normative power.

But the reader also notices that Waldemar is not entirely attuned to this rationale of ultimate class discipline. Waldemar would not have transgressed the nobility's level of tolerance had he pursued his romantic interest in an uninstitutionalized way, as his authoritarian uncle had with Pittelkow. A love affair that crosses the class boundaries in this societal setting of high stratification seems not entirely impossible as long as the propriety that forms class distinctions remains unchallenged. Within this cultural framework Waldemar does not even consider this common practice a viable option, but operates beyond the realm of the rational. Therefore his actions need to be explained in broader terms than those of the rational and self-conscious subject that, by contrast, is embodied so well by his uncle and Pittelkow. They are each paradigmatic figures who, in the Kantian tradition of the Enlightenment, have emancipated themselves from strict orthodoxy. The condition that makes this heresy possible can be found in Kant: it is the division of the public and private spheres.[5] Kant describes an alternative for the bourgeoisie. The nobility, however, according to its decorum, does not rely on the separation of spheres, or if it does, must at least pretend that this separation of spheres does not exist. This makes the relationship between Pittelkow and Waldemar's uncle viable. In order to make sense of Waldemar's wish to legitimate his relationship to Stine, his original motivation must be traced to forces beyond the immediate control of the reflexive mind. Theories of human action that place agencies other than consciousness at their center can help to shed light on this elusive subject.

Our first theoretical source will be the theory of Michel Foucault. Following his primary objective of providing a critique of the way modern societies control their population by sanctioning only certain societal practices, Foucault suggests that the human body above all must be regarded as imprinted by history. Discourse indicates that the relationship between the human body and society ultimately defines normality as a rule of life.[6] "In every society, the body was in the grip of very strict powers, which imposed on it constraints, prohibitions, or obligations."[7] Operating beyond the question of truth and falsity, discourse permits certain statements to be legitimately made, thereby rendering certain types of human conduct possible in the twofold sense of being both comprehensible and acceptable. Ultimately only that which has a place in a discourse is allowed to make sense. Thus, what makes sense is what is socially sanctioned. Meaning therefore is always subject to social change.

The status of the body within the discursive net of socially negotiated meaning changes through history. Foucault distinguishes two basic modes through which discourse has historically acted upon the body: the classical and the modern mode. The classical mode assumes independence of body and soul and therefore subjects the body to direct repression while the soul is addressed independently through representation. The modern mode, on the other hand, constructs a connection between body and soul and so enables discourse to be constitutive to the body. Now considered receptive to discursive strategies, the soul can recruit the body in the interest of society. Physical force becomes obsolete in the face of this far more efficient and economical means of discipline. Foucault writes:

> Discipline "makes" individuals; it is the specific technique of a power that regards individuals both as objects and as instruments of its exercise. It is not a triumphant power, which because of its own excess can pride itself because of its omnipotence; it is a modest suspicious power, which functions as a calculated but permanent economy.[8]

Society's authority is composed of innumerable individual exercises of power that in turn are already consolidated by practices and institutions.[9] Performing a proper function within society therefore results in reproduction of societal power; that is, control. In modern times this control of the body is no longer achieved by direct coercion. It operates at the hidden level of the unconscious. There the agent of social control establishes itself as the memory not only of facts, but also of hidden dispositional behaviors. Its agency is heteronomously activated via a gaze that results in a guilty conscience induced by improper conduct.

What Foucault claims for historical events can be observed in Fontane's fiction as well. Being constructed as a member of an increasingly dysfunctional noble class, Waldemar engages in warfare; one of the few societal domains where nobility is still indispensable. Far from being coarse repression, recruitment for martial activities is achieved by exactly those humble modalities Foucault describes. Waldemar is not pressed into service, but willfully follows the path that the identity-constructive narrative of his class has drawn out for him. Waldemar deliberately becomes a soldier. He goes to war and is severely wounded on the battlefield. He suffers in agony for a long time, but then miraculously recovers. Interestingly enough, he nevertheless enjoys this particular time of his life: "ich war ein Vierteljahr lang der Held und Mittelpunkt der Familie, besonders als die prinzlichen Telegramme kamen, die sich nach mir erkundigten. Ja, Stine, das war meine große Zeit"(301).[10] Despite his misery, Waldemar has not deviated from his class image of a hero. Therefore he receives praise and, since he has internalized the images of happiness that society provides to regulate emotions, enjoys it.

However, his identification with the nobility's narrative of honor and manliness has left deep scars on his body. He is now an invalid. Seen in light of Foucault's theory, this means that his inner attitude, once formed by the discourse of his class, has now been recorded onto his body and taken on a material shape. The body has become a sign within the grammar of society. Constraints and obligations are imposed on the body, establishing the docility-utility relation Foucault calls discipline.[11] "Discipline increases the forces of the body (in economic terms of utility) and diminishes these same forces (in political terms of obedience)."[12]

The interplay of these factors Foucault describes can also be discerned in *Stine*. Waldemar has to discipline himself to maintain his physical health, which requires a mental and emotional regimen. On the surface of Waldemar's body his uncle, the old count, sees his state of mind: "Du bist zerstreut, du hast etwas auf dem Herzen. Und es kann nichts kleines sein, denn ich seh in deinem Gesichte so etwas wie Fieberröte, die mir nicht gefällt"(285).[13] The old count's gaze upon the body evidently serves as an instrument of control. Behaving outside the etiquette of his class is considered unhealthy for Waldemar:

> Laß dir sagen, Waldemar, was du freilich auch ohne mich weißt, da dein Leben an einem seidenen Faden hängt. Also solide! Debauchiere wer kann und mag, aber jeder nach seinen Kräften, und durchschwärmte Nächte sind nicht für jedermann und sicherlich nicht für dich.(285)[14]

After having indicatively stated Waldemar's bodily condition, the uncle switches his speech to the imperative mode. Not without an unmistakable allusion to the anticipated bad conscience of Waldemar does he give his disciplining expert advice: "du bist für immer ins Schuldbuch der Tugend eingeschrieben, oder, um mich deutlicher und doch minder poetisch auszudrücken, du mußt leben wie eine eingemauerte Nonne" (285–6: "You are forever locked into the book of debits of virtue, or, to express myself more clearly and less poetically, you will have to live like an imprisoned nun"). Immediately after this admonition, Waldemar is again reminded of the presence of the gaze: "Und nun sage mir, wenn sichs sagen läßt, woher die roten Flecke?" (286: "And now tell me, if it can be told, where do the red spots come from?"). Waldemar's bodily condition appears as a social condition forged by the interweaving of history, class, and behavior. The body has become the site of social control. In this case the "ledger of virtue," concealed as a seemingly innocent discourse on health, delineates the parameters of societal discourse about acceptable conduct that then regulates behavior and thereby shapes the class to which Waldemar belongs.

In Foucault's theory the power of discourse is omnipresent. In our fictional case the techniques of domination of feudal discourse are indeed omnipresent, but by no means are they omnipotent as well. Otherwise the uncle's admonition would not have been necessary. After the conversation with his uncle, Waldemar still plans to break away from feudal rules of conduct.

At this point we must determine the origin of this resisting counterforce that escapes the power of societal discourse. Obviously, it must be sought where discourse's control is aimed: the body. Here we are confronted with a subversive element within the body over which societal discourse does not exercise control. Foucault's theory for the most part does not account for such accidents. We therefore need to extend our theoretical basis of interpretation to accommodate these types of phenomena that display a body that has not readily fallen prey to discursive strategies. Foucault has received constructive and influential criticism on this problem by Gilles Deleuze.[15] Deleuze faults Foucault's view of the body as a mere recipient of outside influences. He, by contrast, stresses the subversive powers hidden within the body. He conceives of it as a plurality of irreducible dominated and dominating forces which induce conduct. In his view, the body is always the object of competition for domination.[16]

We can observe this competition in the figure of Waldemar. His desire for Stine goes hand in hand with his desire for physical labor. He tells his uncle: "Ich habe nur einfach vor, mit der Alten Welt Schicht zu machen und drüben ein anderes Leben anzufangen" (288: "I simply plan to leave the old world behind and begin a new life abroad"). When Waldemar brings his pastoral phantasms before Stine she keenly notices that this can only be an aesthetic attitude towards life. She replies:

> Wie du dich selbst verkennst. Der Tagelöhnersohn aus eurem Dorfe, der mag so leben und glücklich sein; nicht du. Dadurch, daß man an-

spruchslos sein will, ist mans noch nicht; und es ist ein ander Ding, sich ein armes und einfaches Leben auszumalen oder es wirklich zu führen. (301)[17]

Waldemar's noble upbringing long ago shaped his unconscious. It naively makes him rank physical labor among leisurely activities. The vital complexity that makes up the *Lebenswelt* is reduced to the "human in general," to that which operates along the lines of intrinsic values.[18] Only under this aestheticizing perspective can the difficult relationship between Waldemar and Stine temporarily flourish. Waldemar is clearly unaware of the factors of his conditioning when he earnestly suggests a legitimation of his relationship with Stine. For Deleuze social order and desire are irreconcilable:

> Desire is the system of a-signifying signs with which fluxes of the conscious are produced in a social field. There is no blossoming of desire, wherever it happens . . . which does not call established structures into question. Desire is revolutionary because it always wants more connections and assemblages.[19]

Desire can only be attained in the absence of a subjectivity, since according to Deleuze it is at precisely this point that someone is deprived of the power of saying "I."[20] In its function as a transcending force, desire no longer designates individuals (the results of Foucault's discipline), but rather marks events. These events are constituting processes for emerging assemblages. In this, desire is inherently revolutionary because it produces new relations.[21]

What Stine offers to Waldemar is exactly that niche wherein he can say "I." A glance at Fontane's narrative technique confirms this. Stine's room stands in sharp contrast to Pittelkow's. The reader is not provided with any detailed description of Stine's room; only the most basic furnishings are mentioned. This description evokes an atmosphere of emptiness that provides an unrestrictive space for Waldemar's desire to unfold.[22] During his first unexpected visit to Stine's quarters, Waldemar expresses his intention to help Stine out of her impoverished environment. As the room is flooded with the golden light of the setting sun, he revises his judgment:

> das Kranksein, das eigentlich mein Lebensberuf war, es hat auch seine Vorteile; man kriegt allerlei Nerven in seinen zehn Fingerspitzen und fühlt es den Menschen und Verhältnissen ab, ob sie glücklich sind oder nicht. Und mitunter sogar den Räumen, darin die Menschen

wohnen. Und *hier* lehren mich meine Sinne, Sie können nicht un-
glücklich sein.(263)[23]

Stine's workplace becomes, in Waldemar's transfiguration, the locus
of desire. The social world, with its rules and regulations, is absent
for Waldemar. Since he is not part of the working class, the presence
of Stine's tools do not symbolize a real mode of production to him,
and therefore do not disrupt his idyllic view. The narrator provides
us with a good description of Waldemar's leisurely attitude towards
life. Before his decisive last meeting with Stine, Waldemar visits a
pub near the river: "Dort im Schatten niederzusitzen und zu sinnen
und zu träumen, war das was er liebte" (297: "To sit down there in
the shade, reflecting and dreaming, was what he loved"). Although
nothing escapes his attention, his perspective on modern industrial
life remains merely aesthetic:

> wenn er eine Zeitlang die Qualmwolken aus dem gerade gegenüber-
> gelegenen Borsigschen Eisenwerke hatte hervorquellen und nach der
> Jungfernheide hin abziehen sehen, so gab er seinem Blick mit einem
> mal wieder eine Seitwärtsrichtung und zählte dabei die Brückenpfeiler
> oder die Spreekähne. . . . (298)[24]

The sight of the steel factory means less to him than the spectacle of
the sparrows hopping around his table and picking up the crumbs of
the cake he has especially ordered for them. This is the leisurely lifestyle of the noble class, and along with it come certain expectations
of happiness that cannot be overcome and can only be satisfied
within the framework of this class. Waldemar's knowledge of the
working class does not come from acquaintance but is mediated by
his aesthetic vision of life. From this aesthetic perspective, physical
labor is not associated with inescapable necessity for survival, but
with a means to attain happiness. The phantasm of aestheticized labor forms the first contours of pleasurable images that spring from
the amorphous process of desire. Moreover, it also forms the first
contours of a self-image. In its reference to a pleasureful image, intentionality is constituted, and with its constitution emerges the self-
conscious subject.

According to Deleuze, pleasure always disrupts the inherently
dynamic process of desire:

> But in its most attractive and indispensable forms, it comes rather as
> an interruption in the process of desire as constitution of a field of
> immanence. There is nothing more revealing than the idea of pleas-

ure-discharge; once pleasure is attained, one would have a little calm before desire is rekindled: there is a lot of hatred, or fear, of desire in the cult of pleasure. Pleasure is the attribution of the affect, the affection for a person or subject, it is the only means for a person to "find himself again" in the process of desire which overwhelms him.[25]

This clearly circumscribes Waldemar's position. He is overwhelmed by the various unfoldings of desire and seeks relief in pleasure. He wants to start over and create a new pattern of identity, although his new self-image expresses his desire to remove physical deficiencies that defy a socio-economic foundation for his relationship. The feudal class has already drawn its insurmountable internal demarcation line through the bodies of its members; the demands of Waldemar's peers remain indelible. They are "written into his blood" (301), as he phrases it, and therefore cannot possibly be renounced by himself or anybody else.

Waldemar's desire is that of the romantic, but with the exception that he equates desire and pleasure in an undialectical way, mistakenly ruling out infinity. Aiming at an imaginative world, he makes Stine into a projection screen for his pleasure. The life he does not lead corresponds to the body he does not have. Stine is well aware of the dilemma a legitimation of her relations with Waldemar would constitute, since narcissistic gratification is at the core of Waldemar's desire. After having stated the unrealistic nature of Waldemar's self-image, she points to the dialectic that Waldemar disregards in his proposal: "Und für alles, was dann fehlt, soll das Herz aufkommen. Das kann es nicht, und mit einem Male fühlst du, wie klein und arm ich bin" (301: "And the heart is supposed to provide everything that is still lacking. That it cannot do, and all of a sudden you will start realizing how small and poor I am"). Waldemar is referred back to the framework for happiness that his class provides for him, codified in the ten commandments:

> Der alte Graf ist dagegen und deine Eltern sind dagegen (du sagst es selbst), und ich habe noch nichts zum Glück ausschlagen sehen, worauf von Anfang an kein Segen lag. Es ist gegen das vierte Gebot, und wer dagegen handelt, der hat keine ruhige Stunde mehr, und das Unglück zieht ihm nach. (302)[26]

The power of the class is itself grounded in transcendence, a legitimating narrative too powerful to question. Therefore, Stine's firm rejection of Waldemar's proposal appears consistent within the logic of the theologically legitimatized social order that now appears as a psychological one as well. Only the fulfillment of desire guarantees temporary happiness.

For Waldemar the presumed state of ultimate and infinite happiness of pleasure fused with nature is unattainable. For Waldemar, suicide is the only way out of this predicament. Through his physical destruction he renounces the societal restraints of his class.[27] Nobility, however, uses his suicide to ceremonially reproduce its identity at Waldemar's funeral. The aristocratic mourning ritual at the funeral service is characterized by perfect control of the nobles' bodies:

> In Front erblickte man den alten Grafen, Waldemars Vater, in grauem Toupet und Johanniterkreuz, neben ihm in tiefer und soignierter Trauer die Stiefmutter des Toten, . . . die, was geschehen war vom Standpunkt des "Affront" aus ansah und mit Hilfe dieser Anschauung über die vorschriftsmäßige Trauer mit beinah mehr als standesgemäßer Würde hinwegkam . . . [Graf Konstantins] Haltung war untadelig und gleichfalls von bemerkenswerter Gefaßtheit, ohne die der Mutter ganz erreichen zu können. (310)[28]

In response to Stine's outcry the countess casts a disapproving gaze toward the pillar, behind which Stine had concealed herself during the funeral service.

With tragic irony, Waldemar's body functions in the end as an act of social reproduction. It is an event with provisions in the grammar of societal discourse; taking Stine on as a mistress would have been one too, but a marriage with her would not. Aristocratic power structures do not allow for such subversive "stories outside of history."[29] This constellation formed the scandal that delayed the publication of *Stine*.

Notes

[1] For a thorough account of the novella in Poetic Realism see Walter Silz, *Realism and Reality: Studies in the German Novelle of Poetic Realism* (Chapel Hill: U of North Carolina P, 1965). See also Josef Kunz's collection of scholarly essays on the novella: *Novelle* (Darmstadt: Wissenschaftliche Buchgesellschaft, 1973). The epistemological implications of the novelistic style of writing are examined in Ulf Eisele's "Empirischer Realismus: Die epistemologische Problematik einer literarischen Konzeption," in *Bürgerlicher Realismus: Grundlagen und Interpretationen*, ed. Klaus-Detlef Müller (Königstein: Athenäum, 1981), 74–97.

[2] Paul Heyse, et al., eds. *Deutscher Novellenschatz*, vol. 1 (Munich: Oldenburg, n.d.), xiv.

[3] August Wilhelm Schlegel, *Kritische Schriften und Briefe*, ed. Edgar Lohner (Stuttgart: Kohlhammer, 1965), 218.

[4] It is rather the female character of Pittelkow who comes closest to meeting the standards of a traditional male hero.

[5] Immanuel Kant, "Beantwortung der Frage; Was ist Aufklärung?" in: *Kants Gesammelte Schriften*, vol. 8, ed. Königliche Preußische Akademie der Wissenschaften (Berlin: de Gruyter, 1923), 33–42.

[6] Mark Philip. "Michael Foucault" in Quentin Skinner, ed., *The Return of Grand Theory in the Human Sciences* (Cambridge: Cambridge UP, 1985), 67.

[7] Michel Foucault, *Discipline and Punish*, quoted in *The Foucault Reader*, ed. Paul Rabinow (New York: Pantheon, 1984), 180. The page numbers provided with quotations from Foucault below also refer to this text.

[8] Foucault, 188.

[9] Philip, 76.

[10] English translation: "For a quarter of a year I was the hero and center of the family, especially when the prince's telegrams arrived that inquired about me. Yes, Stine, that was my great time." (Translations of *Stine* in this article are provided by M. Doebeling.) All page numbers in parentheses in the text refer to *Theodor Fontane: Sämtliche Werke*, vol. 3 (Munich: Nymphenburger Verlagsbuchhandlung, 1959).

[11] Foucault, 180–181.

[12] Foucault, 182.

[13] English translation: "You are absent-minded, you want to say something. And it cannot be anything minor, because in your face I see something like a feverish redness that I do not like."

[14] English translation: "Let it be said to you, Waldemar, what I am sure you know also for yourself, since your life is suspended on a silk thread. So, nose to the grindstone! Debauchery is for others; everyone according to his particular strengths, and nights without end are not for everyone, and certainly not for you."

[15] Scott Lash, *Sociology of Postmodernism* (London: Routledge, 1990), 61, 65.

[16] Lash, 64.

[17] English translation: "How you deceive yourself. The day laborer from your village may live in such a way and be happy; not you. Just by wanting

to be without ambition one does not automatically become so. And to imagine a poor and simple life is quite another thing than to lead one."

[18] Erich Langendorf, *Zur Entstehung des bürgerlichen Familienglücks: Exemplarische Studien anhand literarischer Texte* (Frankfurt am Main: Peter Lang, 1983), 197.

[19] Gilles Deleuze and Clair Parnet, *Dialogues* (London: Athlone, 1987), 78–79. Deleuze's materialistic slant is a distinct counterpoint to Foucault's conception of the body as a discursive construct. For our interpretive purposes, however, this qualitative difference can be left aside.

[20] Deleuze, 89.

[21] Deleuze, 96.

[22] See the enlightening comparative study of Fontane's description of the character's inner life by Paul Wessels: "Schein und Anstand: Zu Fontanes Roman *Stine*," in *Formen Realistischer Erzählkunst: Festschrift für Charlotte Jolles,* ed. Jörg Thunecke and Eda Sagarra (Nottingham: Sherwood, 1979), 491–493.

[23] English translation: "Being sick, which was actually the profession of my life, also has its advantages. One grows numerous nerves in ones fingertips and can sense from people and their conditions whether or not they are happy. And sometimes one can even feel it from the rooms in which these people live. And here my senses teach me that you cannot be unhappy."

[24] English translation: "after he had seen the steam clouds coming from the Borsig iron factory, which was straight across from him, and after he had watched them drift off toward the Jungfernheide, he again turned his head to the side counting the pillars of the bridge or the barges on the Spree."

[25] Deleuze, 99–100.

[26] English translation: "The old duke is against it, and your parents are against it (you say it yourself), and I have not seen anything turn out happily that was not blessed from the start. It is against the fourth commandment, and whoever acts against it will never have a peaceful hour again; and bad luck will follow him."

[27] Claudia Liebrand, *Das Ich und die anderen: Fontane's Figuren und ihre Selbstbilder* (Freiburg: Rombach, 1990), 224n.

[28] English translation: "In front one saw the old duke, Waldemar's father, in a grey toupet and cross of the Johanniters. Next to him, in deep and careful mourning, the stepmother of the dead man. . . . She perceived what had happened from the standpoint of an 'affront.' This perception in turn helped her to get over the prescribed period of mourning with almost

more than the dignity appropriate to her station . . . Duke Konstantin's attitude was beyond reproach, and he simultaneously displayed a remarkable resoluteness, without, however, being able to match that of the mother."

[29] See footnote 3.

SARA SHOSTAK
University of California, Los Angeles

The Trauma of Separation:
Public and Private Realms in *Effi Briest*

IN THIS ARTICLE, I EXAMINE THE SOCIALLY constructed dichotomy between public and private realms and its impact on the aristocratic German family of the late eighteenth century. My examination focuses on the family as represented in *Effi Briest*, the most famous novel of Theodor Fontane, written in 1895. Though rarely acknowledged in the literature of this time, the political nature of the family in its role as a socializing institution figures prominently in *Effi Briest*. I will argue that the myth of the family as an apolitical entity was dependent upon an obfuscating ideological framework that maintained that there was a "natural" or at least "necessary" opposition between public and private spheres. This ideological system has been deconstructed and criticized extensively by contemporary feminist scholarship.[1] The demystification of the private realm allows for the examination of those activities which, long masked as "private," "personal," and "intimate" should be considered as public and political: sexuality, marriage, child-rearing. Furthermore, such an examination makes increasingly clear the impact of political contingencies and public responsibilities on familial relationships. The trauma of separation results from internal divisions within individuals and ruptures between individuals wrought by the repressive demands of society.[2]

A demarcation between the public and the private sphere, and the relegation of the family to the private sphere have been integral to conceptions of familial relationships since the division between the *polis* and the *oikos* articulated by Aristotle.[3] The public world has been conceived of as the place for men, "responsible, rational persons who share fully in both private life and the life of the polis and its integral elements or citizens . . . . "[4] Concurrently, the private realm was the world for women, "those who (for whatever reason) are not fully rational and who can only share in the limited goodness appropriate to those spheres."[5] Woman was believed to be capable of participation only in the private realm of the home; she could never experience the "good" of public life. Man, however, as both a member of the family and of the state, could hold status as both a private and a public person. In this intellectual tradition, the public sphere was envisioned as the realm of politics, "the realm of public power, the sphere of justice, and systems of law";[6] while the private sphere was supposedly devoid of such politics, "a private realm of feeling and sentiment, or moral suasion, not subject to laws and not judged by rational standards."[7] This dichotomy, as it has been maintained throughout the centuries, has obscured the struggles for, with, and against socially legitimated power that surround and permeate the family as a political institution that both reflects and sustains the often coercive social relations of society.

In the nineteenth century, the Aristotelian intellectual tradition was carried forward by G. W. F. Hegel, among others, who articulated the distinction between public and private realms as a "natural" phenomenon structured according to the intellectual and ethical potentials of man and woman. In Hegelian philosophy, as in the earlier philosophy of Rousseau, the nature of each gender is assumed to originate in the physical differences between the sexes.[8] These differences determine the realms in which they are each to live:

> Therefore, the exclusion of woman from the economic and political life in the industrial capitalist world is considered to be a necessary result of the natural biological hierarchical division between the sexes.[9]

Man is powerful and active, capable of self-consciousness and therefore:

> has his actual substantive life in the state, in learning . . . as well as in labour and struggle with the external world so that it is only out of his redemption that he fights his way to self-subsistent unity with himself.[10]

In contrast, woman, as she is passive and subjective, is incapable of full self-consciousness and is thus barred from full participation as a citizen of the state. Her world is that of the family, wherein lies her substantive destiny and her ethical value. Woman's life is one which "has not yet attained its full actualization" and is governed by "the law of inward life . . . as a law opposed to public law, the law of the land."[11] Thus, the private realm is separated from the public realm by the supposedly unchangeable and unquestionable reality of the differences between the sexes and the capacities specific to each:[12]

> A core of nature which resists examination, a relationship excluded from the social in the analysis . . . the "obligatory social relationship between 'man' and 'woman.'"[13]

In contrast to the traditional Aristotelian/Hegelian presentation of gender as a natural phenomenon, uninfluenced, at least *expressis verbis*, by society or politics, I adopt as my point of departure an understanding of gender as the social construction and organization of socially and politically relevant categories as they are arrived at primarily but not exclusively from biological sexual differences. Similarly, I propose that the division between public and private realms represents the construction and organization of social reality and social space. Politics, once held to be present solely in the public realm, clearly permeates the construction of all elements of social life:

> It is no longer possible to maintain that there are two spheres of social reality: the private sphere of the family, sexuality, and affectivity, and the public sphere of work and productivity.[14]

The private realm is constructed under the directives of public forces, and even in its most intimate moments is directed toward a public agenda and a public audience.[15] Both the social relations of the family and the masks constructed for them serve specific social goals and political interests: "The language of boundaries masks power . . . [boundaries] are a means of wielding power, shielding power and shielding from power . . . ."[16] The social order, in turn, is upheld through the consent of those positioned within it, through violence to the body or the spirit, or, most frequently, through a complex combination of both. To the extent that individuals internalize the dominant moral framework and social order of their society, the necessity of physically coercing them towards those attitudes and behaviors that perpetuate the social structure decreases. Therefore:

> the relations of individuals to authority . . . give rise in turn to a lasting collaboration of social institutions in producing and consolidating the character types which respond to the relationship.[17]

The existence of the dominant social order depends upon particular institutions, especially the family, to:

> see to it that the kind of human character emerges which social life requires and gives this human being in great measure the indispensable adaptability for a specific authority-oriented conduct.[18]

The family is an agent that is charged with the socialization of the young, and it is responsible for perpetuating the dominant socio-cultural paradigm by instilling it in each successive generation:

> As an agent of society, it served especially the task of that difficult mediation through which, in spite of the illusion of freedom, strict conformity with societally necessary requirements was brought about.[19]

Essential to socialization is the process of internalization, the process by which "the child takes on the significant others [the socializer's] roles and attitudes . . . and makes them his [her] own."[20]

However, no socialization is ever entirely complete.[21] Therefore, individuals may find themselves internally divided against themselves. The "voice of society," the part of their psyche that has been socialized, battles against voices of rebellion coming from those parts of the psyche that have not been entirely indoctrinated into the dominant paradigm.[22] That is to say, the role-identified or role-set parts of an individual's psyche might be separated from and may even stand in conflict with one's deeper feelings and desires. The successful socialization of a child is indicated by a total acceptance of the inevitability of given social roles and realities. This inevitability, if even questioned at all, has typically been justified in terms of divine will, natural law, utilitarianism, or some other legitimating belief system. Thus, individuals are simultaneously encouraged and coerced to abandon any sense of themselves as distinct from the social roles and expectations that are internalized during socialization.

With these observations in mind, we now turn to the character of Effi Briest, who is introduced to the reader when interacting with her mother in their garden of Hohen-Cremmen, in the private realm of the aristocratic home. As has been stated in previous Fontane research, from the very beginning, Effi is portrayed as a wild, impetuous child: "her every movement showed a combination of pertness and grace, while her laughing brown eyes gave evidence of a considerable native wit, high spirits and kindness of heart."[23] The first words she speaks in the novel are a response to her mother's teasing that she should have been a trapeze artist. Immediately, Effi exposes a nascent knowledge of Frau von Briest's role as a socializing agent: "Perhaps I should, Mama. But if so, whose fault would it be? Where do I get it from? Not anyone but yourself."[24] While Effi makes it clear that she knows that Frau von Briest has not properly socialized her as a young woman — "And then why do you put me into this sort of boy's smock? . . . Why don't you make me into a lady?"[25] — this is obviously to her liking. Effi seems far more comfortable with her unusual mannerisms than her mother is: "Don't be so wild, Effi, and so impulsive. It always worries me when I see you like this."[26] According to Horkheimer, it is within the family that "the child's self will is to be broken, and the innate desire for the free development of his [her] drives and potentialities is to be replaced by an internalized compulsion towards the unconditional fulfillment of duty."[27] Effi, however, is sent forth from her childhood with her spirits and her will at least partially intact, conscious of her duties, but not entirely committed to their fulfillment, that is to say, not even close to being entirely socialized.

Adults who take on the role of parents are compelled by internalized roles and expectations. They take on a great burden in their roles as socializing agents, as Kate Millet has explained:

> the chief contribution of the family in patriarchy is the socialization of the young largely through example and the admonition of their parents into the patriarchal ideology's prescribed attitudes towards role, temperament and status.[28]

However, this burden may conflict with the parents' love for their children. Parents are held responsible for constructing every aspect of a child's value system and making sure that it conforms to the dominant social mores. This cultivation of values and preferences knows no bounds and includes even that which was once considered to be the most "governed by nature": for example, an extensive body of literature defines human sexuality as "in fact, completely constructed in culture according to the political aims of the society's dominant class, in order to insure its survival and ideological hegemony."[29] In order to insure proper socialization, the parents may engage a host of pedagogical, disciplinary, and also more routine, daily techniques. The politics of the family impacts all of the relationships within it, as Jane Flax has written: "What is presented ideologically as a private relationship of love is really a social [public] relationship of power."[30]

From the beginning, Frau von Briest is represented as divided against herself, internally separated by her love for Effi and her social role as Effi's mother. This produces a fundamental split in Frau von Briest's identity, one which we later see in Effi as well. To apply Peter L. Berger's formulation, to the extent that Luise and Effi are "well-socialized," their roles

> are not only external patterns of conduct, but are internalized within the consciousness . . . and constitute an essential element of these individuals' subjective identities.[31]

At different moments Frau von Briest may identify more or less with her role as Effi's socializer. When telling Effi of Baron von Innstetten's proposal of marriage, Frau von Briest's voice is completely subsumed by the voice of society:

> It's true that he's older than you, which all things considered is an advantage, and he's a man of character and he's well bred and he has a good situation, and if you don't say no, which I can hardly imagine my clever Effi doing, then you'll have gone as far by the age of twenty as others have at forty. You'll go much further than your mother.[32]

She speaks only of those considerations important to the social order rather than acknowledging the feelings of her young daughter. It is only after Effi and Innstetten are already engaged that Frau von Briest is able to ask Effi about her personal beliefs and feelings about marriage. Effi confides in her mother at this time that she has little interest in "what people call a model marriage." Equality is what is truly important to Effi. Barring the possibility of equality, she values love and tenderness. Though Effi resists her father's belief that love "is just a lot of claptrap," she acknowledges the possibility that she may have to settle for

> wealth, and a lovely big house . . . one where Prince Frederick Karl would come shooting for elk . . . or where the old Kaiser would drive up and have a gracious word for all the ladies.[33]

That is to say, if the emotions and relationships of the private realm are not realizable, Effi at least desires that her private space, her home, will provide her with access, however imaginary, to the public realm. "What I can't stand is boredom," Effi proclaims.[34] This statement ominously foreshadows the dissatisfaction Effi is to experience in her isolating marriage, and this dissatisfaction, in part, leads her outside to her affair with Crampas. Her marriage to Innstetten is a "marriage for reason"[35] from its inception, and later attempts to wrap the arrangement in a private rhetoric of love and romance fail miserably.

Though the von Briests are conscious both of their daughter's still-unbroken spirit and the possibility that Innstetten will be incapable of meeting the needs of their exceptional child, they discuss this only after Effi and Innstetten are already married and on their honeymoon. Frau von Briest believes that Effi talks about love only because she has been enchanted by the romantic rhetoric of the books she has read and the other girls with whom she talks:

> Although she's lively and high spirited and almost passionate, or perhaps because she is all of these things, she's not the sort of girl who is really set on love, at least not what is properly called love. . . . To my mind and according to what she herself says, too, there are two things: love of pleasure and love of ambition.[36]

While Innstetten will be able to satisfy Effi's love of ambition, her mother worries, "But that's only half the story. Her vanity will be satisfied but will her love of fun, her love of adventure?"[37] Old von Briest concerns himself not with the personal qualities of his daughter but rather with the societally produced role which she now inhabits. Her private self is to be subjugated to her public role, he reasons, as he reminds Luise that "Effi's our daughter but ever since 3rd October she's been Baroness Innstetten."[38] Not at all eased by this truth, Frau von Briest warns him that "It's only when a child has fallen into the stream that the council puts up a fence to stop it."[39] Luise von Briest knows that "the wife loses her freedom" in marriage, confined and isolated in the private realm. As Effi has told her friends in the story of her mother's love for Innstetten and her marriage to von Briest: "Well, what's happened was bound to happen, just as it always does."[40]

All of the von Briests' fears are realized when they receive news from Innstetten of Effi's affair with Crampas. However, they are the first to take on the voice of society and to assume the role of socializing agents that they may have neglected during Effi's childhood. Rather than acknowledge the social circumstances that contributed to Effi's "failure" and examine the "rightness" of the marriage that they arranged for her, the von Briests unequivocally blame Effi and cast her out as demanded by the dominant moral framework of society:

> You'll be excluded from the society in which you've been moving up till now. And the saddest thing for us is that you will be excluded from our house too.[41]

As the socializing agents responsible for Effi as a social being, her parents cannot risk even the appearance of complicity in her societally-condemned behavior:

> Not because we are particularly worldly and would look upon it as completely unbearable to have to say good-bye to so-called society . . . but simply because we want to make our position plain and show the whole world that we condemn . . . the actions of our only daughter, the daughter whom we loved so dearly. . . .[42]

It is only when they receive news of Effi's illness from Doctor Rummschüttel that the von Briests' love for their daughter overrides the obligations they feel towards society. Even at this point Luise is torn between her official role and her heartfelt love:

> I love her as much as you do, perhaps more . . . But we've not been sent into this world to be weak and forbearing and show respect for all that's against the laws of God and man and that society condemns and, for the moment at any rate, rightly condemns.[43]

Luise feels that to accept Effi back into their home would be to brush aside the claims of society's current moral code, the code into which she has been indoctrinated and feels responsible for instilling in her daughter. She makes no distinction between that which is ordained by God and that which is constructed by man and society. All are one and the same to her; society's moral order is a manifestation of God's will. She demonstrates what Berger has defined as "bad faith":

> One way of defining bad faith is to say that it replaces choice with fictitious necessity. In other words, the individual, who in fact has a choice between different courses of action, posits one of these courses as necessary . . . faced with a choice of acting or not acting within a certain role program, [she] denies this choice on the basis of [her] identification with the role in question.[44]

This bad faith provides the roles, institutions and expectations of society with a veneer of inevitability, thus insuring their legitimation.

Old Briest, however, finally convinces Luise that "parents' love for their children" is the one thing more important than the laws of society, and reminds her that "if society wants to it can turn a blind eye."[45] While he respects the laws of God, Herr von Briest continues to demonstrate his lack of concern for his obligations to the dictates of the dominant moral order. He tells Luise "you can quote the catechism as much as you like, but don't quote society!"[46] Herr von Briest seems acutely conscious of the socially constructed and therefore temporal nature of society's morality and refuses to equate it with divine decree. Thus, for Herr von Briest, the social constructions of society are less irrevocably legitimate and far less compelling.

However, once Effi has returned to Hohen-Cremmen, her parents are diligent in their once somewhat neglected role as socializing agents. Having accepted their fallen daughter back into their home, it is now their duty to organize the understanding of her "failure" according to Protestant conceptions. As Horkheimer has written:

> For the formation of the authority oriented character it is especially decisive that the children should learn . . . not to trace every failure back to its social causes but to remain at the level of the individual and to hypostasize the failure in religious terms as sin or in naturalistic terms as deficient natural endowment.[47]

The actions of the von Briests insure that Effi will not look outward to society or her marriage in her efforts to understand her misfortune but will rather blame herself. Even when Effi is lying on her death bed, Luise admonishes her for hating Innstetten with words of condemnation: "In a way, forgive me, Effi dear, if I say this to you and at such a moment, you really brought your sorrow, yours and his, on yourself."[48] Again, false boundaries conceptualized between the public and private realms mask the impact of public mores and social expectations on the supposedly private actions of individuals and make it impossible for them to attribute their "failings" to external social factors.

After Effi's death, Luise contemplates her possible responsibility for the course of her daughter's life: "not a day goes by, since that poor child was buried there, without such questions occurring to me. . . . Whether we're not perhaps to blame."[49] When reflecting upon her role in Effi's demise, Luise is brought to acknowledge the power she had as a socializing force in Effi's life. One of the questions that plagues her is: "Whether we ought not to have brought her up differently. . . . "[50] Frau von Briest, unlike her husband, allows herself questions that she did not allow Effi regarding the appropriateness of Effi's marriage to Innstetten: "Whether perhaps she wasn't too young?"[51] However, while it is significant that Luise is at least considering the possibility that there was more to Effi's demise than her moral failure, she still has not gone so far as to question the "rightness" of society's morals and expectations. She, like Effi, is locked within a worldview that places responsibility for all "failure" on individual human action. Guilt is internalized and entirely privatized, rather than accessible and alterable in the public realm of society. Neither Luise nor Effi can look beyond individuals and their private actions to question the public realm of a society that demands certain role-oriented behaviors and punishes others.

Innstetten is consistent in his lack of tenderness and his absence from their life and bedroom: his energy, efforts and attention are entirely outwardly, publicly directed. When Effi accuses him of having sublimated his erotic nature in order to be a more "respectable" politician: "You're really . . . an amorous man, born under Venus. . . . Only you won't show it . . . you think that it won't do and will spoil your career," Innstetten can hardly disagree.[52] Innstetten is totally subsumed by his public role; he has no identity as a private individual.

As a public figure striving for success in the openly public world of politics, Innstetten has allowed himself to be totally controlled by the demands of that world. He is unable to be a private being or have intimate relationships except when such "intimacy" is oriented towards a public audience. Innstetten's total orientation towards the framework of public values is first criticized by Effi upon receipt of his letters during their courtship: "Well, he always starts off with a dash but most of it I could have pinned up in the local bailiff's office, where all the governor's ordinances are displayed."[53] After Effi has been frightened by the ghost and requests that he never again leave her alone in the house, Innstetten reprimands her by reminding her: "I have no choice, I'm an official, I can't just say to the Prince of Princes 'Your Excellency, I can't come, my wife feels lonely.' . . . "[54] Again ignoring Effi's fears of the ghost, Innstetten refuses to move the family out of the house although it terrifies her, stating:

I can't have people in the town saying: Governor Innstetten is selling his house because his wife saw the ghost beside her bed. . . . It would be fatal, Effi. I should never recover from the ridicule.[55]

Effi is hurt by Innstetten's disregard for her fears, a factor that later plays into her affair with Major Crampas: "all you can say to me is that you don't feel like making yourself ridiculous in the eyes of the Prince or the town. That's no consolation."[56] Innstetten refuses to do any of the things that Effi suggests might relieve her fear of the ghost, and insists upon her virtual confinement in the house that inspires her fears.

Ironically, it is only outside of the supposedly private realm Effi shares with her husband that she experiences any sort of intimacy. Effi's affair with Crampas is a defiant rebellion against the rules, morals, roles, and constraints of society, and thus, against Innstetten. Effi will not be bored and will no longer allow herself to be isolated in the home. She constructs an intimate realm in the public world that was denied to her by Innstetten's constant preoccupation with society. Crampas structures much of his seduction of Effi around contradicting Innstetten, the "educator":

Life wouldn't be worth living if things always had to be just as they happen to be. The best of life goes beyond consideration of that sort. Learn how to enjoy it![57]

At first Effi fears the course taken by her relationship with Crampas and prays that God will build a wall around her. However, the wall which goes up surrounds both Effi and Crampas. When Innstetten discovers Effi's adulterous relationship and it becomes a part of his reality, he, of course, brings it into the public domain.

As has been pointed out in previous Fontane scholarship, Innstetten's public exposure of Effi's adultery necessitates, in his world view, a public resolution of this transgression.[58] Innstetten is unable to conceive of the affair as a private matter: Effi has betrayed not only her husband and her vows to him, but has transgressed against all of society's values by violating its moral order. Innstetten's identity is based, in part, upon his colleagues' perception of him as one who upholds "firmness and loyalty" to Protestantism and Prussia and stands as a bulwark against the "rebellion, impudence, and lack of discipline" that characterize what Innstetten calls "these difficult times" under Bismarck.[59] It is because of his loyalty to society that Innstetten feels that he must pursue the duel:

it's got to be done nevertheless. . . . We're not isolated persons, we belong to a whole society and we have constantly to consider that society, we're completely dependent on it.[60]

The source of Innstetten's self-definition as a political, and hence public, man is his belief that:

it's no good transgressing them [the rules and standards of society], society will despise us and finally we will despise ourselves and not be able to bear it and blow our brains out. . . .[61]

His very identity depends upon the existence of a clearly delineated public sphere. Therefore, he is incapable of anything but "idolatry" before the social structure and sacrifices Effi and Crampas to his worship of the same status quo that also defines their roles.

Innstetten's reverence for the normative values of society and his knowledge that much of the role of a parent is to teach, that is, to socialize, inform his decision to make it impossible for Effi to be an influence upon her daughter. He completely alienates Annie from Effi and conditions Annie to be as incapable of intimacy as he is. During their brief visit, Annie's responses to Effi's eagerness to engage her in conversation are cold and mechanical, appropriate to a conversation with a stranger on the street, rather than with one's mother. Effi is furious with Innstetten's impeccable socialization of the child:

He taught the child that; he always was a schoolmaster. . . . He was always thinking of his career and nothing more. Honour, honour, honour. . . .[62]

Effi, in her infidelity, defines herself as an inappropriate socializing agent for Annie, and accordingly, Innstetten takes over the socialization of the child himself and trains the child to be on her guard against her mother. If, as Hegel believed, the family is the ethical root of the state, it is imperative that Effi's "untamed" influence not reach Annie's developing mind and morality.

Effi, still even at the end of the novel, represents a wild, unsocialized spirit seeking freedom from the narrow and restrictive definitions of the female gender and from the private realm in which women of aristocratic families were isolated. The failure of her parents to "tame" Effi's spirit, to properly socialize her, allowed for her continued resistance against established social relations, a resistance which she continued until she died. On various occasions Effi is "redirected" by her parents, her friends and her husband. In Effi's marriage to Innstetten, every aspect of her life is permeated with the public values and expectations that she might have hoped to escape. Because of her rebellion against these values and expectations, she is ultimately denied a relationship with her daughter, which represents punishment for her deviance from the dictates of a rigidly moralistic and repressive society.

In this way, Effi's story is as much about the power of society in overcoming resistance to its moral authority as it is about resistance itself. All of Effi's relationships are impacted by the political repercussions of her "improper" ways of thinking about and interacting with her culture. There is no distinction between the public and private spheres in her life, as the dictates of the political public order structure every aspect of what could be taken to be private. From the moment of her birth, Effi is faced with institutions with the specifically political goal of socializing her into a "proper" young woman. Effi's parents, who genuinely adore their daughter, abandon her for a time in the name of their socio-political obligations. Innstetten, her husband, brings into their home every general political concern that exists in his world of national politics and brings out to the public realm every personal concern. Even her relationship with her daughter is eventually taken from her by a vengeful society, as embodied in the person of Innstetten. Effi's fate illuminates the pervasiveness of political forces within the institutions charged with the formation of personal identities and warns that the ideological hegemony of the ruling class operates not only within institutions but within the minds of individuals. To heal the trauma of separation between public and private realms would be to redefine the ways in which self and society are understood and enacted.

Notes

1 See Jeanne Boydston, *Home and Work: Housework, Wages, and the Ideology of Labor in the Early Republic* (New York: Oxford UP, 1990); Catharine MacKinnon, *Toward a Feminist Theory of the State* (Cambridge, MA: Harvard UP, 1989); Jennifer Nedelsky, "Laws, Boundaries and the Bounded Self" *Representations* 30 (1990); Susan Moller Okin, *Justice, Gender and the Family* (New York: Basic Books, 1989); Christine Stansell, *City of Women: Sex and Class in New York, 1787–1869* (New York: Knopf,

1986); Elizabeth Taub and Nadine Schneider, "Women's Subordination and the Role of Law" in *The Politics of Law: A Progressive Critique,* David Kairys, ed. (New York: Pantheon Books, 1990). Note also that one of the mottos of the American women's movement of the 1970s was "the personal is political."

[2] My analysis has been informed by Jürgen Habermas's discussion of the colonization of the "lifeworld" by the "systems" that destroy its potential for reproduction through normatively based communicative action and consensus building. See Jürgen Habermas, *The Theory of Communicative Action,* trans. Thomas McCarthy (Boston: Beacon Press, 1987). As has been pointed out before, however, Habermas fails to account for the power inconsistencies within the family and its political role as an agent of socialization in his analysis. See Nancy Fraser, *Unruly Practices: Power, Discourse and Gender in Contemporary Social Theory* (Minneapolis: U of Minnesota P, 1989).

[3] Susan G. Bell, ed., *Women from the Greeks to the Middle Ages* (Stanford: Stanford UP, 1975).

[4] Jean Bethke Elshtain, "Aristotle, the Public-Private Split and the Case of the Suffragists," in *The Family in Political Thought,* ed. Jean Bethke Elshtain (Amherst: U of Massachusetts P, 1982), 53.

[5] Ibid, 54.

[6] Ibid, 56.

[7] Ibid, 56.

[8] Cf. Jean Jacques Rousseau, *Emile,* trans. Barbara Foxley (New York: Dutton, 1974).

[9] Joan B. Landes, "Hegel's Conception of the Family," in *The Family in Political Thought,* ed. Jean Bethke Elshtain (Amherst: U of Massachusetts P, 1982), 156.

[10] G. W. F. Hegel, *The Philosophy of Right,* trans. T. M. Knox (London: Oxford UP, 1952), 114.

[11] Ibid, 114–15.

[12] Rousseau, *Emile.*

[13] Teresa DeLauretis, *Technologies of Gender* (Bloomington: U of Indiana P, 1987), 18. In the United States, the same ideology was developed, and then challenged, within the "social sciences." See Rosalind Rosenberg, *Beyond Separate Spheres: The Intellectual Roots of Modern Feminism* (New Haven: Yale UP, 1982).

[14] DeLauretis, 5.

[15] Jürgen Habermas, *The Structural Transformation of the Public Sphere* (Cambridge: MIT Press, 1989) 43–51.

[16] Jennifer Nedelsky, "Laws, Boundaries and the Bounded Self," *Representations* 30 (1990), 177.

[17] Max Horkheimer, *Critical Theory* (New York: Herder and Herder Press, 1972), 97.

[18] Ibid, 98.

[19] Habermas, 47.

[20] Peter Berger and Thomas Luckmann, *The Social Construction of Reality* (New York: Doubleday, 1966), 131.

[21] Ibid, 147.

[22] Ibid, 170–171.

[23] Theodor Fontane, *Effi Briest*, trans. Douglas Parmee (London: Penguin, 1967). All translations from the novel are from this edition.

[24] Ibid, 16.

[25] Ibid, 16.

[26] Ibid, 16.

[27] Horkheimer, 99.

[28] Kate Millet, *Sexual Politics* (New York: Ballantine, 1970), 48.

[29] Joan Scott, *Gender and the Politics of History* (New York: Columbia UP, 1988), 24. See also Luce Irigaray, *The Sex Which is Not One*, trans. Catherine Porter with Carolyn Burke (Ithaca, NY: Cornell UP, 1985).

[30] Jane Flax, "The Family in Contemporary Feminist Thought: A Critical Overview," in *The Family in Political Thought*, ed. Jean Bethke Elshtain (Amherst: U of Massachusetts P, 1982), 266.

[31] Peter L. Berger, *The Sacred Canopy: Elements of a Sociological Theory of Religion* (New York: Doubleday, 1966), 93.

[32] Fontane, *Effi Briest*, 17. German original: "Er ist freilich älter als du, was in allem ein Glück ist, dazu ein Mann von Charakter, von Stellung und guten Sitten, und wenn du nicht nein sagst, was ich von meiner klugen Effi kaum denken kann, so stehst du mit zwanzig Jahren da, wo andere mit vierzig stehen. Du wirst deine Mama weit überholen." *Theodor Fontane, Werke*, vol. 2, edited by Walter Keitel (Munich: Carl Hanser Verlag), 17. All German original quotes of passages from *Effi Briest* are taken from this edition and cited with page number.

[33] Ibid, 36. German original: ". . . nun, dann bin ich für Reichtum und ein vornehmes Haus, . . . wo Prinz Friedrich Karl zur Jagd kommt, auf

Elchwild oder Auerhahn, oder wo der alte Kaiser vorfährt und für jede Dame, . . . ein gnädiges Wort hat" (30–31).

[34] Ibid, 37.

[35] Habermas, 47.

[36] Fontane, *Effi Briest,* 43. German original: ". . . So geweckt und temperamentvoll und beinahe leidenschaftlich sie ist, oder vielleicht auch weil sie es ist, sie gehört nicht zu denen, die so recht eigentlich auf Liebe gestellt sind, wenigstens nicht auf das, was den Namen ehrlich verdient. . . . Sie hat nach meinem und auch nach ihrem eigenen Zeugnis zweierlei: Vergnügungssucht und Ehrgeiz" (37–38).

[37] Ibid, 43.

[38] Ibid, 45.

[39] Ibid, 45.

[40] Ibid, 19.

[41] Ibid, 243. German original: "Die Welt, in der du gelebt hast, wird dir verschlossen sein. Und was das Traurigste für uns und für Dich ist . . . — auch das elterliche Haus wird Dir verschlossen sein" (241–42).

[42] Ibid, 243. German original: "Nicht weil wir zu sehr an der Welt hingen und ein Abschiednehmen von dem, was sich 'Gesellschaft' nennt, uns als etwas unbedingt Unerträgliches erschiene, . . . sondern einfach, weil wir Farbe bekennen und vor aller Welt, . . . unsere Verurteilung Deines Tuns, des Tuns unseres einzigen und von uns so geliebten Kindes, aussprechen wollen . . . ." (242).

[43] Ibid, 251. German original: ". . . ich liebe sie so wie du, vielleicht noch mehr, jeder hat seine Art. Aber man lebt doch nicht bloß in der Welt, um schwach und zärtlich zu sein und alles mit Nachsicht zu behandeln, was gegen Gesetz und Gebot ist und was die Menschen verurteilen und, vorläufig wenigstens, auch noch — mit Recht verurteilen" (263).

[44] Berger, 93.

[45] Fontane, *Effi Briest,* 251.

[46] Ibid, 251.

[47] Horkheimer, 108.

[48] Fontane, *Effi Briest,* 265.

[49] Ibid, 267.

[50] Ibid, 267.

[51] Ibid, 267.

[52] Fontane, *Effi Briest,* 116.

[53] Ibid, 37.

[54] Ibid, 77.

[55] Ibid, 79. German original: "Ich kann hier in der Stadt die Leute nicht sagen lassen, Landrat Innstetten verkauft sein Haus, weil seine Frau den aufgeklebten Chinesen als Spuk an ihrem Bette gesehen hat. Dann bin ich verloren, Effi. Von solcher Lächerlichkeit kann man sich nie wieder erholen" (76).

[56] Ibid, 79.

[57] Ibid, 212. German original: "Das Leben wäre nicht des Lebens wert, wenn das alles gelten sollte, was zufällig gilt. Alles Beste liegt jenseits davon. Lerne Dich daran zu freuen" (220).

[58] Gerhard Kaiser, *Pietismus und Patriotismus im Literarischen Deutschland: Ein Beitrag zum Problem der Säkularisation* (Wiesbaden: F. Steiner, 1961).

[59] Fontane, *Effi Briest*, 111.

[60] Ibid, 213. German original: ". . . weil es trotzdem sein muß. . . . Man ist nicht bloß ein einzelner Mensch, man gehört einem Ganzen an, und auf das Ganze haben wir beständig Rücksicht zu nehmen, wir sind durchaus abhängig von ihm" (223).

[61] Ibid, 213. German original: ". . . und dagegen zu verstoßen geht nicht; die Gesellschaft verachtet uns, und zuletzt tun wir es selbst und können es nicht aushalten und jagen uns die Kugel durch den Kopf" (223).

[62] Ibid, 249. German original: "Das hat er dem Kinde beigebracht, ein Schulmeister war er immer, . . . Ein Streber war er, weiter nichts. — Ehre, Ehre, Ehre . . ." (261).

TILMAN LANG
Hamburg

Cécile: Reading a Fatal Interpretation

THE DELUSIONS AND CONFUSIONS CONFRONTED almost continually by the characters in Theodor Fontane's society novels in-
volve not only erotic and social relationships. The formations and
transformations of technology, and especially media technology, play
a significant role as well. In Fontane's 1888 novel, *Irrungen, Wirrungen* (*Delusions, Confusions*), the Baroness von Rienäcker reflects
upon the variety of media with a certain relish:

> Da setzen wir uns dann und *lesen die Briefe*, die wir doch hoffentlich
> erhalten werden [. . .] Und dann gehen wir zu Tisch und haben
> einen *alten General* zur Rechten und einen *reichen Industriellen* zur
> Linken, und für Industrielle hab' ich von Jugend an eine Passion ge-
> habt. Eine Passion, deren ich mich nicht schäme. Denn entweder ha-
> ben sie neue Panzerplatten erfunden oder *unterseeische Telegraphen*
> gelegt oder einen Tunnel gebohrt [. . .]. Und nach Tische Lesezim-
> mer und Kaffee bei heruntergelassenen Jalousien, so daß einem die
> Schatten und Lichter immer auf der *Zeitung* herumtanzen.[1]

By the end of *Delusions*, the ashes of burned love-letters stand as a
symbol of historically superseded media formations. Fontane's novel
Cécile (1887),[2] written just a few years earlier, presents the literary
consequences of such a reality: a world composed of competing and
conflicting historical orders and self-interpretations. However, the
composition of *Cécile*, with its inclusion of the characters of the
Colonel and the Engineer, does not simply parallel *Delusion*'s figu-
rative polarity of the General and the Industrialist; rather, its shape
derives from the adherence of such oppositions to historically distinct discourse formations operating within the horizon of technological, and particularly media-technological, developments. So to
understand the "logic" of events in the novel — and especially the

logic of its fatal conclusion — within the framework of such a horizon, a few preliminary remarks are necessary.

In *Cécile*, historical and technological media developments are presented as leading to an agonistic conflict in which divergent interpretations and/or systems of reality claim validity and compete for legitimation. But this reading of the novel raises the question of how — that is, in what way and on what level — such developments destabilize given or traditional social orders, particularly when order is understood as systems of communication. Undoubtedly there arises a textualization and thus fictionalization of life-worlds, as Habermas has shown, an experience of the real as an experience of signs, which characterizes every instance of communicative mediation. This seems to be affirmed in Fontane's own description of the ideal novel, "whose figures so array themselves into the figures of real life that we no longer know exactly, in recollecting a specific epoch in life, whether these figures were experienced or merely read about."[3] While these remarks can be read as an appeal for uncompromisingly life-like presentation, they can also just as well be read against the grain as appealing to an incontrovertible techno-logic of signs and a virtual grammatology of the real. And then the question concerning the current or competing reality-models may finally become a question of the "politics of signs," something which constitutes the signature of a given historical-symbolic order.

The Shape of an "Obscure Economy"

In the essay "Structure, Sign, and Play," which has become a classic of contemporary literary theory, Jacques Derrida thematizes the rather complex problem of a politics of signs by distinguishing not only between two ways of interpreting, but also between two interpretations of interpretation:

> There are thus two interpretations of interpretation, of structure, of sign, of play. The one seeks to decipher, dreams of deciphering a truth or an origin which escapes play and the order of the sign, and which lives the necessity of interpretation as an exile. The other, which is no longer turned toward the origin, affirms play and tries to pass beyond man and humanism, the name of man being the name of that being who, throughout the history of metaphysics or of ontotheology — in other words, throughout his entire history — has dreamed of full presence, the reassuring foundation, the origin and the end of play.[4]

These two different interpretations of interpretation are "absolutely irreconcilable even if we live them simultaneously and reconcile them in an obscure economy." Moreover, they "together share the field which we call, in such a problematic fashion, the social sciences" (293). But I recall this all-too-familiar distinction here in order precisely to question its familiarity. The recognizable opposition posed by Derrida is really only part of the story, while the stipulations he attaches to his opposition tend to receive considerably less attention. This comes as no surprise when one considers that the latter conditions seem to undermine or take the edge off what otherwise would appear to be a clear cut distinction. Indeed, having stated the alternative, Derrida goes on to suggest what is required: not so much a choice of one type of interpretation over the other, but rather a reflection upon the common ground of the two absolutely irreconcilable modes and an attempt to conceive "the *différance* of this irreducible difference" (293).

But how are we to approach this common ground or even to conceive its contours more closely? Without addressing the problem much further, Derrida's text gives us at least two clues. In the first place, what he describes is not merely an irreducible difference but the ongoing struggle of the two modes of interpretation to divide up "the field which we call . . . the social sciences." This work of partitioning is no neutral operation. Locked in a process of staking claims and ongoing appropriation, the two modes of interpretation do not merely share the common ground, they dispute it. The common ground appears as a disputed territory, indeed as a kind of battleground.

The temptation arises to make a choice, to take sides, but this only short-circuits the problem. Further reflection reveals that there are more than just two antagonists involved; nostalgic interpretation versus affirmation (Derrida 292).[5] We have a third antagonist, namely the interpretive gesture of Derrida's text itself as it sets the scene of the struggle it only seems to describe. But since this third interpretive gesture is hardly visible, and since Derrida's essay seems to invite the reader to identify its authorial standpoint with affirmative interpretation and with a critical attitude towards the nostalgic yearning for origin, readers have seldom hesitated to associate Derridean deconstruction with Nietzsche.

Although such an identification appears nearly inevitable, it is not as simple as it may seem. What strategy, exactly, is indicated by the name Nietzsche? In "Structure, Sign, and Play" Derrida describes the almost symmetrical reversal of the "saddened, *negative*, nostalgic, guilty, Rousseauistic side" of interpretation: it is "the joyous affirmation of the play of the world and of the innocence of becoming, the affirmation of a world of signs without fault, without truth, and without origin which is offered to an active interpretation" (292). Still, Derrida's description of the Nietzschean side of the opposition hardly coincides with some of the most prominent notes concerning the interpretive attitude and interpretive processes in the *Genealogy of Morals*. In section 12 of the second essay Nietzsche claims:

> daß etwas Vorhandenes, irgendwie Zustande-Gekommenes immer wieder von einer ihm überlegenen Macht auf neue Absichten ausgelegt und, neu in Beschlag genommen, zu einem Nutzen umgebildet und umgerichtet wird; daß alles Geschehen in der organischen Welt ein *Überwältigen, Herr-Werden* und daß wiederum alles Überwältigen und Herr-Werden ein Neu-Interpretieren, ein Zurechtmachen ist, bei dem der bisherige "Sinn" und "Zweck" notwendig verdunkelt oder ganz ausgelöscht worden ist. [. . .] und die ganze Geschichte eines Dings, eines Organs, eines Brauchs kann dergestalt eine fortgesetzte Zeichenkette von immer neuen Interpetationen und Zurechtmachungen sein.[6]

The process of interpretation articulated by Nietzsche, here and elsewhere, coincides less with what Derrida indicated as the second option of interpretation, that is, "the joyous affirmation of the play . . . the *noncenter*" (292), than with an interpretive practice of which such affirmation is a part, but also no more than a part.

No thinker is more aware — even to the point of obsession — of the simulacrum of such innocence than Nietzsche himself. This is precisely the background of his attacks against the Judeo-Christian and Platonic traditions. In Nietzsche's view these traditions played the game of interpretation all the more effectively by denying that interpretation involved any sort of game at all. By concealing the genealogy of its interpretations behind the terms truth, being, and subject, only to name a few, it succeeded in establishing its own authority, driving all competitors off the common ground. Nietzsche himself could not help but be fascinated by such a spectacle. It even forces him to admit some begrudging respect for the traditions: priests and philosophers are the consummate contestants in the agonistic game of interpretation. But their performance is a danger to the game itself. Thus Nietzsche finds himself in the difficult position of condemning those who play the game most perfectly on the grounds that their performance tends to jeopardize its basic rules. The extreme passion that informs Nietzsche's condemnation suggests that it is not the players so much as the game itself that leads to this dilemma.

Nietzsche deals with a similar problem inherent in all agonistic or competitive processes in one of his earlier essays, "Five Prefaces to Five Unwritten Books." In the section "Homer's Contest" he analyses the manner in which the Greeks approached the dilemma and interprets the tradition of *ostracism* as a means by which they sought to safeguard the "necessity of competition" against itself. Thus the "original meaning of ostracism" can be glimpsed,

> des Ostrakismos, wie ihn zum Beispiel die Ephesier bei der Verbannung des Hermodor aussprechen. "Unter uns soll niemand der Beste sein; ist jemand es aber, so sei er anderswo und bei anderen." Denn weshalb soll niemand der Beste sein? Weil damit der Wettkampf versiegen würde und der ewige Lebensgrund des Hellenischen Staates gefährdet wäre.[7]

The gesture of exclusion appears to be a necessity, a move designed to save the agonistic process from its own entropic tendencies.[8] This is all well and good as long as we can distinguish clearly and cleanly between the contestants and the umpire, that is, the transcendental position that decides on the necessity of exclusion. But what if the judges, referees, and legislators themselves become competitors and interpreters? Whose task is it then to exclude the very best? Or is it these best, in the end, who decide whom to exclude and thus assume the exclusive third position?

These are only some of the questions to be encountered in considering Nietzsche's remarks; a more immediate consequence of his concept of interpretation is that it is much more, and different, than a "fröhliche Bejahung des Spiels" (joyous affirmation of . . . play). If the concept of games and play fits at all, then only, perhaps, as a power-play that belies any simple opposition of action and reaction. Interpretation as defined by Nietzsche always begins with reinterpretation. Which is to say simply that every interpretation begins by reinterpreting a previous interpretation. Thus it can never be innocent in the sense of being disinterested and free of presuppositions.

Rather it is based on interest and on debt, in the moral, economic, and informational senses of the terms. Derrida's essay "Structure, Sign, and Play" follows this practice implicitly while not preaching it explicitly. Distinguishing between the nostalgic and the affirmative modes of interpretation as two "absolutely irreconcilable" options, Derrida does not forget to add that "we live them simultaneously and reconcile them in an obscure economy" (293). And if this economy is indeed obscure, then it is doubtless due to our being under its sway; as its contestants and referees, we are still searching for its rules.

Before turning to Fontane, let us attempt to trace this third option of interpreting interpretation, namely the "obscure economy" in which the closure of any interpretation's referential frame is always in excess of itself, or uses excessive force, as a necessary condition of its claim to validity.

Nietzsche's view of interpretation as the dilemma arising from a "general agonistics" (Lyotard), together with Derrida's notion of an "obscure economy," can be strategically reformulated in terms of Saussure's theory of signs. In his *Course in General Linguistics,*[9] Saussure argues that the value of a signifier is determined not by what it represents but by its diacritical-differential relations to other signs, which he calls its milieu. The process of signification is disengaged from that of representation, that is, from extralinguistic entities, and the value of a term is accounted for only via its "pure difference" from other terms of the entire sign-system. But how is this system itself, *la langue*, to be determined? To assume such a precisely delineated system as its object, linguistics must finally call into question its very argument that value is to be determined only negatively as pure difference. The determination can be taken as a determination only if the unlimited play of differences is limited precisely so that the determination can take place.

Saussure tries to find his way out of this predicament by introducing certain positive oppositions that serve to maintain the character and stability of the system. In the course of his argument, the notion of these "determinate oppositions," in turn, serves to recombine what was previously kept apart:

> Although both the signified and the signifier are purely differential and negative when considered separately, their combination is a positive fact; it is even the sole type of facts that language has, for main-

taining the parallelism between the two classes of differences is the *distinctive function* of the linguistic institution. (*CGL* 120; italics added.)

Saussure's shift from difference to opposition takes on an important dimension. Namely, the distinctive function that justifies the linguistic institution lies in maintaining the parallelism and thus guaranteeing the integrity and stability of language as a system of signs. But what is meant by a linguistic institution?

Language as a system is defined by two elementary perspectives: first the synchronic perspective, which defines language as a "system of pure values which are determined by nothing except the momentary arrangement of its terms" (*CGL* 80). Second — if this synchronic perspective is indeed more than a linguist's sheer fiction — we have the foundation of this perspective, which surprisingly enough is not purely intralinguistic. "Synchronic linguistics [is] concerned with the logical and psychological relations that bind together coexisting terms and form a system in the collective mind of speakers." Diachronic linguistics, on the other hand, "stud[ies] relations that bind together successive terms not perceived by the collective mind but substituted for each other without forming a system" (*CGL* 99–100). The surprise is that the "system of pure values" and the momentary arrangement of its terms is now dependent on something *outside* that momentary state, namely on the perception of a collective mind. In this way the synchronic system is distinguished from diachronic systemlessness and given priority over the latter. Saussure accordingly defines the synchronic-systemic aspect of language, which is "the true and only reality to the community of speakers" (90), in relation to the consciousness of those who use it as speakers. In order to know to what extent "a thing is a reality, it is necessary and sufficient to determine to what extent it exists in the minds of speakers" (90). Saussure does not mean here individual speakers but rather the sum of them as a linguistic community. The synchronic linguist thus envisions a communal consciousness and sets out to gather the testimony of its speakers in order to determine what is real for this collective consciousness and what is not. To do this, the linguist must also observe some "facts of language" while ignoring others, since

> their succession in time does not exist insofar as the speaker is concerned. He is confronted with a state. That is why the linguist who wishes to understand a state of things must discard all knowledge of

everything that produced it and ignore diachrony. He can enter the
mind of speakers only by completely suppressing the past. (*CGL* 81)

In order to recognize, the linguist must ignore; to enter the minds
of speakers, something else must be suppressed. Basically, to understand what speakers do, the linguist must do what Saussure assumes
speakers do when they speak: forget time, history, development,
change. Saussure gives no indication of doubt that the organizing
principle of language is communication and understanding, even
though he is arguing that the very process of signification is a differential articulation not reducible to the expression of meaning.

Saussure himself exhibits the tendencies of his linguist. In order
to install a describable institution of language he ignores the forces
responsible for its development and internal structuring process. By
establishing an absolute and irreconcilable opposition between synchrony and diachrony, he justifies a more general reduction of difference to opposition. If diachronic facts are seen as a "blind force"
(*CGL* 89) then their exclusion becomes a necessary condition for
delimiting the intelligibility and order of the synchronic system. This
limitation enables him to transform the play of differences into a
transparent order of oppositions. Saussure began with the insight
that the identity of a term is determined only by what is outside of
it, but then tried to describe that outside in terms of diachronic
forces that function both to contain the internal coherence of a synchronic system and simultaneously serve as its delimitation. This
logic ends up taking the limits and the describability of the social institution of language for granted, rather than interrogating the process that institutes it. Nevertheless, the crucial point here remains the
process of systematic exclusion that renders the play of differences
intelligible in the first place. From this perspective, Saussure's in-
junctions to disregard, ignore, and completely suppress the past and
all becoming and change must be seen as a defense against the unsettling implications of his own principle of "pure difference," that
is, the basic notion of language as a system. As his own chess-game
example illustrates, difference and diachrony are not identical but
intimately related.

What I have tried to suggest up to this point, with reference to
Saussure, is that synchrony and diachrony mark lines of battle in the
field of language theory the same way Derrida's modes of interpretation do: always ending up, namely, in the third position of an "ob-

scure economy." In each case, pure difference is incorporated into the system itself as its founding principle. It is this agonistic inner tension that renders systematicity itself problematic. So what does this have to do with our point of departure?

An "expression of an existing [social] arrangement" (*CGL* 92) is articulated both by Nietzsche on the level of interpretation and by Saussure on the level of linguistic systems. Indeed, confronted with the progressive implementation of new, differential paradigms of signification, this concept becomes virulent in the epistemological discourses of the nineteenth century and manifest particularly in the developments of media technology. Still, insight into the Derridean obscure economy only becomes possible once the traditional semiotic theory of "coinage" and a conventionalized use of signs is replaced by a radical semiology[10] which is oriented towards radicalizing diacritically differential significations. It is here that the idea of play first comes into question. Only contextually relativized values are allowed, and their ephemeral status is enhanced because their foundation is the very source of their dissolution. Hence in the second half of the nineteenth century the natural sciences increasingly conceive of their object field in terms of semiotic relationships: consider, for instance, Mendelejew's periodic table of chemical elements, or Frege's observation that "signs have the same meaning for thinking that the discovery of using the wind to sail against the wind had in seafaring."[11]

Media-technological developments in information transmission and storage allow the semiological reference-paradigm and its "pure difference" to manifest themselves within the field of interactive and communicative relations. The pure value system of signifiers that underlies the level of conventionalized sense and meaning becomes apparent when systems of recording and transmitting signals develop that are no longer analog, but digital. For the simple fact is that these modes of communication do not differentiate between sense and nonsense, but merely transmit specific combinations of signifiers. A decisive factor here is the breaking of a "familiar totality of references" (Heidegger) that occurs through digitalization when the primacy of understanding words and meanings is supplanted by the calculation of signifying units. By freeing up the prospect of a logic of signifiers, the technological media evoke the strangeness of signs. From this stems a heightened awareness that signs do not simply de-

ploy pregiven meanings, but rather are subject to a differential organization that drives every semiologically constructed reality-
model[12] to exceed its own boundaries or to include both these
boundaries and their destabilizing beyond. It is at this point that all
processes of interpretation, explanation, and decoding likewise appear as problems of delimitation, enframing, and exclusion.

The Death of the "Straight Man":[13]
Story of a Fatal Interpretation

Literary-textual theory and the analysis of epistemological discourse
both indicate and describe a semiological rupture in the nineteenth
century.[14] In doing so they set the stage for reformulating the question of the conditions and possibilities of interpretation, thus the
interpretation of interpretation. In particular, it is a question regarding the relation, or rather the *inescapably* conflicted connection
between orders of reference and orders of representation, or, put
differently, between affirmative versus nostalgic interpretation.[15] In
literary works, this problem is presented in the thematization of interpretive processes as processes of appropriating the real, particularly when such processes are situated in the context of media-
technological networks. To the degree that interpretation is dependent upon these networks, the possibility of a position of "analytical
mastery"[16] takes center stage. This is the case in Fontane's novel *Cécile*.

It is neither surprising nor an exceptional insight that in Fontane's late novels especially we encounter the fragility of a social order petrified into mere conventionality. We also find, in the place of
an orderly historical narrative, a polyperspectival simultaneity of epi-
sodic narration. The structure of a public life transformed by inno-
vations in media and information technology is reflected in the
changes in individual communicative relationships.[17] For Fontane,
postal, telegraphic, and finally even telephonic modes of communication function unmistakably as models of the society from which
they spring[18] — consider, for example, the subterranean transmis-
sions of the Stechlinsee. The irritations arising within a traditional
order of discourse can be understood against the historical horizon
of media-technological networks. Corresponding insight into the
"reality" of an "infinite context" (Blumenberg) also emerges as the

negation of the possibility of closed, grounded structures. Fontane's strategic deployment of media can thus be shown to be a procedure of drawing attention to the implications that an informal media-technological order of knowledge, such as the order of the real, can have for acts of interpretive reality or appropriation. For all these would then appear neither as aspects of an ontologically grounded centrality or authenticity, nor a closed, readable meaningfulness of history. Gundermann's conclusion in *Der Stechlin*, that in tele-graphic communication, "'Mr.' . . . has become nonsense," is sufficient commentary. They would appear, rather, in the light of specific decisions made within the "power play" of interpretation.

Underlying these observations is the thesis that Fontane's later novels — and *Cécile* exemplifies this — can precisely be situated within the semiological shift described above. This shift is expressed both by the differential status of objects of experience within the cognitive process and by the reformulation of communication-as-information processes. Fontane's strategic deployment of various media thereby organizes not only the sequence of events in the novel, but also assumes a structural dimension.

Media Strategies

Cécile is the story of an impossible and ultimately fatal amorous liaison between Robert von Leslie-Gordon, a civil engineer, and Cécile, the wife of Colonel a. D. von St. Arnaud. Leslie-Gordon meets the couple during a stay at Thale, a spa in the northern Harz mountains, and right away the novel reveals itself to be the story of an interpretation, as changes in the status of information and interpretation become a measure of the erotic attraction between Gordon and Cécile.

Already in his first encounter with Cécile, Leslie-Gordon is both intrigued and irritated by her appearance, social manner, and radiance. This quickly assumes the form of an intense, virtually detective-like interest in this beautiful but melancholy and hysteria-prone woman. His attraction and curiosity, as well as inconsistencies, contradictions, and enigmas in her appearance and behavior finally bring him to write a letter to his sister requesting information about Cécile. Then, just at the point that the relationship between Gordon and Cécile threatens to cross the bounds of social propriety, a telegram from his company calls him away from Thale. Some time later,

Gordon returns to Berlin and pays a visit to Cécile in her apartment. Daily visits ensue while her husband, St. Arnaud, regularly spends his time at the club pursing his passion for gambling. Gordon's relationship with Cécile takes on renewed intensity. Gordon playfully enjoys writing love letters that cover Cécile like a "cloud of rose petals" (368) but go unanswered nonetheless. Finally, after being invited to dinner at St. Arnaud's home, Leslie-Gordon receives the letter from his sister containing the requested information about Cécile's "story." His impression of her thereupon becomes the "novel" about Cécile, the former royal mistress, and about the St. Arnaud misalliance in which Cécile is unhappily trapped. This knowledge and the novel that results from his attempts to solve the enigma transforms the referential horizon of his observations and his attitude toward Cécile as well. Gordon becomes direct, making certain demands on her, and finally they break up. Once more, Gordon is called away by a telegram from his company. When he again returns to Berlin months later, he encounters Cécile at the opera, accompanied by one of her partners, Privy-Council Hedemeyer. In a fit of jealousy Gordon confronts her, first in her lodge and then later at her home. St. Arnaud reacts to this presumptuousness, which involves more than just an implicit claim upon Cécile, by challenging Gordon to a duel. Gordon is killed in the duel, Cécile subsequently takes her own life, and St. Arnaud flees to Italy to escape prosecution.

A reading of the story that focuses for once not on Cécile but on Fontane's secret protagonist, Leslie-Gordon,[19] soon encounters behind the almost trivial tale of love and jealousy a complex system of social relationships based upon informal connections and interruptions. Indeed even the term *Zivilingenieur*, an uncommon professional designation, points to this stratum of organization and control. Fontane is certainly both referring to the Anglo-Saxon concept of the civil engineer, historically distinguished from military engineering and technology,[20] and he is also alluding to the concept of a "social engineer" who represents the scientific-technological thinking and instrumental pragmatism that characterized a certain Anglo-Saxon mentality in the nineteenth century. Leslie-Gordon embodies the natural scientist and the communications technology specialist as well. As a worldly and well-traveled man, he produces, as Cécile remarks, "ever-new connections and *contacts*" (366). In this way she uses a social language game that is itself permeated with information technology to interpret Gordon's specific profession. He is a "cableman and international wire-puller," that is, a telegraph cable layer and information technician. His business is electronic telegraphic technology — the technology and economics of information through cable — whose ultimate goal is the establishment of a telecommunications network.[21] In short, the reduction of an economy of time, space, and information to one of just time and information.

In the figure of Leslie-Gordon there is, as already indicated, a system. Fontane has also oriented his implementation of contemporary media technology developments on a concrete historical figure: down to the most minute facets of the story, Leslie-Gordon is modeled on the family history of Werner and Wilhelm Siemens, the natural scientists and media technicians.[22] Unmistakably, Wilhelm Siemen's brother-in-law Lewis-Gordon, a partner in the English cable company Newall & Co., served as the namesake for Leslie-Gordon, and aspects of the latter's fictional life story also can be traced to the former's biography.[23] Moreover, this fictional biography itself appears to be a montage of the lives of the two brothers, Wilhelm Siemens and Werner von Siemens.[24] Thus we learn of Leslie-Gordon that, prior to leaving the service on account of exorbitant gambling debts, he had, like Werner von Siemens, served with the "Pioneers in Magdeburg" (366). Further parallels emerge from their professional careers. Thus the civil engineer, like the Siemens brothers, lays "a cable through the Red Sea and the Persian Gulf. . . . Somewhat later he entered Persian service and, after overseeing the construction of a telegraph connecting the country's two major cities, entered Russian service" (367).[25]

The choice of an information technician as the protagonist upon whom and whose profession the novel's social order is based can be understood partially in terms of Fontane's own stated purpose:

> Cécile ist doch mehr als eine Alltagsgeschichte, die liebevoll und mit einem gewissen Aufwande von Kunst erzählt ist. Wenigstens *will* die Geschichte noch etwas mehr sein; sie setzt sich erstens vor, einen Charakter zu zeichnen, der, soweit meine Novellenkenntnis reicht (und das ist nicht sehr weit), noch nicht gezeichnet ist, und will zweitens den Satz illustrieren, wer 'mal drinsitzt,' gleichviel mit oder ohne Schuld, kommt nicht wieder heraus.' Also etwas wie Tendenz. Auch das, wenigstens in dieser Gestaltung, ist neu.[26]

This "character," whose spatio-temporal conception of a world of social obligations is elevated to an existential duty, is doubtless represented by Cécile. The web from which whoever "gets caught up in it" cannot escape is supplied by the media engineer Leslie-Gordon. Similarly he marks the point of transition where the network of social obligations merges with the network of telecommunications connections. Caught up in these interweaving social and telecommunications networks, these two characters practice a form of relationship whose stability is limited.

The close modeling of its protagonist after a pioneer of electronic media and telegraphic networking allows us to assume that the sequence of events in the novel is oriented largely on economies of communication and the flow of information. Relations within the social system are steered by connections in the postal-telegraphic network. So how does this information technology manifest itself, and what results from this deployment of media?

From the beginning of the novel the effects of media technology are registered in the way Gordon detects inconsistencies and inanities in his social-discursive surroundings: namely telegraphically. He is able, like Maxwell's mirror-galvanometer, to pick up even the minutest signals. But precisely because Gordon picks up signifiers and not meanings, what he receives makes little sense in terms of conventional social discourse. As he later states: "I am confronted with an enigma, or at the very least with something indefinite and unclear, which I would like to see clarified" (361). Even at the beginning he assumes that behind the relationship of Cécile and St. Arnaud is hidden "a novel. He is more than twenty years older than she. . . . And then retired, such a brilliant and decorated officer!" (321–22). "She has a story, or he does, or both, and the past is now casting its shadow" (419).

The goal of his search is to uncover that very information about Cécile's past that she, in turn, knows must remain concealed as the condition of maintaining her relationship with Gordon. Thus she explains her desperation to her confidant, the Court Chaplain Dörffler:

> Er weiß nichts von der Tragödie, die den Namen St. Arnaud trägt [. . .] Aber wie lange noch? Er wird sich hier rasch wieder einleben, alte Beziehungen anknüpfen und eines Tages wird er alles wissen. Und an demselben Tage . . . (438)[27]

Cécile's "But for how long?" gives an indication of what follows. What Cécile is hiding is what Gordon is looking for, so that his erotic irritations — "She's got me a little twisted, in a very peculiar way" (361) — which are a "world of conflicting emotions" (419), can find some relief. The cluelessness of an information technician confronted with a "woman's heart" (418) stems from the fact that he is simply unable to find a referential framework or story within which to situate meaningfully the various elements of speech;[28] namely, Cécile's eloquent inventory of physiological signals, such as blushing, twitching corners of the mouth, fainting spells. He is unable to bring clarity to the game of erotic signifiers. Almost "fooled by [his] own science," which has replaced understanding with an anthropometric "spectral analysis of persons" (418), Gordon makes it clear that only finding this novel within the novel will provide a coherent framework, which is the condition for solving the enigma and thus for interpretation. Yet even Gordon's attempt to tap into a shared recollection of the relationship between authorship and love fails because of Cécile's "naive modicum of education." Instead of instigating a merging of hearts, as Goethe's Werther achieves in the appeal to Klopstock's ideal-paternal authority, all Cécile manages to say during the visit to Klopstock's home in Quedlinburg is, "It's so green" (349). Once again, the intertextual irony reveals what is really at stake here. The information technician is again at a loss, for his attempt fails to achieve an understanding of *their* situation based upon shared intersubjective references.[29] Faced with the impossibility, furthermore, of seeking recourse in a Platonic love that would violate no laws, the information technician finally deploys his knowledge of information technology, whereby he also makes use of a delaying tactic.

Gordon is a gambler. Although he no longer incurs debts through gaming, as a civil engineer he incurs debts in other ways, namely debts in the telecommunications network. Thus Cécile judges his past: "But I do find that laying a wire or a cable on some unknown coast (and what coast wouldn't be unknown, for me!) is finally just as trivial as getting into debt" (359). This becomes understandable if we consider, first, that the integration and utilization of a (tele)communications network is always based on a fundamental indebtedness, on the impossible accounting or ineluctable debt of accumulated information.[30] Second, Gordon incurs debts by the requests to his sister for further information about Cécile and St. Arnaud. He does not, as would be expected, reach her via telegraph; rather, he entrusts the question of the truth about Cécile to the time-consuming postal service. He justifies this to himself by reasoning that the post will better find his sister in her travels, by means of forwarding addresses,[31] but from the perspective of a telegraphic logic of time and information Gordon incurs *temporal debts*.

By delaying a solution to the puzzle of that suppressed "story," Gordon's postal ruse assumes the function of holding the momentary status of his relationship to Cécile suspended. From the perspective of information technology, Gordon's trick constitutes a simple procedure for minimizing system entropy. And Gordon is enough of an information technician to recognize that the conditioning factor for maintaining that relationship is this very sum of unstructured or unreconstructable data,[32] that is, the sum of his non-knowledge about Cécile's past.

Unlike letters, the telegram's pointing finger is a dematerialized "sign in the original sense."[33] It also serves to delay matters in the novel by displacing the recipient. As announcements, telegrams are technical signifiers whose function is to transmit, "not knowledge, primarily, but an indication."[34] As exemplary forms of "full speech" they compel the recipient to move, making of him a veritable subjectum of the network. Their value is thus based on their effectiveness, not on the semantic content of the message. In this way they resemble, as Gordon remarks in passing, a direct command. Gordon's subsequent remark, that the "most trivial sentences are always the truest" (475), reads in this context like an insight into the economy of telegraphic signs. As one contemporaneous account explains, "the thought that is given sensory expression in one location is reproduced sensibly at some distant location without any object having been transported along with it."[35] Thus the message increasingly becomes the medium itself. The telegraphic style and its characteristics, the reduction of adjectives and particularly of all personal pronouns, is assumed by the telegraphic message as a "direct function of available channel capacities."[36] In this elimination of all style determining elements is manifested the ironic revision of Buffon's verdict, the style makes the man. The telegraphic message ignores all stylistic self-expression and hence all privacy, as well as authorship and origin — thus Kafka could not be surprised, years later, when a telegraphic declaration of love went unanswered, since technological communications are like ghosts, who "swallow up" all his "kisses in writing" en route.[37]

Gordon's delaying procedure has a double organization in which each of the variants at first seems to supplement the other. For either the information-to-be-sent, which will answer the question and solve the undecidability of the relationship with Cécile, is delayed as long as possible in the network itself, or the network itself displaces the recipient of this information. The telegraphically manipulated displacement, which originates elsewhere as de-individualized speech, thus exemplifies how communication is pressed, or Morsed, through systematic passages that operate like a bottleneck of signifiers.[38] Epistolary discourse, meanwhile, maintains a remnant of individuality, style, and authorship.

Despite this game of displacements and calculated deferrals, the letter from the sister arrives with merciless inevitability. With it comes Cécile's so carefully concealed "story" about the prince's mistress, the misalliance with St. Arnaud, and the earlier death by duel of a member of the regiment. Considering the fact that it also marks the turning point in the narrative, this letter's appearance suggests that the problem of the contingency of information, and likewise of the time and place of the addressee, comprises only a part of this story's logic.

Had Fontane wanted to explicate *only* information technology *avant la lettre* — that is, by following solid scientific principles whereby the level of information increases and the system of social relations undergoes entropy, allowing those figures who are already caught up in the informal system, in accordance with the second law of thermodynamics, to die of heat[39]— then his whole game of exchanges between the postal and telegraphic systems would have quickly run dry. But if the arrival of the long sought novel-within-the-novel is grasped as originating merely within a field of readings and pre-texts and thus as a case of contingent reality, then on the other hand the fatal outcome of the story can hardly be explained adequately. For all indications point to the conclusion that what happens does not result exclusively from the letter received, but also emerges from within a field of interpretive encounters with that message. The comment that the letter brings "few good prospects," namely, can be tied both to its content and to Gordon's hermeneutic praxis. Does not Fontane's narrative, with its inevitably returning letter, not explicate the idea of an inescapable "obscure economy"? For ultimately that "obligatory" indeterminacy which Cécile calls the "advantage of a [never-ending] life of travel" (366), and which she stylizes into a utopia of livable disorder, explodes, ruptured by a determinacy that violates those very conventions of social obligation.

Haecceitas:
Unavoidable Eternal Return to Sender?

As much as Fontane's novel distinguishes itself by this interplay of two modes of communication belonging to different formations of discourse and media technology, the question remains whether the narrative's turns can be explained by this conflict. Particularly, there is the fatal culmination of events: the postal request for the 'truth' about Cécile that eventually returns to sender. "A letter always arrives at its destination," Lacan remarks provocatively in suggesting that the question of whether a message has arrived always depends upon the possibility — or impossibility — of unequivocal meaning.[40] A message is always measured by its eventual reappropriation. Let us therefore return briefly to our starting point.

We recognize now that the concept of exclusion is the condition for upholding a systematic status quo and a balance of probabilities. We encountered this in the Nietzsche quote about *ostrakismos*, and it reappears in Fontane's novel in its sociological and media-technological formation. The exclusion through concealment of her own prehistory is Cécile's condition both for upholding the relationship with Gordon and for integrating herself into the social order generally. The latter is something Cécile strives for, as she herself implies, at the price of a total obligation to this order, along with the necessity that she forget her past:

> . . . die Gesellschaft hat mich in den Bann getan, ich seh es und fühle es, und so leb ich denn von der Gnade derer, die meinem Haus die Ehre antun. [. . .] Ich habe nicht den Anspruch, den andre haben. Ich will ihn aber *wieder* haben . . . .(486)[41]

Cécile's postulate of self-obligation to duty — that keyword of Prussian behavioral culture — simultaneously serves as a means of suppressing, delimiting, and excluding wishes that could endanger the everyday order of things. And as the preceding reflections have also made clear, the stability of relations depends on keeping the level of information in society's flow of communications low, primarily by excluding all diachronic aspects of becoming and change. In the novel *Cécile* accordingly deals with signifiers most sparingly: she is silent, speaks little, or else sends out predominantly psychological signals. And the change in circumstance that destabilizes this small, Fontanesque social system does in fact follow from an increase in the level of available information. However, the change in circumstances in the network of social relations is only realized when this new information, as a quantity of signifiers, is accorded an authority and unequivocal meaning. Only this allows an interpretation or reinterpretation of the social order. What is the value, then, of the letter Gordon receives? Does it simply include what was previously excluded?

These questions can be answered only if we consider Gordon's hermeneutic discovery of meaning. The interpretability of Cécile and the social reality that surrounds her is not so much grounded on the intuitive cognition of either a "woman's heart" or the meaning of a social order as it represents a procedure of multi-variable deduction, particularly as it is based on intermediary reports. Gordon's deductions are not just reached automatically as increased definiteness in the "gibberish" (Fechner) of signs; they are also decisions, their knowledge is conjectural and appeals to a certain behavior through which the prescriptive character of signs is realized. The letter Gordon receives and which helps him to interpret thus also becomes a metaphor of limitation and closure.

Nearly contemporaneous with the writing of Fontane's novel, the scientific pragmatist Charles Sanders Peirce reformulated the cognitive process as a process of signification. He arrived at a necessarily decisionistic principle of interpretation, which he named, following the Scholastic concept, the *haecceitas* of the sign.[42] He orders the process of interpreting reality according to the concepts of decision and event, which determine the direction taken in interpreting signs.[43] Replacing the objective relation of an "intuitive cognition" with the primacy of thinking as a system of semiological references — "it follows that every thought must address itself to some other, must determine some other since that is the essence of the sign" — "haecceitas" designates a point of interruption in the infinite semiosis, a moment of decision that focuses complete attention. This is the instant when the sign's "givenness" becomes apparent amidst the totality of a referential context that itself withdraws from scrutiny; it is this that directs a specific action: "the action, or trans-action, is the place where the *haecceitas* brings the play of semiosis to a halt."[44]

Peirce thematizes the virtually unlimited quality of semiosis and recognizes that meanings can be produced only through the delimitation of references. To the degree that these delimitations have no objective grounding, moreover, they must be based upon cultural or intersubjective functional patterns, habits, and their paradigmatic shifts are based on "habit changes." For Peirce the certainty remains, however, that such delimitation is unavoidable; any attempt even to conceive of an infinite referentiality of signs would be a contradiction in terms. Such alterity could only be conceptualized as the other of cognition, the very negative of knowledge. Precisely because every thought is based on signs and thus necessarily determined by a previous cognition, for instance, the testimony of others, such testimony is able even to "convince a man that he himself is mad."

To avoid such madness, interpretation, as Derrida remarks in relation to Peirce, "should always take the situation of the marks into account, in particular that of utterances, the place of senders and addresses, of framing and of socio-historical circumspection, and so forth."[45] If limitation or closure both name the decision for and the triggering of a semio-pragmatic action, then in response one can either submit the event to what Derrida calls a programmatological reading, or else one can take the process in the affirmative and demonstrate its power, which is always the power of a necessary misreading.

If in conclusion we cast a glance from this perspective at Leslie-Gordon's interpretive practice as a search for "marks" and a reading of signs, he seems to demonstrate the power of necessary misreading. This is because Gordon regards the letter — despite the fact that it is also a matter of layers of testimony from others, and the letter is really a letter within a letter — as a conclusive signifier. Almost as a sort of counterpoint to the laconic telegraphic style, whose digitally

minimized signifiers render the question of sense or nonsense obsolete, the letter from his sister is rife with appraisals, innuendoes, and
illustrations. Even as they provide assurance of the letter's individuality and authorship, they require even more interpretation. Gordon's belief that he can determine the origin of its statements seems
to him to be enough in this case to guarantee their referential
"truth." Thus we notice only at second glance how Gordon has
condensed the letter's uncertainties and ambiguities into "lover of
princes, favorite *in duplo*, inheritance passed from uncle to nephew!
And the chamberlain in between . . . " (461). On all these points,
the letter contains only vague innuendoes. Gordon reads the letter as
though it says what he says it says. That the letter says what Gordon
says (or claims) it says emerges as the effect of a combinatory art of
signs whose author is in some part Gordon himself, and this helps
him position himself more securely. For despite all resistance
Gordon is unable to escape the obsessive force of this phantom-like
combination of signs. Although he tries not to let it show, "still he
let three days go by without calling on the St. Arnauds" (465). And
furthermore:

> Aller Krankheit und Resignation ungeachtet oder vielleicht auch
> gesteigert dadurch, war etwas Bestrickendes um sie her gewesen, und
> diesem Zauber aufs neue hingegeben, war er schließlich doch einer
> Sprache verfallen, die zu mäßigen oder gar schweigen zu heißen er
> nach dem Inhalt von Clothildens Briefe nicht mehr für geboten ge-
> halten hatte. (472)[46]

Overtly criminological, as if piecing together the clues, Gordon concludes:

> Deshalb schrak sie so zusammen und wandte sich ab als wir in die
> gespenstischen Fenster guckten. Und schon vorher, in Quedlinburg,
> als ich über die Schönheitsgalerien und die Gräfin Aurora so tapfer
> perorierte [. . .] *Nun klärt sich alles* . . . Arme, schöne Frau! (465)[47]

But if we ask what really does become clear, we must conclude that
it is actually not very much. Perhaps all we really learn here is that
the letter itself makes possible deception and confusion about what
is read versus what one authors oneself. Such confusion, which ne-
glects the chain of tradition and transmission, is the prerequisite for
Gordon to discover in Cécile the mirror image of his own erotic impulses. Thus what seems at first to be a shocking revelation is in-

verted and transformed into the legitimate basis for an implicitly formulated erotic demand.

Gordon believes, once the complete "picture" of Cécile is at his disposal, that he understands the meaning of her behavior and her nervous reactions. These are symptoms of a constrictive social integration that channels love into an order of representations. Taking Cécile's illness and weakness into account, Gordon believes he knows the "ABC's of the soul" better than she:

> Und diese dummen Tropfen; weg damit samt der ganzen Doktorensippe. Das brüstet sich mit Ergründung von Leib und Seele, schafft immer neue Wissenschaften, in denen man sich vor Psyche nicht retten kann, und kennt nicht das Abc der Seele. Verkennung und Irrtum, wohin ich sehe.[. . .] Sie sind eingeschnürt und eingezwängt [. . .] Sie müßten es wieder blühen sehen, lebendig, wie damals. (469–70)[48]

Gordon's speech about the "ABC's of the soul" clearly recalls Gustav Theodor Fechner's psychophysics and aesthetics, in which "communications from the soul" are explained in strictly mathematical terms.[49] To Gordon's further arguments about unfolding new life-forces under conditions of enjoyment and harmonious (natural) relations, Cécile responds, in a similar Fechnerian vein, that after all the "confusions" she has been a part of she yearns for a state of "innocence" (471) and something "approaching a stable situation." But everything that converges in Fechner's theory remains divided for Fontane. Once more we realize that Gordon's image of Cécile is a fantasy constructed according to his own wishes. For only *after* the devastating revelations does he find her captivating and only after that does he get carried away with the idea of discovering her pure womanhood (*Weiblichkeit*). The details of this procedure are only hinted at: "You, one who is such complete womanhood, and . . . " (471).

The change in Gordon's position regarding Cécile occurs when he finds an overtly Oedipal solution to the riddle,[50] but soon this becomes merely a narcissistic assurance of his own power, importance, and value. The reduction of Cécile to an aspect of pure womanhood that he opposes to the "He-woman, a sort of amazon" itself becomes a metaphor, ironically, for the sort of male narcissistic satisfaction traditionally expected to be provided by someone in the role of a mistress. Thus what Gordon sees *ex post facto* are just so many indications of her attraction: "When I think back, she herself confessed it to me" (466). And characteristically, when he receives her goodbye letter after he has pressed himself upon her all too passionately, his degree of self-misrecognition is indicated by the fact that he does not primarily notice the implicit threat, that "separation or *something worse* is approaching," by which she means St. Arnaud's prohibitive role as the third party, but instead is "most agitated by the unabashed confession of her attraction" (474).

On the other hand, in a letter to Cécile, Gordon is expressly cognizant that his image of her might contain fantasized or substituted qualities. At the same time, he also admits that this coincidence of fantasies with the order of everyday life can hardly be endured:

> Ich soll mich zurückfinden in den Ton unserer glücklichen Tage, schrieben sie mir gestern. Mit Ihnen am selben Orte, dieselbe Luft atmend, würd ich es nie gekonnt haben; aber in dieser Trennung werd ich es können oder es lernen. [. . .] Denn in der Fremde nehmen wir, zurückblickend, das Bild für die Wirklichkeit, und die Sehnsucht, die uns sonst quälen würde, wird unser Glück. (477)[51]

These reflections come about after a telegram has called Gordon away from the scene once more. Telegraphic displacement reveals to Gordon "what is good and understanding in me" (475). What is "good and understanding," namely the necessity of substitution, is once again not the responsibility of the subject. For it could hardly be more clearly stated that it is a telegraphic understanding that forbids a real consummation between Gordon and Cécile. Mandating instead the "joy of substitution," this remains but a "cheerful dream." But if understanding here means accepting denial and substitution, or else, as Cécile says, "something worse . . . approaching," still in the end it is the suspension of deferred understanding and the collapse of substitution that leads to catastrophe. Gordon's fantasies explode when he encounters Cécile again, accidentally, at the opera with Privy Councilor Hedemeyer. Gordon's "vanity is injured" (487) to such a degree because he feels deceived for having accepted denial and substitution. The "womanhood of this beautiful woman" can no longer serve as a mirror of his own wholeness and omnipotence. The immediate result of such irritation is aggression: "Gordon suffered hellish agony; brooding over his revenge, his only uncertainty was whether in the given moment (and the moment had to occur) he would rather act as the 'bad conscience' or as 'Mephisto'" (479). The victim of his own interpretation of her, he paradoxically accuses her of remaining true to *his* interpretation of her story as a mistress of princes: "We remain true to our nature, that is our only fidelity. . . . You belong to the moment and change with it. And whoever has a moment . . . " (487).

As a contest between two claims for legitimacy, the subsequent duel takes place, the narrator notes, mainly because "the fear of [St. Arnaud], of this man of determinations, did not have sufficient deterrent effect" (490). But the point made by the story is that neither side prevails. Not Gordon, because the connection between deferred denial and the claims of a reality interpretation is never vindicated on the personal, everyday level of social order; not St. Arnaud, because his practice of personally punishing transgressions as a way of asserting the legitimacy of his own claims belongs to an obsolete courtly epoch. At the end the scene is empty, signifying what all are lacking: Cécile chooses suicide; Gordon is killed in the duel; St. Arnaud flees to Italy, into exile. Finally only letters are sent, reporting on the deaths of the participants.

Fontane's novel thus seems to end with the exclusion of everyone who raises an interpretive or ordering claim to reality. But this only shows that the absence of objective decidability and the disallowal of *one* interpretation of reality claiming ultimate justification is the signature of what has been called Fontane's realism. If precisely that interpretation, which is based on the more individualized communication of letter-writing, fails because it depends on mastery and a violent interpretation, then this demonstrates Fontane's own combination of diagnostic precision with an ethical intent.[52]

It is a familiar idea that the interpreter of signs can become the dupe of textual undecidability and therefore be drawn into identifying with one partial viewpoint and suppressing all others. That this fact can be observed from within the horizon of the difference between postal and teletechnical communication, however, has not yet adequately been taken into account. What I have tried to indicate here is that Fontane's novel implicitly questions the possibility of gaining a "power of decree" over knowledge by dwelling *within* that very difference.

Translated by Eric Schwab

Notes

[1] Theodor Fontane, *Irrungen, Wirrungen*, in *Sämtliche Werke*, pt. 1, vol. 2, ed. Walter Keitel (Munich: Hanser, 1962), 429. English translation by William L. Zwiebel in: Th. Fontane, *Delusions, Confusions* and *The Poggenpuhl Family*, The German Library, vol. 47, ed. Peter Demetz (New York: Continuum, 1989), 117–118. English translation: "Then we'll sit down and *read one another the letters*, which I hope we'll be receiving. . . . And then we go to lunch and we'll have a *general* on our right and a *rich industrialist* on our left. I've had a passion for industrialists ever since I was a girl. And it's a passion that I'm not in the least ashamed of, because either they've invented some new armor plating, or laid an *undersea telegraph*, or drilled a tunnel. . . . And after lunch, we'll have coffee in the reading room with the venetian blinds lowered so that the shadows and light always dance about on one's *newspaper*" [italics added].

[2] Th. Fontane, *Cécile*, in *Sämtliche Werke*, pt. 1, vol. 3. All further citations in the text refer to this edition. Passages from *Cécile* have been translated for this article by Eric Schwab.

[3] Th. Fontane, *Erinnerungen, ausgewählte Schriften und Kritiken, Sämtliche Werke*, pt. 3, vol. 1, 568.

[4] Jacques Derrida, "Structure, Sign, and Play in the Discourse of the Human Sciences," in *Writing and Difference*, trans. Alan Bass (Chicago: U of Chicago P, 1978), 292. Further quotations from this essay cited with page number in brackets and where necessary, "Derrida."

[5] On affirmative interpretation as a "joyous" affirmation of play, cf. Jacques Derrida, "Sporen. Die Stile Nietzsches," in Werner Hamacher ed., *Nietzsche in Frankreich* (Frankfurt am Main, Berlin: Ullstein, 1986), 129–165.

[6] Friedrich Nietzsche, *Zur Geneologie der Moral. Werke*, vol. 2 (Munich: C. Hanser, 1960), 818. English translation from F. Nietzsche, *On the Genealogy of Morals* and *Ecce Homo*, trans. Walter Kaufmann (New York: Vintage, 1969): "whatever exists, having somehow come into being, is again and again reinterpreted to new ends, taken over, transformed, and redirected by some power superior to it; all events in the organic world are a subduing, a *becoming master*, and all subduing and becoming master involves a fresh interpretation, an adaptation through which any previous 'meaning' and 'purpose' are necessarily obscured or even obliterated. . . .

And the entire history of a 'thing,' an organ, a custom can in this way be a continuous sign-chain of ever new interpretations and adaptations. . . . "

[7] Nietzsche, "Fünf Vorreden zu fünf ungeschriebenen Büchern," *Werke* vol. 3, 1003. English translation: "as it was declared, for example, by the Ephesians upon banning Hermodor. 'Among us, nobody shall be the best; but if someone is, then let him be elsewhere, among others.' For what reason should nobody be the best? Because then the competition itself would be defeated and the eternal foundation of life for the Hellenic nation would be endangered."

[8] I use the systemic notion of entropy as an indicator of the particular level of probability and equilibrium in a system. We will come back to this notion later.

[9] Ferdinand de Saussure, *Course in General Linguistics*, trans. Wade Baskin (New York: Philosophical Library, 1959). Further quotations from this translation cited in brackets and where necessary the abbreviation *CGL*.

[10] "A radical semiology would therefore arise in the discursive encounter with the realm of things — the logos's other — as a theory of universal order. With its help, not only could the concept of language be unfolded but also its opposite, the world of extra-linguistic things." Rodolphe Gashé, "Das wilde Denken und die Ökonomie der Repräsentation," in: Lepenies/Ritter, eds., *Orte wilden Denkens* (Frankfurt am Main: Suhrkamp, 1970), 365.

[11] Gottlieb Frege, *Begriffsschrift: Eine arithmetisch nachgebildete Formelsprache des reinen Denkens* (Halle 1879; repr. Darmstadt 1974), 107.

[12] On the concept of reality models, cf. Siegfried J. Schmidt, "Medien, Kultur, Medienkultur," in Siegfried J. Schmidt, ed., *Kognition und Gesellschaft: Der Diskurs des radikalen Konstruktivismus* 2nd ed. (Frankfurt am Main: Suhrkamp, 1992), 425–451.

[13] I have borrowed the concept of "straight men" from Barbara Johnson. On its application, cf. Barbara Johnson, *The Critical Difference* (Baltimore: Johns Hopkins UP, 1981).

[14] In nineteenth-century epistemological discourse, a new semiological *paradigm of reference* emerges from the description of information processes. This paradigm is expressly immune to the theoretical demarcations of knowledge, i.e. between the human and the natural sciences. This is just as valid for abstract sciences like mathematics as for the social sciences; it is exhibited, for instance, in Fechner's psychologically conceived "other" realm of semiological references.

[15] On the matter of the practice of an obscure economy as an exclusion procedure, cf. Shoshana Felman, "Turning the Screw of Interpretation," in *Writing and Madness: Literature/Philosophy/Psychoanalysis* (Ithaca: Cornell UP, 1985), 141–247. Also published in *Yale French Studies* 55-56 (1977): 94–207.

[16] On the concept of "analytical mastery" cf. Barbara Johnson, "The Frame of Reference" in *The Critical Difference*, 110–147, esp. 110.

[17] I am thankful to Monika Plümer (Mag. Arbeit, Göttingen 1989) for pointing out that in Fontane's novels, especially in *Der Stechlin*, numerous symbols and motifs of mass-media developments can be found. On this, cf. also Eda Sagarra, *Theodor Fontane "Der Stechlin"* (Munich: Fink, 1986).

[18] Jürgen Habermas has already pointed out that the telegraph's invention revolutionized "the organization of the totality of information-services," and was accompanied by a decline in the "cohesiveness of public communication." Cf. Jürgen Habermas, *Strukturwandel der Öffentlichkeit* (Neuwied: Luchterhand, 1962), 221, 194.

[19] All monographic studies up to this point deal more or less exclusively with the figure Cécile, and most often from the aspect of the representation of women. Cf. Inge Stephan, "'Das Natürliche hat es mir seit langem angetan': Zum Verhältnis von Frau und Natur in Fontanes *Cécile*," in Grimm/Hermand, eds. *Natur und Natürlichkeit* (Frankfurt am Main, 1981); Ursula Schmalbruch, "Zum Melusine-Motiv in Fontanes *Cécile*" in: *Text & Kontext* 7-8 (1979/80): 127–144; Cornelie Ueding, "Utopie auf Umwegen. Zwei Szenen in Fontane's *Cécile*" in G. v. Ueding, ed., *Literatur ist Utopie* (Frankfurt am Main: Suhrkamp, 1978), 220–253; Winfried Jung, "Bilder, und immer wieder Bilder . . . " in *Wirkendes Wort* 40 (1990): 197–209.

[20] Particularly in English usage the "engineer" per se is military personnel, while "civil engineer" is its civilian derivative. The conceptual history of the term "engineer" itself indicates its origin in the military complex as the stepping-off point for the construction of social and communicative infrastructure. In the German language context the concept has, with only a few unimportant exceptions, little use. Cf. *The Oxford English Dictionary*, vol. 3, 1989.

[21] On the history of telegraphic technology in the eighteenth and nineteenth centuries, see Rolf Oberliesen, *Information, Daten und Signale: Geschichte technischer Informationsverarbeitung* (Reinbek: Rowohlt, 1982), 82–165; also Volker Aschoff, "Die elektrische Nachrichtentechnik im 19. Jahrhundert" in *Technikgeschichte* 33/34 (1966).

[22] In the context of her analysis of *Der Stechlin*, Eda Sagarra points out Fontane's interest in the Siemens' family history, and she is also one of the few who have remarked about his incorporation of new media and communicative processes, through which a "new sort of consciousness of historical simultaneity" comes into play. Cf. Eda Sagarra, *Theodor Fontanes "Der Stechlin,"* 27, 39, and 81ff.

[23] Cf. William Pole, *Wilhelm Siemens* (Berlin: Springer, 1890), 129–132. The fact that in the novel's fictional biography Leslie-Gordon is born in Edinburgh while the real-life civil engineer Lewis-Gordon also come from Edinburgh confirms this intentional parallelism.

[24] On these parallels cf. Werner von Siemens, *Lebenserinnerungen* (Berlin: Flemming & Wiskott, 1922) 99–100; see also Sigfried von Weiher, *Werner von Siemens: Ein Leben für die Wissenschaft, Technik und Wirtschaft* (Göttingen: Musterschmidt, 1974).

[25] Cf. Pole, 178: "The Indian government suggested laying an undersea cable from Kurachi through the Persian Gulf. Through their agent, Colonel Stewart, they consulted with the Siemens brothers about this project, and in October 1862 Werner and Wilhelm sent them back a report on it. Another line was designed in this way: the Indian government extended their connection over land from Bushire to Teheran; the Persian government then continued it from there all the way to Djulfa, on the Russian border, from which point the Russians continued the line from the Circassian region all the way to Southern Russia, where it could once again be connected to the European telegraph system."

[26] Fontane, letter to Paul Schlenther of June 2, 1887. In the letter, Fontane expresses his gratitude for Schlenther's evaluation of the novel, while at the same time, in the passage quoted here, setting this evaluation aright by pointing out what Schlenther evidently neglected: the social realm and its complex networkings. English translation: "Cécile is really more than just an everyday story told with charm and a certain degree of artfulness. At least the story *wants* to be more than that: firstly it sets out to depict a character who, as far as my knowledge of the novel goes (and that is not very far), has not yet been depicted; secondly it means to illustrate the phrase, that whoever 'gets caught up in it,' no matter whether or not by fault, 'never gets out of it.' Thus something like a tendency [*Tendenz*]. That too, at least in this shape, is new."

[27] Fontane, *Cécile*. English translation: "He knows nothing of the tragedy that carries the name St. Arnaud. . . . But for how long? He will quickly regain his familiarity here, resume his old connections, and one day he will know everything. And on that day . . ."(438).

[28] On the difference between "full speech" and "empty speech" a priori, cf. Jacques Lacan, "The function and field of speech and language in psychoanalysis," in: J. Lacan, *Écrits: A Selection*, trans. Alan Sheridan (New York: Norton, 1977), 30–113.

[29] On the loss of linguistic-hermeneutic understandability in this case, cf. Marion Doebeling, "Theodor Fontane im Gegenlicht. Essays, Kopien, Konfigurationen" (Diss., UC Davis, California, 1990), 216–17.

[30] Cf. Nietzsche's reflections on the impossible innocence of interpretation in the first part of this essay; cf. also Samuel Weber, "The Debts of Deconstruction and Other Related Assumptions," in Joseph Smith and William Kerrigan, eds., *Talking Chances: Derrida, Psychoanalysis, and Literature* (Baltimore: Johns Hopkins UP, 1984), 33–66.

[31] Cf. *Cécile*, 359: "Little sister has likely taken off on a summer jaunt and is somewhere in the mountains, in Landeck or in Reinerz or even in Bohemia. But so what? The postal service will find her. What else is Stephan for?"

[32] In 1904 Ludwig Boltzmann was inspired, on the basis of his previous research, to apply the principles of statistical mechanics to the statistics "of animated beings, of human society, of sociology." Cf. L. Boltzmann, *Populäre Schriften* (Braunschweig/Wiesbaden: Vieweg, 1979), 222. It is worth noting that the concept of entropy later attained decisive significance in theories of information.

[33] Cf. Sagarra, *Theodor Fontane*, 82.

[34] Martin Heidegger, *Prolegomena zu einer Geschichte des Zeitbegriffs. Collected Works*, vol. 20, part II, *Lectures 1923–1944* (Frankfurt am Main: Klostermann, 1979), 280.

[35] Quoted in Volker Aschoff, "Die elektrische Nachrichtentechnik," 403, n.1. Generally linguistic usage at the end of the nineteenth century also grouped the telephone in the telegraphic genus.

[36] Friedrich Kittler, "Telegrammstil," in H. U. Gumbrecht and K. L. Pfeiffer, eds., *Stil: Geschichten und Funktionen eines literaturwissenschaftlichen Diskurselements* (Frankfurt am Main: Suhrkamp, 1986), 358–370, esp. 361.

[37] Franz Kafka, *Briefe an Milena* (Frankfurt am Main: Fischer, 1983), 412.

[38] This follows, in a general sense, Jacques Lacan.

[39] Cf. Boltzmann, "Über statistische Mechanik" in *Populäre Schriften*, 220.

[40] Lacan, "Le séminaire sur 'La Lettre volée'" in J. Lacan, *Écrits I* (Paris: Éditions du Seuil, 1966), 19–75.

[41] Fontane, *Cécile.* English translation: "Society has me in its power, I see it and I feel it. I live therefore only by the grace of those who do my house the honor. . . . I cannot claim the rights that others have. But I want to have them back" (486).

[42] Charles Sanders Peirce, *Collected Papers* (Cambridge: Harvard UP, 1931–35; repr. Cambridge: Belknap, 1993). Further quotations from this text in brackets cited with "CP."

[43] The first series of essays laying the groundwork for a semiology of thinking were published by Peirce in 1868.

[44] Umberto Eco, *Lector in Fabula* (Munich: Carl Hanser Verlag, 1987), 55.

[45] Derrida, "My Chances/Mes changes," in Smith and Kerrigan, eds., *Talking Chances,* 27.

[46] Fontane, *Cécile.* English translation: "Despite all her illness and resignation, or perhaps even enhanced by this, there was something captivating about her. Surrendering himself anew to this spell, he eventually fell into a language that bore in mind the contents of Clothild's letter, and which he would not temper or even silence, since he considered such restraint no longer warranted" (472).

[47] Fontane, *Cécile.* English translation: "This was why she started with fright and turned away when we were looking into the haunted windows. And even before that, in Quedlinburg, as I so bravely perorated about the galleries of beauty and Countess Aurora . . . *Now it all becomes clear . . .* poor, lovely woman!" (465)

[48] Fontane, *Cécile.* English translation: "And these silly drops — get rid of them, along with that whole tribe of doctors! They boast of fathoming body and soul, constantly invent new sciences so full of psyche you can hardly move, and yet don't know the ABC's of the soul. Misconception and error, everywhere I look. . . . You're all laced up and fenced in. . . . If you could see yourself blossoming again, alive, like before" (469–70).

[49] Cf. Gustav Theodor Fechner, *Vorschule der Ästhetik* (Leipzig: Breitkopf/Härtl, 1876). Further quotations from this text in brackets cited with "Fechner."

[50] Oedipus's well-known solution to the Sphinx's riddle consists in Oedipus recognizing the riddle's parts as segments in a man's lifetime; with this solution, he is able to stake his claim both to the Theban throne and, unwittingly-incestuously, to the Queen.

[51] Fontane, *Cécile.* English translation: "I should find a way to return to the tone of our happier days, you wrote me yesterday. To be in the same

place with you, breathing the same air as you, I never would have been able to; but separated like this I will be able to, or will learn. . . . For once we are away, looking back, we take the image for reality, and the yearning desire that otherwise would torment us becomes our joy." (477)

[52] On this point, cf. Norbert Mecklenburg, "Einsichten und Blindheiten. Fragmente einer nichtkanonischen Fontane-Lektüre," in *Text & Kritik: Theodor Fontane* (Munich: Text & Kritik, 1989), 149–162.

RANDALL HOLT
Stanford University

History as Trauma:
The Absent Ground of Meaning
in *Irrungen, Wirrungen*

WRITTEN LESS THAN TWO DECADES AFTER THE unification of Germany under Bismarck, Theodor Fontane's novel *Irrungen, Wirrungen* (1888; translated as *Delusions, Confusions,* 1989) offers a late realist rendering of some of the larger cultural concerns within Wilhelmine or Prusso-German culture during the closing decades of the nineteenth century.[1] While the realist text may not provide an unproblematic representation of reality during the period, it can reveal not only some of the intellectual and cultural anxieties of its author, but also those of the context which it claims to represent and in which it is produced. Thus, Fontane's novel constitutes not only a critique of its socio-cultural constellation, but also exposes its own implication within that system. As recent scholarship has demonstrated, the realist text self-destructs by reflecting on its own fictional underpinnings, yet at the same time, it also uses the very same narrative strategies to cover and enforce its prejudiced view of the world.[2] It is precisely this reflection in Fontane's writings that exposes and displaces the instabilities experienced within the highly transitory socio-cultural landscape of the Second German Empire.[3] Historian Wolfgang Mommsen notes that the "loss of dynamism in the social sphere that resulted from the creation of the semi-constitutional German Empire was closely mirrored in the cultural realm."[4] Thus, the malaise of late-nineteenth-century Europe may be observed in the text of the realist novel where, if it can no longer fulfill earlier emancipatory programs, it at least tries to maintain a socio-political status quo. Russell Berman has persuasively argued that the internal malaise of realism represents an aesthetic corollary to the demise of liberalism and its faith in meaning, language, and discursive exchange.[5] And indeed, Fontane chronicles this dissonance while at the same time attempting to construct literary meaning vis-á-vis cultural disorder. In *Irrungen, Wirrungen,* this stabilization of social order and meaning is arrived at by Fontane through the use of extraliterary detail, whereby reference to nonliterary realities outside the text is employed to prevent the collapse of meaning within it. Although Fontane relies upon this proliferation of detail, of description, throughout his œuvre, in *Irrungen, Wirrungen* he attempts to figuratively prescribe order and meaning through the excessive specificity of social space. By examining the construction of social boundaries and space within Fontane's text, I seek to reveal the sites wherein the seemingly uncanny epistemological and ontological instability provoked by modernity are displaced and repressed by the realist imagination in the name of locating meaning outside the hegemonic yet unstable realm of Prusso-German culture.

Ostensibly, the novel's narrative revolves around the affair between an aristocratic officer, Baron Botho von Rienäcker, and a lower-class seamstress, Lene Nimptsch. Botho enjoys the hospitality and the superior simplicity of social relationships characteristic of a premodern past that Lene and her working-class circle represent. Pressured by his family's precarious financial and social position, Botho marries a wealthy heiress and ends the affair with Lene, internalizing the social imperative to maintain order in the face of the growing disturbances within traditional social structures. While both Lene and Botho acquiesce to the rigid boundaries of Wilhelmine social constructions, Lene's understanding and stoic acceptance of the impossibility of a lasting union with Botho is contrasted with his confusion over his ongoing emotional entanglement long after the affair has ended. That Fontane ambivalently stages the novel's thematic concern along spatial lines reflects broader cultural implications regarding the simultaneous desire for order and its transgression, which transcend the relatively simple narrative.

The opening lines of the novel indicate Fontane's exacting spatial precision of realist detail, "In the middle of the 1870s, just at the crossing of the Kurfürstendamm and the Kurfürstenstraße, diagonally across from the 'Zoological'" (3). In marked contrast to the experience of error and confusion suggested by the novel's title, this topographical specificity attempts to provide a sense of stability perceived as absent in the social realm. As the social and political changes created by the rapid pace of modernization taking place in imperial Germany provoked a sense of confusion, literary realism resorted to the use of even greater preciseness of detail to evoke, if not stabilize, meaning. The use of proper names, not only of places but also of things, reflects the realist gesture of producing a sense of order to counteract the unsettling experience of pervasive cultural change. Indeed, whereas realism earlier in the century sought to present the essence or inherent meaning through narrative description, the crisis of meaning rendered by societal changes at the close of the nineteenth century appears in realism as a strategy of at once revealing meaning and obscuring it. The opening paragraph of *Irrungen, Wirrungen* is worth quoting at length,

> An dem Schnittpunkte von Kurfürstendamm und Kurfürstenstraße, schräg dem 'Zoologischen' gegenüber, befand sich in der Mitte der siebziger Jahre noch eine große, feldeinwärts sich erstreckende Gärtnerei, deren kleines, dreifenstriges, in einem Vorgärtchen um etwa hundert Schritte zurückgelegenes Wohnhaus trotz aller Kleinheit und Züruckgezogenheit von der vorübergehenden Straße her sehr wohl erkannt werden konnte. Was aber sonst noch zu dem Gesamtgewese der Gärtnerei gehörte, ja die recht eigentliche Hauptsache derselben ausmachte, war durch eben dies kleine Wohnhaus wie durch eine Kulisse versteckt, und nur ein rot- und grüngestrichenes Holztürmchen mit einem halb weggebrochenen Zifferblatt unter der Turmspitze (von Uhr selbst keine Rede) ließ vermuten, daß hinter dieser Kulisse noch etwas anderes verborgen sein müsse, welche Vermutung denn auch in einer von Zeit zu Zeit aufsteigenden, das Türmchen umschwärmenden Taubenschar und mehr noch in einem gelegentlichen Hundegeblaff ihre Bestätigung fand.[6]

Despite the exacting description of old Dörr's "castle" and its precise location on the outskirts of Berlin, Fontane also suggests the presence of something, of "its main part," which somehow remains obscured or hidden. Within the exacting delineation of social space, Fontane displaces an earlier nineteenth-century notion of a poetic or transcendental meaning — culturally suspect in a period dominated by materialism and empiricism — and thereby re-inscribes a locus of meaning absent in bourgeois/aristocratic Berlin/Prussian society but retrievable at its social margins. The narrator notes that the "main part" was "hidden by this very dwelling as if by a stage

[back]drop." Thus, realism stages the very meaning it claims is present yet obscured. The implicit promise of the realist enterprise is to reveal exactly what is obscured, and Fontane proceeds to take his reader into the homes and lives of both his aristocratic and lower-class characters. However, this promise is soon subsumed by the accumulation of surface detail. Indeed, this simultaneous gesture within realism testifies to the complex and contradictory economy of desires receiving currency within the Prussian culture of Berlin in the age of the Second Empire.

Fontane's poetic realism evokes a latent romanticism in the novel's *Märchen* or fairy-tale quality staged behind the back drop of an excess of details.[7] Indeed, the surface realism of the text with its extreme precision, in the wake of the materialization of nineteenth-century European culture and the primacy of the world of objects, serves to legitimate poetic or transcendental meaning. The turret, the broken clock, and the circling birds and barking dogs are all details which invoke earlier literary conventions. "In the middle of the 1870s" substitutes for "once upon a time," while the broken clock represents this suspension of real time. Moreover, after Botho ends the affair, Lene develops a white streak in her hair. As Frau Dörr notes, "My God, Lene, right there on the left. But naturally, sure, that's where it is . . . it's gotta' be on the left" (112). On an excursion into the countryside, Lene makes a wreath of wild flowers for Botho. The narration makes the reader aware of the particular flowers by naming them. However, the naming does not create so much an effect of realism as it points to the symbolic significance that the flowers possess. Lene, reluctant to bind the wreath with a strand of her hair, recalling the old saying that "hair binds," is reduced to superstition by Botho. Yet, being symbolically "bound" points to the psychological entanglement of the title which Botho experiences long after his liaison with Lene has come to an end.

Fontane litters his narrative with symbolic details; however, he combines the realist detail of the central narrative with a symbolic context, and one reinforces the other. Thus, while Fontane maintains textual unity through the use of extraliterary, hierarchical codes of place and name, *Irrungen, Wirrungen* also relies upon a covert, symbolic or poetic level of signification. The references to the realm of the fairy tale such as Dörr's "castle," Lene's status as a foundling, and Frau Dörr's joking remark that perhaps Lene is a "princess" all call attention to the fictionality of the text as well as the contingency of meaning when confronted by epistemological uncertainty. And indeed, this recourse to a secondary level of symbolic reference indicates the problematic status of the exchange of meaning in the realist enterprise as an expression of broader cultural trends in the late-nineteenth century. As Russell Berman observes,

> in the context of increasingly radical social conflicts, the hierarchical organization of society loses its appearance as a natural order . . . meaning can be guaranteed only by an external imposition of symbolic order, organizational forms grafted arbitrarily onto the perceived confusion. Such external codes of meaning do not merely embellish the central narrative but grant it a stability which, left on its own, it could not attain. Reality is no longer the carrier of an immanent meaning, and order becomes meaningful and orderly only because of the imposition of heterogeneous matrices.[8]

In *Irrungen, Wirrungen,* Fontane at once attempts to represent this loss of immanent meaning and to impose a matrix of external order. The breakdown of the meaningful order of social structures thus requires the arbitrary imposition of spatial and hierarchical codes as well as disguised symbolic or poetic contexts. Yet this loss of meaning also raises the possibility of alternative readings or constructions of "reality." Indeed, one of Fontane's minor characters who voices decidedly romantic notions on pleasure and the imagination, Serge, a friend of Botho's among the cavaliers, asserts that in the "final analysis all pleasure is nothing but imagination, and whoever's got the best imagination has the greatest pleasure. Only the unreal has any true value and is really the only reality" (46). Here, one of the novel's marginal figures suggests a perspective which would undoubtedly have appeared suspect or marginal to most of Wilhelmine society.[9] Indeed, this relocation of the pursuit of happiness to the realm of the imagination suggests the inherent failure of bourgeois liberalism and a rationalist and materialist system of exchange. Moreover, this notion affirms the contingent nature of reality, and that "reality" itself is an arbitrary imposition of the imagination rather than a social experience or structure.

However, this reflection upon fictionality both in the textual and contextual worlds is obscured throughout the novel by the desire to impose order, a desire which is conducted through the language of the characters as well as the narrative. To clearly maintain the social class divisions that are threatened in the novel, Fontane marks the speech of his characters by the use of dialects. The aristocracy, for whom oral and written language are virtually equivalent, exhibit normative speech, while those beyond the Prussian imperial center speak in dialects. The speech of the Jewish Viennese Frau Salinger, for example, is represented by Fontane with a broad, intentionally humorous Austrian accent, while the lower-class characters speak in regional Berlin dialect. The speech of Lene and others of her class is depicted as fragmentary, signifying a more spontaneous connection to their emotions and unconsciously expressing a certain authenticity. Indeed, it is Lene's directness and lack of pretense in both her verbal and written communications that arouses Botho's admiration for her. After reading one of Lene's letters, Botho takes a pencil to it marking the errors. Rather than being pedantic, Botho notes that the letter is "just like Lene herself, kind, true, dependable, and its mistakes make it only all the more charming" (34). Thus, the language of the lower class is infused by Fontane with a simplicity and authenticity inviting and reassuring to the upper classes. Yet the narrative also largely elides the very realities under which the working class is living. Although lower-class characters such as Frau and Herr Dörr are gently satirized, the lower class, especially as represented by Lene, is regarded as a representative of authentic and idyllic experience by the aristocratic Botho.[10] He refers at one point to Chamisso's poem "The Old Washerwoman" and notes that "every class has its honor" (19). Botho counters the skepticism expressed by Mother Nimptsch and the Dörrs by asking rhetorically, "How do you live? Like the Good Lord in Paradise itself! For one thing you've got this house and this hearth and then you've got the garden" (20). Thus, while Fontane lamented the decline of the aristocracy and the rise of the nouveau riche middle class, he came ultimately to view the world of the working class as "more genuine, more true and more full of life" than the bourgeoisie.[11] The conspicuous absence of representations of the bourgeoisie in the novel attests to the perceived failure of middle-class liberalism and its legal-rationalist belief in an economy of exchange. Despite the fears of worker uprisings in this period, the lower class is strangely romanticized and identified as the repository of an orderly or idyllic otherness by the middle and upper classes, whose cultural and political unconsciousness registers the disturbances of social order by the processes of modernity.

Fontane's trademark use of conversation precisely demonstrates the unequal exchange of information as a substitute for meaning. In response to Frau Dörr's comment about the difficulty of establishing a dialogue, Botho conducts pseudo-conversation for the amusement of Lene's lower-class peers. Yet this enactment is no more false than that within the circles of the social elite. Botho concedes that:

> . . . eigentlich ist es ganz gleich, wovon man spricht. Wenn es nicht Morcheln sind, sind es Champignons, und wenn es nicht das rote polnische Schloß ist, dann ist es Schlößchen Tegel. . . . Es ist alles ganz gleich. Über jedes kann man ja was sagen, und ob's einem gefällt oder nicht. Und, ja, ist gerade so viel wie, nein." (23)[12]

This exchange of social currencies reflects a meaninglessness in which opposites collapse into one another. Regardless of the bankruptcy of the content of information, meaning now resides largely in the social convention of empty exchange for the aristocracy. Watching Lene and Botho parting at the garden gate, Frau Dörr recalls her own affair with a member of the aristocracy in her youth. As she and mother Nimptsch watch the young lovers part, Frau Dörr offers a running commentary:

> Und nu sagt er ihr was ins Ohr, und sie lacht vor sich hin. Aber ganz rot is sie geworden . . . Und nu geht er. Und nu . . . wahrhaftig, ich glaube, er dreht noch mal um. Nei, nei er grüßt bloß noch mal, und sie wirft ihm Kußginger zu . . . Ja, das glaub ich; so was laß ich mir gefallen . . . Nei, so war meiner nich." (6) [13]

The internal contradiction in Frau Dörr's commentary reveals not only the collapse of distinction between oppositions but also that her own past social experience differs fundamentally and confusingly from Lene's situation in the 1870s.

The breakdown of meaning and of communication not only between but also *within* the classes is attested to by the movement of Botho from the margins of society along Unter den Linden to the cultural center of Imperial Berlin. Although Botho's uncle Kurt, a conservative East Prussian Junker, is humorously dealt with in the narrative, it is he who is most highly aware of the precarious position of the social order in the wake of rapid industrialization. Lunching with Botho and his friend Lieutenant von Wedell in a private club, the old Junker demands "Fresh air gentlemen, fresh air! This beautiful Berlin of yours . . . has everything, except fresh air" (38). However, the old conservative from rural East Prussia, sensitive to the urban environment, is speaking figuratively as well. For he registers the rather claustrophobic conditions of the modern city with its smoke-belching factories and the surrounding environs of the workers, which are virtually elided in the textual world of Fontane's novel. In a discussion on politics with Botho and Wedell, the old Junker's attacks on Bismarck highlight the weakness of liberal exchange. Botho's own liberal equivocation provokes his uncle to exclaim: "I don't understand you, Botho. What's that supposed to mean, 'one can say that?' Why it's the same as saying, 'one *can't* say that'" (39). It is the conservative who rejects the liberal weakening of distinctions between the positive and negative, seeking, rather, authentic exchange. Ironically, the conservative becomes the advocate of free speech: "But you're silent gentlemen. I beg you, speak up. Believe me, I can listen to other opinions and put up with them. I'm not like he [Bismarck] is. Speak up, Herr von Wedell, speak up'" (40). However, Wedell, a liberal, pro-Bismarck, and anti-conservative, responds with a "might before right" adage that parallels the blood-and-iron *Realpolitik* of Bismarck's own antiparlimentarism. Whereas the liberal Botho had earlier also sought genuine exchange in the earthly paradise of the lower-class home of Lene, he increasingly comes to perceive the threat of transgression against social order that is represented by his personal relationship with Lene. Thus Fontane's novel "echoes the experiences of German political culture" where the "liberal ideology of exchange and debate collapses in on itself and renounces these ideals just as it renounces the possibility of happiness."[14]

Botho had formerly sought an alternative to the disturbances of modernity outside the imperial center, at its outskirts, but these disturbances are increasingly experienced there as well, as the center expands its social and cultural hegemony toward the margins. Although Lene's home is located at the periphery of Berlin, she too has felt the exertion of social and cultural conventions that lead Botho and her to confine themselves to the Dörr's garden or the fields around Wilmersdorf instead of strolling boldly down the "Slanderer's Boulevard" or the main promenade of the nearby Zoological Garden. In order to consummate their affair, Lene and Botho must find private space beyond even the periphery of Berlin. Botho decides upon Hankel Depot, at that time a landing and excursion site located on the River Spree, six miles east of Berlin.[15] For

Lene, the "only thing that mattered . . . was to get out in the open for a change, as far as possible from the bustle of the city in God's free and open spaces" (61). With the movement outside of Berlin and a change in social space comes a personal change as well. The narrator notes that a "resolute quality, something almost severe, that otherwise lay in her character, seemed to have been taken from and had given way to an otherwise foreign tenderness" (62).

Later that evening, while waiting for Botho in their room in the inn, Lene notices a color lithograph with the inscription: "*Si jeunesse savait.*" Lene recalled having seen it in the Dörrs' home and that seeing it made her feel "put out. Her delicate sensuality felt violated by the lewdness in the picture, as if it represented a distortion of her own feelings" (73). In realist fashion, Fontane, while dealing precisely with desire and sexuality, displaces these aspects in the text. "To free herself of such an impression, she went to the gable window and opened both sides to let in the night air." This maneuver, however, echoes the realist strategy in *Irrungen, Wirrungen* of a displacement of a particular disturbing element into the realm of nature or what is construed as natural. Both Lene and Botho construct their ephemeral happiness through recourse to patently romantic visions. Sitting at the window, Lene notes that only

> Eine tiefe Stille herrschte; nur in der alten Ulme ging ein Wehen und Rauschen, und alles, was eben noch von Verstimmung in ihrer Seele geruht haben mochte, das schwand jetzt hin, als sie den Blick immer eindringlicher und immer entzückter auf das vor ihr ausgebreitete Bild richtete. Das Wasser flutete leise, der Wald und die Wiese lagen im abendlichen Dämmer, und der Mond, der eben wieder seinen ersten Sichelstreifen zeigte, warf einen Lichtschein über den Strom und ließ das Zittern seiner kleinen Wellen erkennen. (73)[16]

The following morning, in response to the innkeeper's inquiry as to their night's rest, Botho states that with the "new moon shining right into our window and the nightingales singing so softly that you could just about hear them, well, who couldn't sleep with all that as if in paradise" (76). Significantly, whereas Lene perceives "deep silence," Botho, in addition to the moonlight, perceives barely audible nightingales, a staple of earlier Romantic poetry. Thus the underlying symbolic context which reinforces the surface detail with meaning also serves as a reservoir of displaced disorder.

Not unlike the Dörrs' garden, which also lies beyond the imperial center, Botho refers to this place as "paradise." Jokingly, Botho voices the hope that no steamer loaded with passengers is looming at the depot, asserting that that would "really be an expulsion from paradise" (76). However, their expulsion comes not from hordes of strangers, but rather from the arrival of three of Botho's most intimate friends: Pitt, Serge, and Balafré, and along with them their courtesans. The narration informs the reader that the "whole thing was an intrusion, perhaps even one that had been planned. Nevertheless, the more this seemed to be the case, the more necessary it was to put up a good front" (78). Paradoxically, the attempt to move outside the constraints of Wilhelmine society results in an encounter where its representatives simply serve to remind both Lene and Botho of the impossibility of a continued liaison.

Botho and his friends' use of nicknames, or more precisely, code words by which to address themselves and others, once again points to the instability of identity. The courtesans are introduced to Lene in code, each bearing the name of a character from Schiller's *The Maid of Orleans*. Earlier, when Botho attempted to explain the nicknames to Lene, coming to the name Gaston, Lene noted that she recalled the name from the play *The Man in the Iron Mask*. Although Botho thinks she will be amused when he reveals the fact that Gaston is his nickname, Lene responds: "No, I'm not laughing. You've got a mask too" (57). And indeed, the iron mask that Botho wears is that of an authoritarian state and society to whose social conventions he will ultimately conform.

The episode of the intrusion is quite significant, and perhaps reveals unconsciously the subversion of social boundaries that Botho himself has transgressed, provoking his subsequent ending of his affair with Lene and his desire for order embodied in the form of marriage to Käthe. The questionable social status of the "ladies" contrasts markedly with their names: what are in effect prostitutes are designated by the code names of nobility. However, as Lene and Botho's discussion suggests, these nicknames are in essence masks that conceal authentic identity. Indeed, the episode enacts at a subdued level the Bahktinian notion of the carnivalesque where boundaries are transgressed and hierarchies subverted.[17] The character identified as Queen Isabeau, for example, is described as "extremely well upholstered in the posterior," and is said to "[distinguish] herself almost as much through her loquaciousness as her rotundity" (78). While certainly not a full-blown example of the carnivalesque, which had largely been repressed throughout the nineteenth century by bourgeois social conventions, Isabeau's concern with the intake of food and the effect of the outing upon her bodily comfort do suggest grotesque distortion of or intrusion upon the idyllic inter-lude earlier envisioned by Botho. Still, the social stability and authenticity of identity ensured by the precision in delineating place and name is undermined. Whereas naming was once viewed as of-fering a sense of order of people and objects through classification, the carnivalesque "masks" assumed by the characters now subvert the presumed means of ascertaining authentic identity. When Lene asks Queen Isabeau about the strange names used by the gentlemen, the latter replies that it's "nothin' but a lot a' put-on anyway . . . . Who's it gonna hurt? They all don't have nothing to reproach them-selves for and each one of them is just the same as the other" (82–83). Yet this exchangeability reflects the very social disorder of crossed boundaries and the accompanying sense of confusion that forms the thematic concern of the novel.

Shortly after the Spree outing, Botho ends the affair with Lene, yet he still feels himself bound to her. Confused and disturbed, Botho rides his horse out into the surrounding countryside in order to clear his thoughts. There, in the novel's only overt reference to industrialization, he comes upon a factory where, with his "sense for the unsophisticated, [he] was enchanted at the sight" of the "the lower classes, the 'happy people.'" Yet Botho ambiguously locates the very traits whose absence has created such confusion in himself and, by extension, in society.

> Arbeit und täglich Brot und Ordnung. Wenn unsre märkischen Leute sich verheiraten, so reden sie nicht von Leidenschaft und Liebe, sie sa-gen nur: "Ich muß doch meine Ordnung haben." Und das ist ein schöner Zug im Leben unsres Volks und nicht einmal prosaisch. Denn Ordnung ist viel und mitunter alles. Und nun frag ich mich: War mein Leben in der "Ordnung"? Nein. Ordnung ist Ehe. (93) [18]

Botho concedes to the wishes of his mother and uncle to marry Käthe, thereby stabilizing the Rienäcker estate and internalizing the imperative of a society for order over passion. Although Botho char-acterizes Lene as having the "best combination of all, common sense and passion combined," as the narrative proceeds, the possibility of a supplementary relation between these elements becomes increasingly precluded. Fontane clearly sets up a dichotomy between Lene and Käthe, contrasting the two largely through their differing modes of communication. Whereas, for Botho, Lene's style represents "simplicity, truthfulness, and straightforwardness," Käthe, though good humored and a clever conversationalist, betrays a fundamental lack of authenticity. While it was "perhaps possible to exchange a passably reasonable word with Käthe, it was by no means possible to exchange a serious one." Botho's recognition of Käthe's inability to "distinguish between significant and insignificant matters" disturbs him, and despite the outward order his marriage provides him, "now and again a sense of dissatisfaction came over him" (107–8). Käthe voices her own dissatisfaction with the speech habits of Botho and, by extension, the seriousness of German men, for she says, "Our men, your friends included, are always so thorough. And you're the most thorough of all, which sometimes really depresses me and tries my patience" (161). Ultimately, the thematic concern of the novel is the confrontation between social order and personal happiness also being confronted in German culture in the wake of unification and imperial expansion.

Significantly, the narrative ends shortly after Käthe's return from a curative retreat; here the text is marked not only by the pattern of unequal exchange perpetuated in Botho's married life, but also by the instability against which the realist use of the literary detail had sought to defend. The novel's closing chapters consist in large part of Käthe's fragmentary and seemingly trivial recounting of her stay at the spa. Recalling some of the colorful characters she encountered on her trip, Käthe tells Botho that she will finish telling him the story about that "Russian woman, who naturally wasn't Russian at all." Like identity, the order of place now comes into question as well. Käthe notes that although the Russian woman had no doctor, "everyday she was over in Frankfurt or in Wiesbaden or even in Darmstadt and always on somebody's arm" (165). Whereas the first part of the novel is marked by an excessive precision, the confusion and instability implied by the title have now become pervasive; even order secured by seeming enforcement of social boundaries disintegrates. Thus, the social order of society, like its aesthetic counterpart, literary realism, actually obscures the very order it seeks to restabilize. Yet this maneuver also obscures the fact that order is itself a social construction, and that this recognition provides a disorienting but liberating ground upon which alternative constructions might be entertained.

Shortly before Käthe's return home, Botho rides out along the canal where he had found the courage to part with Lene three years earlier. There he encounters a minor character in the narrative, fellow officer Bozel von Rexin, who seeks out his advice on a particular "affair." Rexin confides a situation that parallels Botho's own: although engaged to a girl of the upper class, he is in love with one from the lower class. Like Botho, he yearns for the "simple things, for a quiet, natural way of life, where one heart speaks to another, and where one has the best thing one can ever have, honesty, love, freedom." All this Rexin contrasts to the "boring and straight . . . conventions and formalities of our society" (152). While Rexin considers "distinctions" to be "nothing but sham," he is also aware of the social repercussions of transgressing those artificial bounds of distinction. He confesses that he can't simply break with convention, he doesn't want to hurt his parents nor does he wish to leave military service at "twenty-seven to become a cowboy in Texas or a waiter on some Mississippi steamboat"; rather, he proposes a "middle course." This middle course parallels a strategy that is not only Botho's, but also Fontane's: that of constructing some sort of transcendental meaning against the extremes available within the social and cultural milieu. Despite the unhappiness he experiences after having opted for the order metaphorically promised by marriage, Botho now rejects the affair of the heart. He also rejects the middle way because when "you make your peace with society and family, then comes the real misery. Then you've got to sever something that has become intertwined and interwoven. . . . And that hurts." Moreover, Botho warns "keep away from this middle course. Look out for such halfway measures. . . . It *never* leads to anything good" (153). Botho's position insists on the inherent dangers and the ultimate impossibility of supplementing order with passion in late-nineteenth-century Prussian culture. Anxiety over disturbance-provoking traits such as passion and epistemological uncertainty are uncannily displaced by the realist imagination onto a bucolic, idealized realm of the lower class. While this class is represented as existing outside the destabilizing effects of modernity, paradoxically, their availability to the upper class is also viewed as symptomatic of the epistemological and ontological instability attendant to that same experience of modernity. Moreover, Fontane critiques the extremes of Wilhelmine society, which virtually preclude the possibility of an alternative "middle course." However, the demands of society are such that deviance outside of the accepted course implies an entanglement that ultimately requires that one sever the authentic part of one's self.

Thus, in *Irrungen, Wirrungen* Fontane critically exposes the reactionary nature of Prusso-German society in a period of transition during the 1870s and 1880s. Yet he also symptomatically displays the realist impulse to stabilize the latent social and cultural disorder perceived as immanent within that society through the imposition of a rigidly ordered and precise use of literary detail. Promising to reveal what is obscured, the realist enterprise itself obscures while at the same time it exposes the very absence of a ground upon which meaning may be constructed. Although the textually marginal characters of Serge and Rexin suggest alternatives to the conventions of the cultural center, the exchange between Botho and Rexin on the "middle course" perhaps suggests the difficulty of enacting transformative alternatives within a society anxious about the assault on traditional boundaries by the forces of modernity.

The most prominent exclusion in the novel is that of the liberal middle class. In Germany this class was never a completely unified social entity; it was increasingly fragmented by political blows from Bismarck, and even more so by the explosive takeoff of industrialization.[19] The alternative to this struggle of nineteenth-century liberalism is located in the lower class; however, their social realities are largely elided as well. The dissatisfactions with the hegemonic center of Wilhelmine culture sent many in search of premodern stability and meaning, which it located in its other: the marginalized working class, which simultaneously attracted and repelled bourgeois sensibilities.[20] The designation of a "fairy tale" in reference to the peripheral realm of the Dörrs' "castle" and its inhabitants exposes a realist displacement of the uncanniness of modern experience. At the same time, the novel also calls attention to its own fictionality and that of late-nineteenth-century realist paradigms, which will ultimately collapse in on themselves. Indeed, what realism obscures is the very constructedness of meaning; it represents the natural or universal order, thereby denying an epistemological relativity that undermines intellectual certainty. In response to the dislocation of social and cultural meaning by modernization and modernity, the Prusso-German cultural imperative sought a solid epistemological and ontological ground within the realm of the social other. However, rather than represent Prusso-German culture as a unified entity, Fontane also renders the contestatory elements within it, revealing the ambivalent currents operating within the culture of Imperial Germany which at once desire social order and meaning *and* their opposites. Thus, at the center and margins both of the text itself and the society in which it was produced, *Irrungen, Wirrungen* renders the response to the experience of modernity in late nineteenth-century Prusso-German culture as a historical trauma that ultimately may not be displaced or disregarded, despite the degree of specificity with which social space may be inscribed.

Notes

[1] Theodor Fontane, *Delusions, Confusions*, trans. by William L. Zwiebel (New York: Continuum, 1989).

[2] Robert Holub, *Reflections of Realism: Paradox, Norm, and Ideology in Nineteenth-Century German Prose* (Detroit: Wayne State UP, 1991), 18.

[3] Comprehensive studies of the relations between culture and politics in late Prussian history remain to be written, however, for more general overviews, see Gordon A. Craig, *Germany 1866–1914* (Oxford: Oxford UP, 1978), 180–213; Eric J. Hobsbawm, *The Age of Empire 1875–1914* (New York: Random House, 1989).

[4] Wolfgang Mommsen, *Imperial Germany 1867–1918: Politics, Culture, and Society in an Authoritarian State*, trans. by Richard Deveson (London: Arnold, 1995), 128.

[5] See Russell Berman, "The Dissolution of Meaning: Theodor Fontane," in *The Rise of the Modern German Novel: Crisis and Charisma* (Cambridge: Harvard UP, 1986), 134–160.

[6] Theodor Fontane, *Irrungen, Wirrungen*, in *Sämtliche Werke*, vol. 3 (Munich: Nymphenburger Verlagshandlung, 1959), 95. English translation: "In the middle of the 1870s, just at the crossing of the Kurfürstendamm and the Kurfürstenstraße, diagonally across from the 'Zoological,' could still be found a large vegetable garden, stretching a distance away from the street. Despite compactness and seclusion, its small three-windowed dwelling, located some hundred paces back, could nevertheless

still be made out quite easily from the passing street. Everything else that belonged to the whole spread of the truck garden, in fact what was really its main part, was hidden by this dwelling as if by a stage drop. Only a small wooden turret, painted red and green, with its clock face half-broken away — of the clock itself naught can be said — led one to suspect that behind this stage drop something else might indeed be hidden, a suspicion likely to find confirmation in the flock of pigeons which from time to time circled the tower, and ever more so, in the occasional barking of a dog."

[7] On the romantic and classic elements in Fontane, see Horst Turk, "The Order of Appearance and Validation: On Perennial Classicism in Fontane's Society Novel *Schach von Wuthenow*" in the present volume.

[8] Berman, *The Rise of the Modern German Novel*, 146.

[9] On minor or secondary characters and their place in challenging or suggesting alternatives to accepted societal roles and structures in Fontane's fiction, see Sabine Cramer, "*Grete Minde*: Structures of Societal Disturbance," forthcoming article.

[10] The fascination with the lower classes by realist artists can also be witnessed in the visual arts, such as in the works of Max Liebermann and Adolf Menzel's "unofficial" paintings. On realism in art see Linda Nochlin, *Realism* (New York: Penguin, 1971).

[11] Katharina Mommsen, *Gesellschaftskritik bei Theodor Fontane und Thomas Mann* (Heidelberg: Stiehm, 1973), 19–29, quoted in Wolfgang Mommsen, *Imperial Germany 1867–1914*, 128.

[12] Theodor Fontane, *Irrungen, Wirrungen*, in *Sämtliche Werke*, vol. 3 (Munich: Nymphenburger Verlagshandlung, 1959), 112. English translation: " . . . it doesn't make even the slightest difference what you talk about. If it's not mushrooms, its champignons and if it's not the red Polish castle, why then it's Tegel Castle. . . . It's all the same, really. And you can say something about every one of those things for sure, whether it pleases you or not. And yes means just as much as no." (22)

[13] Theodor Fontane, *Irrungen, Wirrungen*, in *Sämtliche Werke*, vol. 3 (Munich: Nymphenburger Verlagshandlung, 1959), 97. English translation: "And now he's whisperin' somethin' in her ear, and she's laughin' to herself. But she's started blushing all over. . . . And now he's goin'. And now, why really, I think he's comin' back again. Nope, nope, he's just waving one more time, and she's blowin' him a kiss. . . . Yes, sir, that's the thing for me . . . nope, mine was never like that." (6)

[14] Berman, *The Rise of the Modern German Novel*, 156.

[15] It was here that Fontane wrote a number of chapters for *Irrungen, Wirrungen* in May 1884.

[16] Theodor Fontane, *Irrungen, Wirrungen*, in *Sämtliche Werke*, vol. 3 (Munich: Nymphenburger Verlagshandlung, 1959), 154. English translation: "Deep silence prevailed. Only in the old elm tree could a rustling and whispering be heard. Everything left from the unpleasantness which had just touched her soul now disappeared, as she looked more closely and with growing delight at the scene spread out before her. The water flowed quietly on, forest and field lay in an evening twilight, and the moon, which was just again showing its first sicklelike form, cast a ray of light over the river so that one could make out the gentle undulation of its waves."(73)

[17] For a discussion of the subversive potential of Bahktin's notion of the carnivalesque in culture and literature, see Peter Stallybrass and Allon White, *The Politics and Poetics of Transgression* (Ithaca: Cornell UP, 1986). By the late nineteenth century, the carnivalesque was largely repressed as bourgeois social conventions and constraints were internalized. However, this and other works of the period increasingly reveal the latent presence of repressed carnivalesque impulses. Thus, the intrusion of socially subversive figures such as the prostitute and the carnivalesque tropes of the lower bodily strata and of masks subtly presages the return of the repressed others of bourgeois society that would mark high modernist works such as Joyce's *Ulysses*.

[18] Theodor Fontane, *Irrungen, Wirrungen*, in *Sämtliche Werke*, vol. 3 (Munich: Nymphenburger Verlagshandlung, 1959), 171. English translation: "Work, daily bread, and order. When our Brandenburg folk marry, it's not passions and love they talk about. They just say, "I've just got to have my order." And that is a beautiful trait in the life of our people and not at all a prosaic one. Order means a great deal, sometimes it's everything. And now I ask myself: Has *my* life been in order? No. Order is marriage."

[19] Mommsen, *Imperial Germany*, 146.

[20] See Stallybrass and White, *The Politics and Poetics of Transgression*, 1–6.

WILLI GOETSCHEL
Columbia University

Causerie: On the Function of Dialogue in *Der Stechlin*

BY NOW IT IS A SUFFICIENTLY KNOWN FACT that Theodor Fontane's *Der Stechlin* (1897) consists primarily of conversations. Fontane himself pointed this out,[1] Fontane critics have reiterated it,[2] and a glance into the novel confirms it.

Dialogue in Fontane's novels has also become a theme in Fontane research. It has undergone monograph-length studies, in addition to being mentioned *en passant* with some degree of obligatoriness.[3] Occasionally, more critical judgments have also surfaced. Yet even Conrad Wandrey — who in this regard was hardly one to mince words, and thus was universally chastised — saw the manner in which Fontane's last novel degrades human beings to mere functions of their conversations as just an accidental defect of an author in his waning years.[4]

Remarkably enough, no critical inquiry into the function and position of dialogue in Fontane has been undertaken; instead, statistical and stylistic analyses have been deemed sufficient.[5] But purely language- and style-oriented analysis unaccompanied by critical reflection on the role of those speaking must, at least since Martin Buber's *I and Thou* and *Dialogue*, be seen as no longer adequate on its own.[6]

Werner Weber has pointed out Fontane's "veil of talking," whereby he talks on and on in order not to have to say anything: "In *Der Stechlin* we encounter not only the art of keeping silent; art itself keeps silent. . . . "[7] Fontane's art, he concludes, is the art of "not letting oneself . . . get involved."[8]

The conversations in *Der Stechlin* are not genuine dialogue in Buber's sense; on the contrary, they are paradigms of causerie and representations of what Buber termed "misencounters" (*Vergegnun-*

gen). In order to prove this thesis, we shall turn first of all to theories of conversation and consider their significance for an understanding of Fontane. Since Fontane's skeptical side has been compared with Montaigne's,[9] and since the connection between skepticism and dialogue is a fundamental one, let us briefly consider Montaigne's opinion of conversation. In the third book of his *Essais*, in the essay "De l'Art de Conferer" (On the Art of Conversation), he writes: "Le plus fructueux exercice de nostre espirit, c'est à mon gré la conference . . . je consentirois plustost, ce crois-je, de perdre la veuë que l'ouir ou le parler."[10] Montaigne, the Seigneur de Montaigne who for more than a thousand pages talks on and on about God and the world: is he not a relative of Herr von Stechlin? Both are skeptics who talk to themselves, albeit that the one is listened to by his reader, the other by his servants.[11] And if Montaigne has already noted that, in reading certain writers, it is less their knowledge of a subject that interests him than their manner ("leur façon")[12] — this is also the very thing Fontane intends.

W. Martin Lüdke refers to Max Horkheimer's essay on Montaigne as one study that is particularly instructive for a critical understanding of Fontane's old Dubslav.[13] Indeed, Horkheimer's analysis of the function of skepticism not only reminds one, throughout, of the elder Stechlin; it also points the way to a more adequate appreciation of Dubslav's skeptical humanism, which is still so often, and widely, acclaimed. On the one hand, Horkheimer exposes the bourgeois moment of such skepticism as the veiled legitimation of the status quo: "If there is no truth, then it is not smart to risk oneself for it."[14] On the other hand, he distinguishes Montaigne's philosophical orientation from the modern form of skepticism, which is hardly more than a reactive reflex to real change: "The peace that the liberal skeptic has concluded with the authoritarian order is not an expression of humanist praxis, but rather its renunciation."[15] For "he who attacks ideology without explicating its basis is practicing bad, or much rather no critique, however sophisticated it may be."[16] This is precisely what conversation or causerie consists of, *per definitionem* — and this is developed probably to its highest artistic potential in the house, or rather "castle," of Stechlin.[17]

Moritz Lazarus, who was a friend of Fontane, was one of the first to demand a scientific examination of conversation. He recognized conversation primarily as a function of self-expression for the person leading it.[18] "How numerous are our authors?" he asked. And the answer: "The number of conversants is as great as that of the people [*Volk*]. . . . It is not in what is written or what is read, but in speaking that the spirit of the people *lives* with its language."[19] And: "Literature relates to conversation much the way genuine *creativity* relates to the simple, yet also real *life*."[20]

Georg Simmel's formal-sociological analysis of conversation reads like a description of Fontane's *Stechlin*:

> Das Entscheidende ist hier die ganz banale Erfahrung auszudrücken: daß im Ernst des Lebens die Menschen um eines Inhaltes willen reden, den sie mitteilen oder über den sie sich verständigen wollen, in der Geselligkeit aber das Reden zum Selbstzweck wird, aber nicht im naturalistischen Sinne, wie im Geschwätz, sondern in dem der *Kunst* des Sich-Unterhaltens, mit deren eigenen artistischen Gesetzen; im rein geselligen Gespräch ist sein Stoff nur noch der unentbehrliche Träger der Reize, die der lebendige Wechseltausch der Rede als solcher entfaltet. Alle die Formen, mit denen dieser Tausch sich verwirklicht: der Streit und der Appell an die von beiden Parteien anerkannten Normen; der Friedensschluß durch Kompromiß und das Entdecken gemeinsamer Überzeugungen; das dankbare Aufnehmen des Neuen und das Ablenken von dem, worüber doch keine Verständigung zu hoffen ist — alle diese Formen gesprächhafter Wechselwirkung, sonst im Dienste unzähliger Inhalte und Zwecke des menschlichen Verkehrs, haben hier ihre Bedeutung in sich selbst, das heißt in dem Reize des Beziehungsspieles, das sie, bindend und lösend, siegend und unterliegend, gebend und nehmend, zwischen den Individuen stiften . . . Damit dieses Spiel sein Genügen an der blossen Form bewahre, darf der Inhalt kein Eigengewicht bekommen: sobald die Diskussion sachlich wird, ist sie nicht mehr gesellig. . . .[21]

As a function of sociability, conversation is therefore not an expression of individuality; rather, it is the socialization of precisely that which stages itself *as* individuality *within* the framework of the social.

The aesthetic component is thus already determined by conversation's own dynamics. Because of this, aesthetic interpretations regularly lose sight of the social aspect,[22] which is in fact decisive for the aesthetic dimension of conversation. For precisely this aspect is crucial with regard to the pragmatics of narrative intention — if conversations are to even have such an intention beyond just celebrating an aesthetic surplus. As Simmel formulates:

> Nicht als ob der Inhalt der gesellschaftlichen Unterhaltung gleichgültig sei: er soll durchaus interessant, fesselnd, ja bedeutend sein — nur

daß er nicht an sich den Zweck der Unterhaltung bilde, daß diese nicht dem objektiven Resultat gelte, das sozusagen ideal außerhalb der Unterhaltung bestünde. Äußerlich mögen deshalb zwei Unterhaltungen ganz gleich verlaufen, *gesellig*, dem inneren Sinne nach, ist nur diejenige, in der jene Inhalte, mit all ihrem Werte und Reize, doch nur an dem funktionellen Spiele der Unterhaltung als solcher ihr Recht, ihren Platz, ihren Zweck finden, an der Form des Redetausches mit ihrer besonderen und sich selber normierenden Bedeutsamkeit. Darum gehört zum Wesen der geselligen Unterhaltung, daß sie ihren Gegenstand leicht und rasch wechseln könne; denn da der Gegenstand hier nur Mittel ist, kommt ihm die ganze Austauschbarkeit und Zufälligkeit zu, die überhaupt den Mitteln gegenüber dem feststehenden Zwecke eignet. So also bietet, wie gesagt, die Geselligkeit den vielleicht einzigen Fall, in dem das Reden legitimer Selbstzweck ist. [23]

With this description, Simmel has named the rules of the game whereby a conversation is conducted — and these count for Fontane as well.[24]

Let us now look briefly at the general place of language in *Der Stechlin*. For right at the start the reader is confronted with a procedure that has distinct linguistic implications: the disengagement of the name "Stechlin" from reality. The lake is called "Lake Stechlin," the castle "Castle Stechlin." "And just as everything around here bore the name Stechlin, so naturally the lord of the castle himself did as well. *He too* was a Stechlin."[25] Thus from the very beginning of the novel, language is effectively removed from reality. Like the lake and the castle, Dubslav too is introduced as something static.

Rather than a conversation or a dialogue, the subsequent passage — the novel's first direct speech — contains *ways of speaking*. Traces of the novel's genesis can still be detected here.[26] It is the suppressed characterization of an attitude which can "transform weaknesses into strengths"; endowed with "ironic self-regard, because by his very being he [Dubslav] generally placed a question mark after everything"; with "humanity coming from the heart" and the "inclination . . . to let five be even." What Fontane presents here are all mere attitudes, habits, but not virtues of action. For Dubslav, small talk is important, and he enjoys "always leaving his listener in doubt as to whether he's meant it seriously or jokingly" as the narrator tells us at the beginning of the novel.

The first conversation of two persons face-to-face, as short as it is, takes place between father and son Hirschfeld. And it likewise does not develop any sort of action, but instead serves as an illustration, breaking off abruptly with: "The conversations between father and son often led in this direction. . . . " ("In dieser Richtung gingen öfters die Gespräche zwischen Vater und Sohn": 13) — and then the narrative switches to Stechlin's sister Adelheid. The next conversation, the first extended one, is carried out between Dubslav and Engelke and serves to profile the former by using the latter as his bland foil. And with this the first chapter comes to a close. The second brings us a scene that is hardly more colorful. After snippets of his conversation from the ride up to Castle Stechlin, Woldemar rushes up to his father but then has nothing better to say than: "Erlaube, lieber Papa, dir zwei liebe Freunde von mir vorzustellen: Assessor von Rex, Hauptmann von Czako."[27] This is — one is well aware — etiquette, the sign of good breeding. But it also implies that a more informative approach to such dialogue — and one more adequate to Fontane — will not so much search for the contents of these conversations as investigate more carefully what function these conversations actually serve. Such an approach will therefore also include — just as importantly — what goes unsaid.

That Fontane plays his own game with language in *Der Stechlin* is well known.[28] Still, hardly any attention has been paid to the rules of that game. But it is only through a better understanding of these rules that an adequate critical interpretation becomes possible. A key word here, for instance, would be the specific concept of *action*, of the deed. Compared to the intellectual effort that has previously been dedicated to this question by Fichte and Moses Hess, Fontane's definition of action looks almost Victorian, or rather *spätbiedermeierlich*. The novel's simple formula might read: the one way to take action is to marry (50).[29] Indeed this was virtually the only action possible in post-1848 Germany, and it was certainly the only option left for Effi Briest.[30] But when Dubslav states this, only then to shift the responsibility for such an outlook onto Adelheid, and when he subsequently feels compelled to regard it with all the irony he can muster — this can hardly be considered a sign of his critical distance. Rather it indicates the opposite: the sheer force of fixation.

Ambivalence should not be misconstrued here as a state of freedom. Instead it should be recognized for what it is: an expression of an inner lack of freedom and a compulsion. Old Stechlin only acts so free with his irony because he is utterly at a loss; admitting the compulsive character of society's rules, his non-binding ambivalence only amplifies the reigning social norms. All that remains a question here is whether or not Dubslav's irony and the narrator's fall together into one. And the insolubility of this question conceals yet a further irony: namely, the author's. For his non-binding attitude comes at the expense of having to make this ambivalence a permanent fixture, a sort of skeptical playpen in which the spirit of freedom can run itself to death — in case it does not choose to merely dawdle in childish self-satisfaction instead.

In *Der Stechlin*, the subject of conversation is treated in a twofold manner: on the one hand, explicitly in numerous remarks from the elder Stechlin and others; and on the other, implicitly in what these conversations say about the novel by the way they function structurally within it. Certainly Dubslav's ambivalence does not make it any easier to evaluate his attitude towards conversation. Statements from him such as: "Und dann sollen wir uns ja auch durch die Sprache vom Tier unterscheiden. Also wer am meisten red't, ist der reinste Mensch"[31] can be read in any number of ways. So that, for instance, the opposite would also be just as true, "since we contradict ourselves continuously, just by speaking" ("denn man widerspricht sich in einem fort": 52). This particular parenthetical aside is one Dubslav never tires of, and he repeats it at least once more (180). When Gundermann explains to Stechlin, "He who lets himself be talked to . . . is weak" ("Wer mit sich reden läßt, . . . ist schwach": 39), this also explicates, *e contrario*, Stechlin's own viewpoint. The same is true for the ironic description of the post-election meal, which turns on the question of the mute Herr von Alter-Friesack's chairmanship: "ob er nun sprechen könne oder nicht, das sei, wo sich's um eine Prinzipienfrage handle, durchaus gleichgültig. Überhaupt, die ganze Geschichte mit dem 'Sprechen-können' sei ein moderner Unsinn."[32]

Whenever such passages appear ambivalently ironic the tone changes undetectably into the ironically ambivalent. For instance, when Stechlin states: "Es gibt nichts, was mir so verhaßt wäre wie Polizeimaßregeln, oder einem Menschen, der gern ein freies Wort spricht, die Kehle zuzuschnüren. Ich rede selber gern, wie mir der Schnabel gewachsen ist."[33] To interpret this passage as evidence of Stechlin's inner freedom — as has so often been proclaimed — would be naive. Simply the expression "die Kehle zuschnüren" (to throttle) is telling enough. The fact that it is used negatively does not weaken its repressed violence. And within the context it is also nothing positive; it is mentioned merely as a concession. It is preceded by the words, "Mein Pastor aber sollte, beiläufig bemerkt, so was lieber nicht sagen. Das sind so Geistreichigkeiten, die leicht übel vermerkt werden. Ich persönlich lass' es laufen."[34] And this is not exactly a song of freedom. More like a quadrille danced to a tune of the *ancién regime* of which Dubslav is so fond. It is the power of a master who deigns to let his subjects live. For Stechlin's "principle" is precisely "live and let live" (322). Sober, "realistic" perhaps (and what exactly is realistic?), but humanistic? Rather the kind of humanism that is well attuned to comfort and conformity.

In any case, one always runs the risk "of gainsaying one's happiness, . . . if one speaks about it too soon, or too much," as Woldemar reasons in keeping his marriage plans a secret. Stechlin agrees with him whole-heartedly. When Lorenzen at one point remarks, in response to Stechlin's chatting, that this is just the thing the Social Democrats also want, the old man demurs: "Ach was, Lorenzenen, mit Ihnen ist nicht zu reden . . . Übrigens Prosit . . . Wenn Sie's auch nicht verdienen."[35] With this, the conversation breaks off. "Pointed sentences should never be taken literally" ("zugespitzte Sätze darf man nie wörtlich nehmen"), Woldemar explains (236). Yet these are precisely what make up the essence of conversation. And whoever takes them at face value, like Lorenzen or Melusine, is headed for disappointment. When Melusine tries to draw her sister into the conversation, Woldemar advises her rather tactlessly: "Ich glaube, Gräfin, wir lassen die Komtesse. Manchem kleidet es zu sprechen, und manchem kleidet es zu schweigen. Jedes Beisammensein braucht einen Schweiger."[36]

What is more important than these various individual statements, however, are the situations themselves in which the conversations take place. This was mentioned above in respect to the novel's first conversations. Now let us take a closer look in particular at how conversations are broken off. Most noticeably, they consistently break off at the moment when the discussion promises (or threatens) to become interesting. This occurs when either an unequivocal opinion on some matter becomes unavoidable if the conversation is to maintain its course, or when an immediate consequence of what has already been said is that saying anything more would transcend the limits of mere speech — either as an internal transformation or as an action. The rules laid out by Simmel are in effect here.

Following all the rules of the art, Dubslav guides the great dinner-table conversation at the beginning of the novel with a sovereign hand. Thus he interrupts Czako when the latter, just after dining on carp and radishes, starts talking about catacombs. And later, when Czako challenges him pointedly, Rex frankly replies, "I can't answer that right now . . . " and instead begins to recount the "story of little Stubbe," a non sequitur — end of conversation (48).[37] Unhappy Czako is cut off again twelve pages later; this time he is not interrupted by Dubslav, but prevented from answering (60).

Old Count Barby finally spills the secret: "A conversation is always interrupted right at its best point."[38] The conversation between Frau Imme and Hedwig is a classic example of talking past each other (147–48). Conversely, both Katzler and Woldemar later try unsuccessfully to change the topic of discussion (178 and 255–56, resp.) — confronted, in each case, by domineering ladies, namely the Princess and Adelheid.

During the trip to the Eierhäuschen the conversation is broken off at the most interesting moment. An attempt is made shortly thereafter to resume the discussion, but this also meets with little success (154–58). There is a sort of playful virtuosity in the way Fontane orchestrates disturbances from outside to prevent Adelheid from voicing her curiosity about Woldemar's marriage plans (160). She does manage to get a word in nonetheless: "marry local and marry Lutheran" (162). The reader who has learned a lesson from Dubslav will be able to understand this correctly. Adelheid's categorical imperative must read: Act in the interests of the homeland, and act Lutheran.

Horkheimer's analysis of skepticism provides a basis for explaining the remarkable fact that Lutheran tradition and Dubslav's skepticism accord so perfectly, time after time. It also explains, conversely, why Lorenzen's Gospel nevertheless does not accord with Dubslav's ideas: "The Gospel is hence the negation of that skepticism wherein action is a matter of taste or a question of individual discretion. The skeptic regards humaneness as a sort of personal ornament, a peculiarity of temperament, like the instinct for traveling."[39]

What all these conversations have in common is that they cannot (any longer) be mastered by merely verbal means. They inevitably refer to some extralinguistic context. Lake Stechlin can also be seen as a metaphor that points to this extralinguistic context. So it is also important to take a closer look at the role of who does the speaking — or, frequently, who just chats.

It has been rightfully observed that these conversations are much more epic than dramatic in their construction.[40] They are not "dialectical" in the Platonic sense of the art of leading discussions; rather, what we encounter in *Der Stechlin* is the additive principle of sentences: the art of conversation as a technique of dissimulating ennui. But by shifting the emphasis from the dramatic-dialectical to the epic-monotonous, Fontane re-orients dialogue in an important way. What was an element of the action (either as an action itself, or as the cause of action) becomes instead an object of contemplation and reflection. The function of those playing the speaking parts is transformed accordingly: from participants in dialogical interaction and conflict, to narrative (and narrating) side-by-side.

The situation in *Der Stechlin* can thus be compared to the frame-narrative in the *Decameron*: a retreat into interiority in the face of a threatening world, and conversation as a parlor game for distraction. Yet what Boccacio represents as just the frame, Fontane allows to become fully fused with the narrative as a whole (therein marking a transition into the twentieth century). One could argue that his characters are conceived from the outset as nothing but voices.[41] While most of the conversations are systematically broken off whenever they threaten to escalate from idle talk into actual discussion and dialogue, there is one conversation in particular that seems to assert — even content-wise with its utopian theme — the real possibility of a genuine dialogue: the encounter between Melusine and Lorenzen. It is the only time in the novel that two free persons come face-to-face on equal terms. During its course, each contributes equally to the discussion. And it is the only one that is carried out to its logical end. But something new also enters the conversation. Their dialogue intends something, it wants something.[42] The conversation as end-in-itself fades away, and along with it the externally imposed rules that allow it to only be such. Instead, this conversation is free and able to determine itself.[43] Thus when Melusine calls it a "revolutionary discourse" (274), the reader can assume from the novel's particular sensibility for language that her remark applies to more than just the conversation's content.[44] Revolution and revolutionary discourse are thus seen as intricately connected. What is revolutionary is the free — and here this also means autonomous — discourse itself.

Whereas in the previous conversations what is said is meaningful only to the extent that it remains mere causerie, this conversation is significant because what is said actually means something, indeed has its own, self-sufficient meaning. Although the dialogue occurs shortly before the wedding and relates to it, it also distinctly mirrors this event and thereby serves as the novel's anti-marriage.

Yet even the context of engagement and marriage that frames the Melusine-Lorenzen dialogue is developed only on the very margins of language. The passage in chapter 25, whose utter ambivalence marks it as perhaps the most Fontanesque in the novel, constructs events through essentially non-verbal or verbally indirect means. Accordingly, Fontane ends the conversation — and the chapter — with a rare word from Armgard, who, following some thoroughly irrelevant small talk, confesses to her sister: "Ich glaube fast, ich bin verlobt."[45] The wedding that follows is remarkably colorless; here, strangely enough, the two conversationalists Barby and Stechlin suddenly have nothing to say (292). Neither of these fathers is capable, in any case, of sharing a good word when their children finally take action. Giving the toast is left up to Frommel, a clergyman.[46]

Alongside the social conversations at dinner, while riding or strolling, voting, visiting, and so on, all of which are conducted in a way that complies with the rules of Simmel's analysis, the discussion between Melusine and Lorenzen is certainly not the only one carried out between just two persons. Some of these two-party dialogues are played out within larger group discussions and thus do not differ from social conversations; they are just that on a smaller scale. However, some one-on-one conversations do take place at the conclusion of the novel on the occasion of Dubslav's impending death. In Dubslav's last conversations with Hirschfeld and Koseleger, a new tone comes to the fore that sets these conversations apart and creates its own sort of contrast to the dialogue between Melusine and Lorenzen. Where a common interest, a *volonté générale*, brought Melusine and Lorenzen together, the egotistical, particularistic interests and intentions that the participants reveal in these later personal encounters demonstrate their incapacity for personal dialogue. Hirschfeld, Koseleger, and Chief Forester Katzler's wife all make egocentric, economic, political, and confessional demands instead.[47] Even Dubslav's disappointment about these scenes is itself just a repression of his own guilt in the matter — the real reason he is so upset. His resignation shows signs of self-righteousness. His self-pity is only pity for his impoverished self, even though he presents it as an old man's wisdom — something he is still just wise enough to pull off.

When Adelheid finally shows off her familiarly unpleasant side, only Agnes is able to drive her away (345–54). Krippenstapel brings along his best honeycomb, but his rather touching affection for his fellow man is able to express itself only in broken form: "The tithe, if I may say so, *was* really something finer than money."[48] Uncke's visit is also rather sad (363–65); with its monologues trailing off in static silence between the two, it is a characteristically successful Fontane dialogue — or rather double monologue.

Only the two conversations with Lorenzen manage, in the face of death, to free themselves from the previous tone of small talk and approach something like a personal dialogue. One of these conversations closes with Dubslav's telling remark: "You're probably right" ("Sie sollen recht haben": 344). Following this visit Dubslav has a good night. And likewise, after the second of these concluding conversations with Lorenzen, "the old man felt almost rejuvenated . . ." ("fühlte sich der Alte wie belebt . . .": 370).

Parallel to all this runs the Agnes episode. "Lil'" Agnes stands as much for the natural and the angelic as the political. As an impressionable woman-child, she represents the still-pure potential of human existence and thus of human relationships as well.[49] To the dying Dubslav, Agnes becomes a sort of guarantor of hope for the breakthrough he never had during his lifetime and which he no longer has the opportunity to realize. But even here his attempt at an authentic encounter is interrupted by the destructive intrusion of the repressed, making it instead Dubslav's final "misencounter."

As Dubslav feels "that the end is approaching," he professes his insight in one last monologue — only then to take back half of what he says:

> Das "Ich" ist nichts — damit muß man sich durchdringen. Ein ewig Gesetzliches vollzieht sich, weiter nichts, und dieser Vollzug, auch wenn er "Tod" heißt, darf uns nicht schrecken. In das Gesetzliche sich ruhig schicken, das macht den sittlichen Menschen und hebt ihn. Er

hing dem noch so nach und freute sich, alle Furcht überwunden zu haben. Aber dann kamen doch wieder Anfälle von Angst, und er seufzte: "Das Leben ist kurz, aber die Stunde lang." (372) [50]

The recognition that the "I" is nothing and the "eternal Law" everything does not enable Dubslav to die. Not only is it insufficient consolation, it also provides no real certainty. Such self-encouragement alone is not enough to banish his anxiety. Finally, with a sigh and a modified quotation on his lips, he passes away. [51]

With the exception of the one between Melusine and Lorenzen, all the dialogues show themselves to be externally determined, conversation as pure sociability — causerie. The frame, the rules, the ends are all pre-set. As Lacan put it: "La loi de la conversation, c'est l'interruption." [52] Conversation will always break off at the point in an encounter where genuine dialogue would have to begin. So that ultimately, "der Humanität zuliebe beschränkt das Gespräch sich aufs Nächste; aufs Stumpfste, Banalste, wenn nur ein Inhumaner anwesend ist." [53]

The "virtuosity of saying" — this is true for Fontane as well as his protagonists — "reveals its danger and weakness precisely in the tract-like sentimental tone it strikes in moments when ideology and content become crucial." [54] Irony, self-irony, and utter seriousness blend at times into one and the same tone. As a purposiveness without purpose (*Zweckmäßigkeit ohne Zweck*) in sociability, as an external determination governing an interest-beholden personal dialogue that can never advance to true dialogue, all of these conversations remain inescapably restricted to the realm of the aesthetic. Only in genuine dialogue is the purpose self-determining and thus able to achieve meaning for itself. To read *Der Stechlin* as a self-thematization of the author and of writing means to assert this structural analogy: between beauty as freedom in appearance and as a purposiveness without purpose, and conversation as purpose-free and hence likewise purposeless causerie. The function of conversation could then come into focus as an eminently critical and self-critical challenge by literature itself to the possibility of dialogue under the given circumstances. Read with the aesthetics of German Idealism in mind, *Der Stechlin* can then be understood as voicing its critical, or rather skeptical, post-idealist reservations against an aesthetics of containment.

Translated by Eric Schwab

Notes

[1] In a letter to Adolf Hoffmann, May/June 1897. Cf. Theodor Fontane, *Dichter über ihre Dichtungen*, ed. R. Brinkmann (Munich: Heimeran, 1973) vol. 2, 474–75.

[2] Cf. the sources cited below.

[3] Works that have dealt with this include: Mary-Enole Gilbert, *Das Gespräch in Fontanes Gesellschaftsromanen* (Leipzig: Mayer & Müller, 1930); Ingrid Mittenzwei, *Die Sprache als Thema: Untersuchungen zu Fontanes Gesellschaftsromanen* (Bad Homburg: Gehlen, 1970); Ekkehart Rudolf, "Über die Darstellung des redenden Menschen in den epischen Prosadichtungen Theodor Fontanes," *Wissenschaftliche Zeitschrift der Friedrich-Schiller-Universität Jena* 7 (1957/58): 393–428; Heiko Strech, *Theodor Fontane: Die Synthese von Alt und Neu. 'Der Stechlin' als Summe des Gesamtwerks* (Berlin: E. Schmidt, 1970); Kurt Wölfel, "Man ist nicht bloß ein einzelner Mensch," *Zeitschrift für deutsche Philologie* 82 (1963): 148–65; Hans-Martin Gauger, "Sprachbewußtsein im *Stechlin*," *Bild und Gedanke: Festschrift für G. Baumann*, ed. Günter Schnitzler (Munich: Fink, 1980); Pierre Bange, *Ironie et Dialogisme dans les romans de Theodor Fontane* (Grenoble: Presses Universitaires, 1974); Claudia Liver, "Glanz und Versagen der Rede. Randbemerkungen zu Fontanes Gesellschaftsroman," *Annali Studi Tedeschi* XXIV, 1–2 (1981): 5–33; Wolfgang Preisendanz, "Zur Ästhetizität des Gesprächs bei Fontane," *Das Gespräch*. Poetik und Hermeneutik XI, ed. Karlheinz Stierle and Rainer Warning (Munich: Fink, 1984); Heinz-Helmut Lüger, "Stereotypie und Konversationsstil. Zu einigen Funktionen satzwertiger Phraseologismen im literarischen Dialog," *Deutsche Sprache: Zeitschrift für Theorie, Praxis, Dokumentation* 17 (1989): 2–25; Glenn A. Guidry, *Language, Morality, and Society: An Ethical Model of Communication in Fontane and Hofmannsthal*, University of California Publications in Modern Philology 124 (Berkeley and Los Angeles: U of California P, 1989); Norbert Mecklenburg, "Figurensprache und Bewußtseinskritik in Fontanes Romanen," *Deutsche Vierteljahresschrift* 65 (1991): 674–94; and N. Mecklenburg, "Im Vorfeld modernen Erzählens: mündliches Wissen und Dialogizität bei Theodor Fontane," *Mündliches Wissen in neuzeitlicher Literatur*, ed. Paul Goetsch (Tübingen: Gunter Narr, 1990). Pertinent chapters or comments can also be found in: Richard Brinkmann, *Theodor Fontane: Über die Verbindlichkeit des Unverbindlichen* (Munich: R. Piper, 1967); Peter Demetz, *Formen des Realismus: Theodor Fontane. Kritische Untersuchungen* (Munich: Carl Hanser, 1964); Katharina Mommsen, *Hofmannsthal und Fontane* (Bern: P. Lang, 1978).

[4] Conrad Wandrey, *Theodor Fontane* (Munich: Beck, 1919). On *Der Stechlin*: 300–11.

[5] Cf. Gilbert; Eugen Koltai, *Untersuchungen zur Erzähltechnik Theodor Fontanes: Dargestellt an den Werken* "Vor dem Sturm," "Irrungen, Wirrungen," *und* "Effi Briest," (Diss., New York: New York University, 1969); Katharina Mommsen, "Vom 'Bamme-Ton' zum 'Bummel-Ton.' Fontanes Kunst der Sprechweisen," in *Formen realistischer Erzählkunst: Festschrift für Charlotte Jolles*, ed. Jörg Thunecke and Eda Sagarra (Nottingham: Sherwood, 1979); cf. also Rudolph, Lüger, Gauger.

[6] Martin Buber, *Werke I* (Heidelberg: Lambert Schneider, 1962). Cf. also the writings of Hermann Levin Goldschmidt: *Philosophie als Dialogik. Frühe Schriften. Werke I*, and *Freiheit für den Widerspruch. Werke 6* (both Vienna: Passagen, 1993); *Dialogik. Philosophie auf dem Boden der Neuzeit* (Frankfurt/M.: Europäische Verlagsanstalt, 1964), and *Haltet Euch an Worte: Betrachtungen zur Sprache* (Schaffhausen: Griffel, 1977), in which Goldschmidt discusses Buber and Franz Rosenzweig and outlines the significance of conversation. On the question of the openness to conversation and the capacity for it, cf. also Maja Wicki-Vogt, "Von den notwendigen und den nicht-notwendigen Widersprüchen einer freiheitlichen Gesellschaft," *Wege des Widerspruchs: Festschrift für H. L. Goldschmidt*, ed. Willi Goetschel, J. Cartwright, and M. Wicki (Bern: Paul Haupt, 1984), 78–79.

[7] Werner Weber, "Theodor Fontane," in *Berliner Geist: Fünf Vorträge der Bayrischen Akademie der Schönen Künste* (Berlin: Propyläen, 1963), 140, 141, 148–49. On the subject of small talk in *Stechlin* cf. also Gauger, 313–14. Certainly, whoever is inclined to consider Stechlin's "good-natured skepticism" and his "good-natured, well-styled indifference" as unproblematic indications of his humanism (cf. Gauger 313–14, 322) invites the suspicion that they have fallen in with the prevailing tone of Fontane criticism and thereby overlook the repressive and violent moment of any aestheticism or indifferentism.

[8] Weber, 142. On Fontane's silencing technique as a gesture of political critique, cf. Gisela Brude-Firnau, "Beredtes Schweigen: Nichtverbalisierte Obrigkeitskritik in Theodor Fontanes *Stechlin*," *Monatshefte* 77 (1985): 460–68.

[9] By Heiko Strech, among others. Klaus Matthias does not ever mention Montaigne in his essay, "Theodor Fontane — Skepsis und Güte," *Jahrbuch des Freien deutschen Hochstifts* (1973).

[10] Michel de Montaigne, *Oeuvres complètes*, Bibliothèque de la Pléiade, ed. A. Thibaudet and M. Rat, (Paris: Gallimard, 1962), 900. English translation: "The most fruitful exercise of our spirit, for my taste, is the conver-

sation . . . I would sooner consent — this I believe — to lose my sight than my hearing or speech."

[11] Cf. also Montaigne's dedication to the reader, 9.

[12] Montaigne, 906. The decisive passage reads: "nous sommes sur la manière, non sur la matière du dire. Mon humeur est de regarder autant à la forme qu'à la substance, autant à l'advocat qu'à la cause, comme Alcibiades ordonnoit qu'on fit" ["we are concerned with the manner, not the matter of speech. My inclination is to pay as much attention to the form as to the content, as much to the speaker as to the cause, just as Alcibiades directed us to proceed"] (906).

[13] Cf. W. Martin Lüdke, "Was Neues vom alten Fontane. Historischer Prozeß und ästhetische Form am Beispiel von Fontanes letztem Roman 'Der Stechlin,'" *Diskussion Deutsch* 9 (1978).

[14] Max Horkheimer, "Montaigne und die Funktion der Skepsis," *Gesammelte Schriften IV*, ed. A. Schmidt (Frankfurt am Main: Fischer, 1988) 242.

[15] Horkheimer, 270, cf. also 280.

[16] Horkheimer, 276.

[17] The Lord of Montaigne thus differs from Herr von Stechlin and his proverbial love for ironic superlatives in that the latter does indeed, out of an ambivalent sense of superiority, continually call each and everything "the best," and in so doing only plays along with the language game. Montaigne, however, concludes his essay on conversation: "Tous jugemens en gros sont lâches et imparfaicts" ["All judgments that generalize are lax and imperfect"] (922).

[18] Moritz Lazarus, "Über Gespräche," rpt. in Claudia Schmölders's anthology, *Die Kunst des Gesprächs* (Munich: Deutscher Taschenbuchverlag, 1986).

[19] Lazarus, 283.

[20] Ibid.

[21] Georg Simmel, "Die Geselligkeit (Beispiel der reinen oder formalen Soziologie)," in *Grundfragen der Soziologie* (Berlin: de Gruyter, 1970), 61–63. English translation by Eric Schwab: "The decisive element has to be expressed here in terms of utterly banal experience: that in the seriousness of life people talk for the content's sake, for what they want to communicate or reach an agreement about; whereas in sociability talking becomes an end in itself, indeed not in the naturalistic sense of idle chatter but in the sense of the *art* of entertaining oneself with conversation. This is something that has its own set of artistic rules: in a purely sociable con-

versation the content is nothing but the necessary vehicle for the stimulation that unfolds in the course of the lively mutual exchange of talking as such. All the forms through which this exchange realizes itself — argument and the appeal to norms recognized by both parties, reaching peace through compromise and discovering commonly held convictions, gratefully taking up new subjects and steering away from those where finally no agreement can be expected — all these forms of conversational reciprocity, which otherwise serve innumerable contents and purposes of human intercourse, achieve here a significance unto themselves. It is this stimulating play of relations — engaging and disengaging, dominating and submitting, giving and taking — that these forms institute between individuals. . . ." About Simmel himself, cf. the introduction by Heinz-Jürgen Dahme and Ottheim Rammstedt in Georg Simmel, *Schriften zur Soziologie* (Frankfurt am Main: Suhrkamp, 1983).

[22] Cf. Preisendanz, "Zur Ästhetizität des Gesprächs bei Fontane." What Mecklenburg describes as "dialogicity" [*Dialogizität*], however, are only forms and features of orally-communicated knowledge (1990). To view the space where interpersonal encounters occur as the locus of Fontane's critique of society is something that, remarkably enough, goes unheeded even here. This space also cannot be thematized and critiqued by means of current discourse analyses. In opposition to the trendy proliferation of such drastically denatured deployments of the meanings of dialogue, dialogics, and dialogicity, we must keep in mind that any usage that ignores the expressly critical intent of such terms cannot expect to accomplish more than a repetition of purely positivistic research. For Guidry, though, the interpretive *Wünschelrute* swings toward the opposite extreme: he sees conversation as reducible to an ethical core: "In Fontane and Hoffmannsthal, distorted communication seems to be attributed to an unethical disposition of character as well as immoral ways of relating to others" (Guidry, 125). The possibility that in Fontane the crystallization point of the social is represented precisely in the intimacy of the interpersonal sphere is something that falls by the wayside in an interpretation constructed around the ethical. But it is in those very moments in which a critique of communication emerges that we should look for Fontane's narrative impetus. On the philosophical concept of dialogics, cf. the literature cited in note 6, and also Willi Goetschel, "Formen des Widerspruchs: Zur Diskursausdifferenzierung in der Neuzeit," *Widersprüchliche Wirklichkeit*, ed. E. Fischer, H. Herzka, and K. Reich (Munich: Piper, 1992), 78–97.

[23] Georg Simmel, "Die Geselligkeit," 61–63. English translation by Eric Schwab: "In order for this play to preserve satisfaction in mere form, the content must not take on any weight of its own; the moment the content of a discussion becomes important, it is no longer sociable. . . . Not as if

the content of a sociable conversation were unimportant; it may well be interesting, engaging, or even meaningful. Only it cannot by itself comprise the purpose of the conversation, which is not about arriving at an objective result that (so to speak) would exist ideally outside that conversation. Hence two conversations may follow the exact same course externally; but still, only that conversation is *sociable* in the narrow sense in which such content — for all its importance and charm — serves only the purpose (at least its only rightful purpose) of a functional interplay and a form of verbal exchange with its own self-regulating meaning. Therefore one inherent quality of sociable conversation is the ability to change the subject easily and quickly; since the topic of conversation here serves only as a means, it has the full exchangeability and contingency that means assume with regard to a fixed end. Thus sociability offers, as we stated, perhaps the only case in which talking is a legitimate end in itself."

[24] Cf. Brigitte Hauschild, *Geselligkeitsformen und Erzählstruktur* (Frankfurt am Main: Peter Lang, 1981). In her chapter "Gespräch als Repräsentation und Vollzug des Wirklichen," Hauschild offers a good overview of conversation types and their occurrence in Fontane's novels: "In the conversations of *Stechlin*, the continual change of topics and the virtually limitless field of inquiries make the particular theme almost irrelevant. It is never dealt with 'thoroughly,' but instead is taken as the excuse for speaking one's mind and as the point of transition to whatever topic comes next" (151). However, it seems to me that the claim that "in the representation of the conventional the critique is implicit" remains to be proven. If skepticism is a given in Fontane's representation of the conventional, it is still necessary to determine more carefully how and to what extent this is able to transform itself into a critique. The undecidability of this question offers us a distinctive example of Fontane's ambivalence.

[25] Theodor Fontane, *Der Stechlin*, ed. W. Keitel and H. Nürnberger (Munich: Carl Hanser, 1968; Ullstein Taschenbuch Verlag, 1976), 9. Page numbers in brackets will refer to this edition of *Der Stechlin*. All English translations are by Eric Schwab. German original: "Und wie denn alles hier herum den Namen Stechlin führte, so natürlich auch der Schloßherr selbst. Auch *er* war ein Stechlin."

[26] Fontane developed his characters by reference to manners of speaking. Cf. Julius Petersen, "Fontanes Altersroman," *Euphorion* 29 (1928).

[27] Theodor Fontane, *Der Stechlin*, 18. English translation: "Please, dear Papa, allow me to introduce to you two dear friends of mine: Assessor von Rex, Captain von Czako."

[28] Cf. Max Rychner, "Theodor Fontane," *Welt im Wort: Literarische Aufsätze* (Zürich: Manesse, 1949), 269; Hans-Heinrich Reuter, *Theodor Fon-*

tane, 2 vols. (Munich: Nymphenburger Verlagshandlung, 1968), 855, 859; Mittenzwei, 165–66 and passim; Gauger, 313–14.

[29] Cf. also Fontane's *Irrungen, Wirrungen*, where (in chapter 14) Botho's mother writes in a letter to her son that action is equivalent to marriage — of one's equal, naturally. On Fichte and Hess, cf. Moses Hess, "Philosophie der Tat," *Philosophische und sozialistische Schriften 1837–1850*, ed. W. Mönke, 2nd ed. (Vaduz: Topos, 1980), 210–11.

[30] On Germany after 1848, cf. Georg Lukács, "Der alte Fontane," *Deutsche Realisten des 19. Jahrhunderts* (Berlin: Aufbau, 1952), 262–307.

[31] Theodor Fontane, *Der Stechlin*, 23. English translation: "And language is also supposed to be what distinguishes us from animals. Thus whoever talks the most is the most purely human."

[32] Ibid, 192. English translation: "whether he could speak or not was, when it came to a question of principles, entirely unimportant. In general, this whole business about 'being able to speak' was just modern nonsense."

[33] Ibid, 55. English translation: "There is nothing I would find so hateful as police measures, or to throttle a man who likes to speak freely. I myself like to talk any way my old snout sees fit."

[34] Ibid, 54–55. English translation: "But my Pastor — by the way — should really not have said such things. That kind of overly clever remark is too easily taken in the wrong sense. I'll let it go, personally."

[35] Ibid, 70. English translation: "Oh come on, Lorenzen! There's no point talking with you . . . Anyways, cheers . . . Even if you don't deserve it!"

[36] Ibid, 155. English translation: "I believe, Countess, we should leave the Contessa alone. For some, it is fitting to speak, and for some it is fitting to be silent. In any moment of togetherness someone must keep silent."

[37] On the story of Stubbe as a possible allusion to Lou Andreas-Salomé, cf. Paul Irving Anderson, "*Der Stechlin*. Eine Quellenanalyse," in *Fontanes Novellen und Romane*, ed. Christian Grawe (Stuttgart: Reclam, 1991), 266, note 50.

[38] The German original reads: "An bester Stelle wird ein Gespräch immer unterbrochen" (134). Cf. Jacques Lacan, *Le Séminaire I. Les écrits techniques de Freud* (Paris: Seuil, 1975), chapter 25, "La vérité surgit de la méprise," 296: "La loi de la conversation, c'est l'interruption."

[39] Horkheimer 247–48, quote 260.

[40] Demetz 179–80; Charlotte Jolles, "'Gideon ist besser als Botho.' Zur Struktur des Erzählschlußes bei Fontane," *Festschrift für Werner Neuse*, ed. H. Lederer and J. Seyppel (Berlin: Die Diagonale, 1967), 91.

[41] Mittenzwei also points this out.

[42] For this very reason it has been dismissed as programmatic, for instance, by Horst Turk, "Realismus in Fontanes Gesellschaftsroman. Zur Romantheorie und zur epischen Integration," *Jahrbuch der Wittheit zu Bremen* 9 (1965): 454–55; Klaus R. Scherpe, "Die Rettung der Kunst in Widerspruch von bürgerlicher Humanität und bourgeoiser Wirklichkeit: Theodor Fontanes vierfacher Roman 'Der Stechlin,'" in Scherpe, *Poesie der Demokratie: Literarische Widersprüche zur deutschen Wirklichkeit vom 18. bis 20. Jahrhundert* (Cologne: Pahl-Rugenstein, 1980), 257. Scherpe likewise does not entirely grant Melusine the capacity for revolutionary discourse. Cf. also Gauger, 315–16. The passage in the novel is on pages 268–69.

[43] Kant's definition of the beautiful as purposiveness without purpose reflects precisely this situation, and thus can be used to clarify what exactly this new element is that enters into the conversation between Melusine and Lorenz and that exceeds causerie as mere ornament: it is, namely, a moral-practical purpose. Cf. Kant's *Critique of Judgment*, esp. A 68–69, and in addition Schiller's *Kallias* letters and his letters *On the Aesthetic Education of Man*.

[44] "And now, after this revolutionary discourse of ours, allow me to return once more to the huts of peaceful folk" [Und nun erlauben Sie mir, nach diesem unserem revolutionären Diskurse, zu den Hütten friedlicher Menschen zurückzukehren: 274]. For the full implications of the usage of such imagery, cf. also Hölderlin's fragment, "Im Walde," in *Werke und Briefe*, ed. F. Beissner and J. Schmidt, vol. 1 (Frankfurt am Main: Insel, 1969), 244.

[45] English translation: "I almost believe I've gotten engaged."

[46] When Gauger speaks of "such a moving engagement" and regards its "almost speechless implicitness" as a moment of happiness (321–22), he manages not only to avoid completely the total ambivalence of Armgard's speechlessness but also the moment of coercion that comes to the fore in such a scene with remarkable precision. Thus when Melusine teases Woldemar in her knowing way, "You are going to make me jealous," and Woldemar responds, "Really, Countess?" Armgard's remark that immediately follows — "Perhaps" — is anything but a confirmation. Instead it means exactly what it says: in this "perhaps" is hidden a knowing resistance to social repression, along with an attempt to take it to the edge — to the extent this is even possible for Armgard. To overlook the divided, even broken quality of this "perhaps" would be a mark of cynicism.

[47] Hirschfeld (315–17), Koseleger (322–26), Frau Katzler (327–30).

[48] "Der Zehnte, wenn ich mir die Bemerkung erlauben darf, *war* eigentlich was Feineres als Geld." My emphasis both in English and German [W. G.]. Theodor Fontane, *Der Stechlin*, 359.

[49] Agnes enters Stechlin's world as Buschen's granddaughter; the latter becomes significant for Dubslav as a "witch" (333, 348, 362). The triple constellation of grandmother-mother-daughter, together with Buschen's apothecary talents, points to the matriarchal order behind this patriarchal world. Agnes's first appearance (226) has the quality of an epiphany — in addition to its unstated erotic dimension. On the progressive-subversive aspect of Bachofen's theory of matriarchy, cf. Hermann Levin Goldschmidt, *Pestalozzis unvollendete Revolution: Philosophie dank der Schweiz von Rousseau bis Turel,* in *Werke*, vol. 8 (Vienna: Passagen, 1995), 189–211.

[50] Theodor Fontane, *Der Stechlin*, 372. Cf. the parallel passage on 148, where Woldemar lectures Lorenzen. English translation by Erich Schwab: "The 'I' is nothing — this must be understood through and through. An eternal Law is fulfilling itself, nothing more, and this fulfillment, even if it is called 'death,' should not scare us. To adapt oneself calmly to the Law is what makes man moral, and elevates him. He dwelt on this for a while and was pleased to have overcome his fear. But then the attacks of anxiety returned, and he sighed, 'Life is short, but the hour long.'"

[51] On the question of quotations as an element of conversation, cf. Hermann Meyer, *Das Zitat in der Erzählkunst* (Stuttgart: Metzler, 1961) 174–75 for uncritical remarks, and Wölfel 164–65 for more critical ones.

[52] Lacan, 296.

[53] Theodor W. Adorno, *Minima Moralia: Reflexionen aus dem beschädigten Leben* (Frankfurt am Main: Suhrkamp, 1980) §118, 242. English translation: "for the sake of humanity, conversation restricts itself to what is closest at hand; to what is dullest, most banal when even only one inhuman person is present."

[54] Wolfgang Wittowski, "Theodor Fontane und der Gesellschaftsroman," *Handbuch des deutschen Romans*, ed. H. Koopmann (Düsseldorf: Bagel, 1983), 433.

SABINE CRAMER
Missouri Southern State College

Grete Minde:
Structures of Societal Disturbance

"ES IST EIN 'CHARAKTERBILD'"
[It is a "character representation"]
— Fontane to Paul Lindau[1]

ALTHOUGH *VOR DEM STURM* (1878) has been viewed as marking the beginning of Theodor Fontane's purely novelistic creativity that would produce, among other writings, the fourteen novels, novellas, and narratives upon which his international fame is based, it is essentially a transitory work, standing between his earlier critical, essayistic, and reflective prose, such as the first volumes of *Wanderungen durch die Mark Brandenburg* (published in four parts between 1862 and 1882) and his later major novels. It is *Grete Minde*, rather, that deserves to be considered the first of Fontane's significant novelistic writings.

Published in 1880, two years after *Vor dem Sturm* — although an extant preliminary sketch of *Grete Minde* predates its publication by four years — *Grete Minde* manifests many of the central characteristics of Fontane's later, more acclaimed novels. Not only does it prove to be exemplary *in nuce* of his later novelistic style, but it also serves to illuminate central aspects of Fontane's use of character and setting. Furthermore, it is his first work to display a clear, conscious distinction in the narrative use of primary and secondary figures, which is the focus of this article. As early as 1866, in the context of a critical discussion of *Vor dem Sturm*, Fontane addresses exactly this point in a letter to Wilhelm Hertz:

> One has to have foreground-, middle-, and background figures and it is a mistake if one moves everything into the full light of the foreground. . . . Right from the beginning the characters have to be drawn in such a manner that the reader knows right away whether they are central or secondary figures. It is not the extent of description that is important here, but rather its intensity that provides the clue. [2]

This passage not only reveals Fontane's consciousness of the different roles his figures are to play and the distinctive levels of their importance, it also emphasizes the significance he attributes to all his figures, regardless of their position as major or minor figures. The intensity with which he endows his figures in his subsequent novels, an intensity which contributes to the effectiveness of their portrayal, is already found, albeit in less defined form, in *Grete Minde*. With the passage of time, his "secondary" figures become increasingly important, particularly in relation to the "primary" figures, so that we can draw a line marking the ascendance of their significance from *Grete Minde* to *Stine*,[3] the novel which in many ways represents the epitome of Fontane's deployment of secondary figures.

The very intensity of Fontane's novelistic figures is closely related to another of the author's fundamental concepts: the search for what Fontane calls "das Eigentliche" ("the essential"), a concept that recurs repeatedly in his letters, exposés, and journals. His attempt to achieve "das Eigentliche" in *Vor dem Sturm* was unsuccessful because he focused not on the individuals themselves who constituted the community and who reflected the forces at work within it, but rather on external incidents and episodes occuring within the community. Fontane's biographer Hans-Heinrich Reuter notes in his critical remarks about *Vor dem Sturm*:

> The two main elements which Fontane later viewed as the basis of his "entire production," "psychography and criticism," were not yet perceivable in an equal manner in his first novel. Psychological penetration — if we may be allowed to translate this term of "psychography" in a simplified manner — remained an analytical end in itself, if not to say an isolated, poetical game; epic training. (548)[4]

In *Grete Minde* and the novels that follow, Fontane's narrative concern matures, and the "essential" becomes merged with issues which draw upon broader human experience. Each individual character, regardless of his or her significance within the novella, is endowed with a rounded, psychologically-defined personality that not only embodies that figure's specific, unique nature and lot in life, but also represents an aspect of the society of the day and, by accentuating distinctions of class, gender, and economic status, illuminates the social and socio-political factors at work within it.

While *Vor dem Sturm* contains only seminal indications of the psychographical and critical tendencies to be found in Fontane's subsequent novels and narratives, *Grete Minde* is successful in drawing a clear picture of the psychological factors that underlie and define the central protagonist's mental state and in delineating the stages of its deterioration. As a result, the novella foreshadows Fontane's ultimate mastery in identifying his fictive figures with what he called a *Psychograph*. Furthermore, *Grete Minde* demonstrates that this technique is not just applicable to the main protagonists, but is consciously and effectively used by Fontane in the portrayal of all his literary figures.

Fontane's concern with the role and portrayal of secondary figures reflects his concept of the novel [5] and his fundamental premise for its thematic focus: "It is the introduction of a great idea, a great moment, into relatively simple lives."[6] This view of the novel evolved in part from his reactions to the negative reception of *Vor dem Sturm*.[7] Thus he wrote to Paul Heyse concerning the unfavorable reception which the work evoked:

> Don't you agree, that besides the novels, such as *Copperfield*, in which we observe a human life from its beginning, those, too, are valid which place instead of an individual a complex time period under a magnifying glass? While I do admit that the greater dramatic interest will always remain with the narratives "with *one* hero," the complex novel with its numerous portraits and episodes can have equal status with the single strain novel, not in its effect but in its artistry, as long as it does not proceed in an arbitrary manner, but rather introduces only such moments which, though they appear momentarily to forget the total work, actually serve it well. (December 9, 1878) [8]

Significantly, this letter to Heyse [9] was written while Fontane was fully immersed in his work on *Grete Minde* and hence is of particular interest for its ramifications for that novella. *Grete Minde* can subsequently be viewed as the first of Fontane's narratives consciously structured with this concept in mind. In accordance with his newly formulated views of the novel, its secondary characters are portrayed in a manner which allows them to establish a socially representative framework for the novella's chief protagonist and the unfolding of the plotline. Each figure in this novella is drawn minutely to present not only his or her unique human fate, a fate which is shown to be both predetermined by heritage and influenced by milieu, but also to reflect the forces at work in the society of that day. By extension, the main characters themselves are shown to be affected, even driven, by the secondary figures, following the premise that no individual can avoid registering the impact of those around them. They thus react passively or actively to the actions and influences of family and friends, colleagues and neighbors, supporters and enemies.

Reflecting Fontane's views, most of the main protagonists are placed in a clearly defined and essentially restrictive social context. While their personal ambitions may lead their actions beyond the boundaries of that context, the protagonists ultimately fail because of the limitations established by societal rules. On the other hand, Fontane grants the secondary figures a greater degree of freedom. These characters' social origins and their position in the social hierarchy of the day are left relatively unspecified, and Fontane grants them greater flexibility in attitude, behavior, and speech; they may even exercise the right to judge, and to criticize their superiors, by class and by individual — as Regine does in this novella. Because of this greater freedom, the role and function of Fontane's secondary figures increase in significance, and they prove pivotal to an understanding of the central concerns of his novels; *Grete Minde* is the first of Fontane's works to illustrate this function of his secondary characters.

My discussion of *Grete Minde* focuses specifically on the secondary figures. Even though these secondary figures have largely been ignored by most critics, they are significant in that they are deployed in this novel for the first time in a manner that would become characteristic of Fontane. The setting of *Grete Minde* in the post-Thirty Years' War era establishes a general tone of turbulence, inherent in the dialogue between societal origin and religious background. Within the work, the larger historical context of the religious quarrels and battles is reflected in detail within the framework of a single family, and the violent and destructive impact of these conflicts is recorded in the lives of specific individuals, corresponding to Fontane's own espoused novelistic intention.[10]

Grete Minde concentrates on the interaction between protagonists and consequently depicts the qualities and roles of the secondary figures only by brief reference. One can nevertheless detect the emergence of what would become a classical novelistic structure in Fontane's future work: the juxtaposition of boldly characterized main protagonists — in this case Grete and Valtin — with subtly delineated secondary figures, as in Trud, Gerdt, Gigas, Zenobia, Regine, and the nuns. Perhaps even more striking, however, is Fontane's deployment of the secondary figures to illustrate and illuminate the societal forces that provide the motivations underlying the novella's plotline. Thus, while the plotline of the novel — reminiscent of popular *Kriminalliteratur* and unusual for a work by Fontane — focuses on Grete's transformation from an innocent girl to a deranged, destructive murderess, Grete is not the force which propels the action. Rather, she is herself propelled and victimized by the forces at work in her society, typified by the work's secondary figures.

Not only does Grete appear predispositioned by her Spanish-Catholic heritage, but she also suffers from the hatred of her elder brother, Gerdt, who himself never forgave their father for having remarried. After the death of Gerdt's mother, his father married a beautiful Spanish woman, whom he loved and cherished, and who bore his second child, Grete. While Fontane's psychological portrayal of Gerdt as a product of familial relationships and their emotional ramifications, complemented by the portrayal of Grete's psychological disposition as a product of different genetic traits, seems to indicate a characterization based upon psychological factors of family, milieu, and heredity, and hence suggests a Darwinistic view of the human being, it is ultimately the social and sociopolitical facts of the historical setting that prove to be the determining factors for human behavior in the world as Fontane depicts it.[11] Indeed, Fontane uses Grete in particular to represent her contemporary world and to register the impact of its societal conflicts. Grete is presented as an essentially passive object in this world. Not only does she suffer under the views and the actions of others, but her behavior is also shown to be directed by external events and circumstances, the result of societal forces made manifest in those around her.

As a result, the course of Grete's life and, correspondingly, the plotline of the novel is not primarily predicated upon her initiation of action but is rather associated with two secondary figures, Trud and her husband Gerdt. They are the people from whom Grete flees, and their harsh and heartless rejection of her and her child creates in Grete a feeling of total hopelessness that ultimately drives her to madness, murder, and suicide. Within the context of the novella, however, Trud and Gerdt's actions and their consequences are not to be perceived as limited to the personal sphere of intra-familial relationships; Trud and Gerdt, as accepted and respected members of their social and religious community, also function within the novella as representatives of that very society.

Trud's characterization as a negative force is already apparent in the novella's opening scene, which she dominates even though she herself is not present. Thus, Grete is reluctant to visit her neighbors' garden, because Trud is "dawider" (against it: 8). [12] Valtin attempts to reduce Trud's power over Grete, which she holds in part through her assumption of a mother role, by reducing her to the status of an equal, saying: "Oh, Trud, Trud. Trud is a sister-in-law and a sister-in-law is no more than a sister" (8). Shortly thereafter, however, he indicates his own attitude to Trud: "I can't stand her" (9). The scene serves to forewarn the reader about Trud, her personality and her actions, and the subsequent course of the novella confirms Trud's role as an essentially destructive and evil one. Thus, Valtin's description of Trud — "Pretty she is, but pretty and mean" (9) — proves to be an apt one. [13]

Although Fontane does appear to attribute some positive qualities to Trud, including physical beauty and intelligence, allowing Regine to characterize her as "still pretty and smart" and as someone who knows "what she wants, fits into the house, and has an elegant manner" (26), when Trud appears for the first time, her outward beauty is contradicted by her mean intentions and sneaky actions, reflections and expressions of her unfulfilled, dissatisfied nature: "A beautiful, young woman, Mrs. Trud Minde, fashionably dressed, but with stern features . . . had been hiding behind a wine trellis" (11). Not only does Trud spy on Grete and Valtin, she even attempts to impugn the behavior of the youngsters in her conversation with Valtin's stepmother. In the process, as the narrative voice notes: "The blood rushed to her head, and envy and resentment gnawed at her heart" (12). Indeed, her actions are presented as a reflection of inner turmoil and the ugliness of her nature: "conflicting feelings, none of them amiable, clashed in her breast" (12). [14]

Trud's rare moments of humane behavior are overshadowed by an innate viciousness that reinforces the negative aspects of her character. Thus she acts "in a fleeting moment of compassion" (22) towards Grete's father; she places her hand on the back of his chair in an attempt to console him in the face of the presumed death of Grete. Yet, even here her hatred of Grete overpowers her: "when she heard Grete's name for the third time from his lips, she turned away again, and paced up and down the room restlessly and ill-tempered" (22). Her secret wish for Grete's death surfaces here, too, for the first time: "Was she dead? It had often been her wish, but this prospect did unnerve her. 'God, Grete' she cried and sank into a chair" (22). [15] This human reflex of *Ehrfurcht* (veneration) when confronted with death and the ultimate transitory nature of life only momentarily overrides her deep hatred of Grete. Fontane consistently lets any trace of humanity in Trud's behavior be almost immediately contradicted either by Trud herself or by the reactions of other figures. Even in the depiction of Trud's relationship to her own child, the expression of motherly love is restricted and limited: "The child was still whimpering softly, and the cradle was rocking rigorously, swinging back and forth, while Trud, leaning over the child, hummed her lullabies quickly and impatiently" (66). [16]

While Trud serves as a manifestation of the societal expectations and attitudes of the village community, her husband Gerdt is more closely aligned with the village's official power structure. He carries on the tradition of the Minde family in his public function as a city council representative. In the course of the novella, he uses this authority to disenfranchise Grete, both officially in front of the city council and privately within the family.

Even though Fontane introduces Gerdt as one who is "in everything the counterpart of his wife" (20), the reader encounters in him a second negative personality whose despicable nature is even more intensely described. Trud's envy of other people's love is matched and exceeded by Gerdt's insatiable greed for money and wealth. His disdainful remarks reduce his wife's and Gigas's religiously motivated criticism of the puppet-show as blasphemous to an expression of the latter's alleged interest in profit: "Yes, that's Gigas; he is afraid for himself and for his pulpit" (21). Here he is in effect attributing his own greed to Gigas. Gerdt's ill-natured personality affects every person with whom he comes into contact. "For his spiteful nature enjoyed nothing more than the anger of others, which did not exclude his wife" (52). [17] Gerdt surpasses his wife in cruelty — and in his case this cruelty is even reflected in his physical ugliness and unrelenting coldness of manner.

The ugliness of Trud's and Gerdt's child is also viewed as a sign of his parentage: "it is and remains just like Gerdt; it is as if it were sculpted directly from his face" (44).[18] Grete's identification of the child as Gerdt's heir also encompasses a projection into the future of the evil her husband personifies:

> For you must know that it is an ugly child, and everything is wrongly positioned and doesn't quite fit together, and I can already visualize him grown, how he will shuffle along, just like Gerdt, and always sit crooked and slouched and how he will stick his legs out far, far from him. Oh, he already has such long, skinny little legs. Like the spider on the wall. (44) [19]

Ultimately even Trud turns against Gerdt, whom she characterizes as the incarnation of heartless evil:

> Do you really think that this witch will sit down next to some country road and die and decay, just to please you? Oh Gerdt, Gerdt, it can bring no good. I might have been allowed to do it, *perhaps* allowed to, because from the beginning we were strangers and enemies. But *you*! You were *not* allowed to. There'll be a disaster! And you yourself conjured it up. For the sake of your good name, you say? Go on, I know you better than that. It was nothing but avarice and greed, a matter of possession and gold! Nothing else (97). [20]

This passage, which follows Gerdt's humiliating rejection of Grete, concludes with her final statement to him with its evocation of Judgment Day: "So fare thee well, and let your reward match your compassion. . . ." (96).[21]

A more positive secondary figure is the Protestant Gigas, who assumes the role of Grete's mentor and serves essentially as a mediator between her and Trud. Whereas the reader's negative judgment of Trud and Gerdt is ensured by the use of direct, almost directive terms, Gigas is granted a subtle, indirect description. The first reference to him by Grete is a negative one, based entirely on hearsay, and the image of him that she enunciates is an unappealing, even frightening one: "His eyes pierce one through and through. And his reddened eyes, which have no eyelashes . . ." (10). Valtin attempts to correct her assessment, describing Gigas as essentially wise, though intolerant in matters of religion: "Gigas is good. As long as there's no Calvinist or Catholic around. Then he immediately becomes angry, all fire and flame" (10).[22]

Gigas enters the narrative proper when Trud introduces him to Grete as her teacher in a scene laden with the potential for discord and hostility. The reader has already been informed of both Gigas's utter abhorrence of Catholicism and Grete's own Catholic origins. As Grete herself notes, "I'm afraid of Gigas . . . I always feel as though he thinks I am hiding something in my heart and am still Catholic from my mother's side" (26).[23] Conflict between these figures seems inevitable. Furthermore, Grete's fear of Gigas, based partially on her own belief, is underscored by Trud's affection for him and her introduction of him. What occurs reveals Gigas to be both perceptive and sensitive to the young girl's anxieties:

> He saw that Grete was trembling and always looked at Trud, not for advice or comfort, but rather because of her own shame and shyness. And Gigas, who not only understood the human heart, but who had also rescued a wealth of genuine love from the embittered religious conflicts, now turned towards Trud and said: "I would like to speak to the child alone" (28).[24]

In the conversation that follows, Grete's fear disappears as she recognizes the openness with which Gigas treats her. She gains respect for the old man, and in turn the religiously radical Gigas even appears willing to tolerate Grete's idolatry (29), at least for the time being. Thus, although he rejects Grete's amulet as a religious symbol for an old, now rejected belief, he lets her keep it as a remembrance of her mother. He understands Grete's own doubts, her inner conflict, and her questioning of her own religious background; he even senses her fear that he might think she is hiding something in her heart. Gigas is able to explain to Grete what he thinks, and takes her seriously, viewing her as an innocent, as yet uneducated child, rather than an innately evil being. Their relationship continues to deepen, and ultimately Grete accepts his tutelage in spiritual matters.

Despite his defense of the young pupil in front of Trud, his apparent desire to form and educate Grete, and even his willingness to tolerate her individual personality and origin, Gigas nevertheless represents within the novel the otherwise recalcitrant position of the Protestant faction toward the Catholics in the aftermath of the Thirty Years' War. The discrepancy between the old Catholic and the new Protestant belief that Fontane develops in *Grete Minde* is highlighted in the description of Gigas's desk:

> On this table, among opened books and stacks of numerous files, though pushed back to the wall with the crucifix, a delicate ebony staircase of five steps rose. It bore — in intended or accidental contrast — a skull on top and, tied around its base, a wreath of red and white roses of his own cultivation (27). [25]

The skull set on top of his desk with its wreath of fresh roses seem to symbolize the unresolved conflict in the coexistence of the old, though still present, "dead" object, and the blossoming of new, innocent life.

The conversation between Gigas and Trud mentioned above not only characterizes him as an essentially impartial and knowledgeable observer but also provides the reader with crucial insights into the forces at work in the community and in the lives of its inhabitants. His understanding of the personalities of the participants and thoughtful analysis of the situations he witnesses serve both to delineate their characters and to illuminate the roots of the impending tragedy. In chiding Trud, for example, he provides a valuable corrective to her view:

> "I cannot follow you, Frau Trud, in what you have told me about the child," Gigas said. "You misjudge her. She has a discouraged heart, not a spiteful one. I saw how she trembled, and the words she intended to say did not want to come over her lips. No, she is a good and beautiful child, like her mother" (30). [26]

Gigas accurately assesses the situation at the Minde household and Trud's role in it when he notes: "For you rule in the house" (31). His response with its pointed query to Trud after her judgmental assessment of Grete — "There is something evil in her" (31) focuses directly on the crux of the problem in Trud's relationship to Grete: "'In all of us, Frau Trud. And there are only two things that tame it: the faith we ask for, and the love we cultivate for ourselves. Do you love the child?' And she lowered her gaze" (31). Her acknowledgment of a deep-seated hatred of Grete, elicited by Gigas and implied by her demeanor, is ultimately confirmed by Trud's only direct characterization of her relationship to Grete, cited earlier, which occurs near the conclusion of the novella: "From the beginning we were strangers and enemies" (97).[27]

The warning inherent in Gigas's advice to Grete, "Look, our good deeds are nothing and mean nothing, because all of our actions are sinful from the very beginning" (29), is intensified by his subsequent words: ". . . you know it well, all seeds that fall from weeds and multiply are a disaster and damage the grain intended for our heavenly barns" (31),[28] words which, in the course of the novella, prove to be prophetic. Gigas's analysis of the factors at play in the community is borne out by subsequent events, and ultimately the forces he identifies lead inexorably to destruction and devastation.

Another significant secondary figure in this novella is Zenobia, a representative of an unaccepted social group: the gypsies. As such, she is sharply set apart from members of the accepted and respected social classes, as even the first reference to her evidences: "They're pagans and Turks. Did you see the woman? And how the long black veil hung from her head?" (17).[29] This brief passage constitutes Zenobia's only characterization, for in contrast to Trud, Gerdt, and Gigas, Zenobia is given no individual personal traits. Furthermore, her participation in the scenes depicted in the novella is limited — she does not take part in the activities and lively conversation of her fellow gypsies in the inn, despite their insistence. Indeed she is only once granted voice in the novella — significantly, it is to ask Grete to play the role of the angel in the staging of the *Sündenfall* (Fall from Grace). Yet her role for the novella itself proves to be crucial: the action of the novella begins with her appearance, and, as the work ends, she has, in a manner of speaking, assumed Grete's role.

Zenobia's relationship to Grete is based in part on their strikingly similar physical appearance. The alien image of the woman and her long black veil singled out among this group of "pagans and Turks" is echoed in the first description of Grete: "Only now did her figure become visible. It was a half grown girl of delicate build, and her fine features and, more particularly, the oval shape and tint of her face suggested foreign origin" (8). The physical similarity between Zenobia and Grete is reinforced by the subsequent description of the actress provided by Trud's and Emrentz's initial observations, as the small band of puppeteers marches into the city: "The woman with the dark complexion, who sat on a horse between the other two,

also bowed deeply. She appeared tall and imposing and wore a diadem with a long, black veil in which numerous little golden stars had
been embroidered" (16).[30] Though never explicitly stated, this description ultimately provides additional insight into Trud's animosity
toward Grete — her own prejudice toward Grete's Spanish heritage
from her Catholic mother.

The similarity between Grete and Zenobia, as well as their inter-
changeability, is accentuated by the two theatrical productions included in the novella: *Das Jüngste Gericht* (Judgment Day) at the
beginning and the concluding *Sündenfall* (Fall from Grace). The
first is a puppet show, and Grete becomes so engrossed in the action
on stage that she feels like she is an intrinsic part of it: "It seemed to
her as if she herself was being called before God's throne; her heart
pounded and her tender figure shook" (19). In the dramatic presentation of the *Sündenfall,* the puppets are replaced by human ac-
tors, granting the performance a heightened dimension of reality. It
is in this setting that Zenobia plays the angel in Grete's stead. Fontane, by means of these two performances, not only creates a frame
for the internal story of the novella but also links these two figures
together in an allegorical fashion. At the end, after Grete's death in
the flames, Zenobia plays her role in the *Sündenfall* play without the
change being noticed by the audience: "No one noticed the change
which had occurred in the cast. Zenobia played the angel" (107).[31]

The last of the secondary figures in *Grete Minde* to be discussed
here appear within small but key sections of the novella: Regine, an
employee in the Minde household, and the two nuns to whom
Grete turns for help after the death of her beloved Valtin. The
seemingly marginal figure of Regine, the housekeeper and maid, has
a significance in the novella far beyond her occupation. As the main
character's closest friend and confidant, and a person characterized
by innate goodness and a deep understanding of human nature, she
stands in strong contrast to the other secondary figures. In Grete's
early years, Regina counters the evil and hatred which the young girl
faces in Trud and Gerdt and provides an island of warmth and secu-
rity in the family setting so fraught with discord and ill-will. Furthermore, because of her long-standing service in the family, she
possesses knowledge of the past which she shares with Grete — and
subsequently the reader. She had been a nursemaid for Gerdt, knew
both his mother and Grete's, as well as their father, and had ob-

served the changes in the household and family over the years. It is she who describes Gerdt's mother as heartless: "she had no love, and the one who has none finds none" (26); and she tells Grete about her own mother, whom she regarded highly: "she was like an angel"; she also emphasizes Grete's father's love for his young and beautiful wife.[32] Equally important for the reader, she also illuminates the basis of Gerdt's behavior toward Grete by relating his reaction when he is first introduced to his half-sister:

> "Look Gerdt, this is your sister." But he did not want to look at you. And when I encouraged him, saying: "Just look at her black eyes; she has those from her mother," he ran off and said: "From *her* mother. But she is not mine."(25)[33]

Regine thus functions in the novel as a supplementary narrator, who not only provides background information about the family's history, but also, as a keen observer of human nature, analyzes the internal relationships between the various protagonists. The segment of the novella entitled "Regine," which portrays her close relationship to her young charge, reveals her personal warmth and gentle nature, the trusting and loving relationship she and Grete shared, and the positive influence she exerted during that period of Grete's life. It also reveals her personal bias — her dissatisfaction with the current regime of Trud and her positive predisposition toward Grete, attitudes which the narrator appears to understand, and even shares:

> She shared this gabled room with old Regine, who had run the Minde household for years. Certainly, ever since Trud had been there, things had changed, but to no one's real satisfaction. Least of all to old Regine's satisfaction. She now sat down *on her darling's bed,* and Grete said: "Do you know, Regine, Trud is mad at me."(24)[34]

When Grete, in a moment of heat and rage, confronts Trud and her heartlessness, Regine warns her: "Child, child, that will turn out badly; that she won't forget" (38). However, Grete rejects Regine's warnings — the narrator notes "Grete had become presumptuous" — and insists instead: "She is afraid of me. Let's see; I'm going to have better days now" (38). Neither Regine nor the narrator respond to this assertion, but when the situation is addressed in the opening line of the next chapter, the use of the subjunctive underlines the illusory nature of Grete's apparent success, thereby indirectly endorsing Regine's appraisal of the situation and her assessment of the combatants:

> And indeed, it was as though Grete had been right. . . . . All resentment
> appeared to be forgotten, and Grete, who, just like all passionate individuals, was as easily won over as she was angered, became accustomed, whenever Gerdt was taking care of business outside of the
> house, to sitting in Trud's bedroom, chatting to her or reading out
> loud, which she particularly enjoyed doing. (38)[36]

The course of the novella confirms the validity of Regine's concern and reveals the superficiality of their apparent harmony. After the death of Grete's father, which occurs shortly afterwards and precipitates changes in the household, Regine's premonitions are realized, and the subsequent chapter records Grete's recognition of the shift in the atmosphere of the house and in her own position:

> She was an orphan, and was to feel it all too soon. In the beginning it
> seemed to work . . . but as Easter approached, things changed in the
> house . . . Trud gave birth to a boy. Now the joy was great, and even
> Grete rejoiced. But not for long. Soon she had to realize that the
> newborn was everything and that she was nothing. . . . (41)[37]

Thus, with Regine, Fontane creates a secondary figure who not only fulfills her societal role as a competent housekeeper and dedicated children's maid, but is also an individual in her own right, one capable of independent thought and analysis, willing and able to make judgments about those around her, including her employers. Within the novella, Fontane uses her as a reliable informant who provides the reader not only with necessary background information, but above all with accurate and reliable assessments of the situation at hand and the likelihood of future developments.

The last figure under scrutiny in this context is the Domina,[38] one of the nuns of Arendsee. The nuns' introduction as representatives of the Catholic Church and, consequently, counterfigures to Trud and Gerdt, sheds new light on the religious controversy that pervades the novella. Although Gigas, viewed from Trud's perspective, embodies the new and, in her eyes, better belief, the more generous feelings and greater freedom of thought and attitude in the novella are granted to the old Catholic faith through its representation by the nuns.

The nuns are first introduced in a conversation between Gerdt and Trud that follows a heated argument between the two, which had ended in violence after both had lost their tempers. Trud and Gerdt decide that Grete must leave the house and, in that context, Trud suggests the Catholic convent in Arendsee:

> I thought of the nuns of Arendsee, that is not too near and not too far. And that is where she belongs. For she has a Catholic heart, in spite of Gigas, and whenever she talks to me, she is looking for the little amulet with the splinter to which she then clings with both hands. And even if she says nothing, her lips still move, and I could swear that she is praying to the Holy Virgin. (65)[39]

The nuns do not appear again until after Grete's return to Tangermünde following the death of her beloved Valtin. When Grete's attempt to have Valtin buried in the Protestant cemetery is thwarted by the refusal of the local pastor, Prediger Roggenstroh, she is directed to the nuns by a sympathetic innkeeper, who describes them as well-meaning, good individuals:

> [Grete] should summon up her courage and ask for the Domina, or, if she were sick (for she is very old), for Ilse Schulenburg. *She* has her heart in the right place and is the Domina's right hand. (83)[40]

Fontane is clearly fond of these representatives of the Catholic church: he depicts them as kind and wise women who indeed do help Grete. He even grants them the ability to predict the future. Significantly, he not only makes them old but also situates them in an almost inaccessible place. Grete has difficulty finding the entrance to the convent and ultimately gains entry only by forcing her way through the hedge, as if there were no actual entrance. Thus Fontane implies that Catholicism is both self-contained and encapsulated against the outside world, and suggests that whoever wishes to enter needs to be determined in order to succeed.

When Grete finally enters the convent's premises and finds the house in which the Domina lives, she learns that there are no longer any nuns, except the Domina and Ilse Schulenburg. Their house is surrounded by vines and evokes the atmosphere of a long-vanished, almost fairytale-like setting:

> And she [Grete] stopped, ducked, and raised herself up again, and it seemed to her as though this luxuriously growing graveyard-wilderness, this pathlessness amid flowers, spun a web of mysterious magic about her. (84)[41]

In addition to her fascination with this almost other-worldly setting, Grete's eyes are captured by the faded paintings in the entrance hall. One painting in particular rivets her attention: it depicts "floating figures of angels who were carrying a corpse" (83).[42] The impact of this particular picture is carefully orchestrated by Fontane through repeated references to Grete's amulet and Regine's characterization of Grete's Catholic mother as "like an angel" (25).

When the nuns themselves are finally introduced, their portrayal is a very favorable one. The Domina presents herself in a straight-forward manner, even noting her physical shortcomings: "stand over here in the light, for my ears no longer serve me, and I have to read your lips" (85).[43] Although Fontane inserts, with an ironic under-tone, an element of friction between the nuns and Prediger Roggen-stroh, which might lead the reader to deduce that their willingness to help was based on an antagonism towards him, this impression is ultimately dissipated by the genuine nature of the kindness and warmth with which the Domina treats Grete.

The Domina, drawing from her personal experiences over some ninety-five years, judges the problems of the day as not particularly unusual in comparison to other hard times, "Yes, child, I have wit-nessed many times, and they were no worse than our own times" (86). And although the conflict between her and Roggenstroh re-emerges in the context of the burial, her personal warmth and con-cern for the others is re-established when the ceremony is over and the Domina addresses Grete, seeking to offer her consolation and expressing concern about her future, "And now, child, tell me where you come from and where you are going. I'm asking for *your sake.* Tell me what you can and want to say" (88). Responding to these words, Grete entrusts the Domina with the entire story of her life, and after Grete leaves the convent, the Domina predicts Grete's im-minent death: ". . . I saw death on her forehead. And take heed, Ilse, she'll not live three more days!" (89)[44]

The Domina's prophecy proves true, and her assessment of the tribulations of the day as not being particularly unusual is validated by the final scene of the novella and serves to reduce the impact of the tragic events precipitated by Grete, ". . . Ilse Schulenburg and the Domina were again sitting by the ivy-covered wall of their house and everything was as usual" (107). The circle is closed, the Domina's prediction has been fulfilled: "Poor child . . . Today is the third day . . . I knew it," and the situation is brought back to the normal routine of their life: "Thus their conversation went" (107). [45]

Not only does her Catholicism designate Grete as an outsider, but the manner in which those around her perceive her, particularly in light of their prejudice against the "old" belief, also proves to be a major force that leads ultimately to the final 'tragedy.' The roots of Grete's downfall lie in the society depicted in this novella; specifically, a society in a state of transition from Catholic to Protestant belief, from "religious" war to "reformed" peace. In this period of political and social change, the broad historical scene is reflected in the individual, familial sphere and embodied in the contrasting figures of Gigas, who stands as a middle figure between the old and the new faith; Trud, who uncompromisingly and relentlessly represents the new belief; and Grete, who, while open to the new faith, clings to the remnants of the old belief as part of her personal, maternal heritage. In the concluding action of the story, not only does Grete die, but she takes her own child, and the child of her two adversaries, Trud and Gerdt, to a fiery death as the blazing village church St. Stephan collapses. Thus the old and the new, the past and the future are subjected to an ultimate Judgment Day, one precipitated by Grete, who is herself a victim of the world she condemns. The concluding lines of the novella return to the scheduled final performance of the puppeteer, "The hall was filled and the applause immense. No one noted the change that had occurred in the cast. . . . Zenobia played the angel" (107). Grete's death loses significance — Zenobia reappears in her stead. The last paragraph of the novella notes only the great success of the play, and the stage is left to a secondary figure: Zenobia.

Grete Minde, in light of its focus on the character study of the secondary figures, represents a turning point in Fontane's novelistic writings. Through their highly individualized portrayal, Fontane both illustrates and illuminates the societal forces at work in their world and delineates the personalities and conflicts central to the novella's plot and crucial for its main protagonist. With this work, Fontane thus establishes the narrative mode that he was to follow and further develop in his subsequent works.

Notes

¹ Letter from Fontane to Paul Lindau, October 23, 1878. (*Theodor Fontane. Briefe in 4 Bde.* Ed. Walter Keiter and Helmuth Nürnberger. [Frankfurt: Ullstein, 1986], Vol. 2, 625.) In an earlier letter to Lindau of May 6, 1878, Fontane had written: "Ich habe vor, im Laufe des Sommers eine altmärkische Novelle zu schreiben. Ort: Salzwedel; Zeit: 1660; Heldin: Grete Minde, Patrizierkind, das durch Habsucht, Vorurteil und Unbeugsamkeit von seiten ihrer Familie, mehr noch durch Trotz des eigenen Herzens, in einigermaßen großem Stil, sich und die halbe Stadt vernichtend, zu Grunde geht. Ein Sitten- und Charakterbild aus der Zeit nach dem Dreißigjährigen Kriege." (568) [During the course of the summer, I plan to write an old-*märkian* novella. Location: Salzwedel; time: 1660; heroine: Grete Minde, a patrician's daughter, who is destroyed because of greed, prejudice, and stubbornness on the part of her family, but even more because of the spite in her own heart. . . . She thus also destroys half of the town. The novella will be a reflection of the mores and characters during the period of the 30 Years' War.]

² Richard Brinkmann and Waltraud Wiethölter, eds. *Dichter über ihre Dichtungen.* Heimeran: Munich, 1973, 188–89. This work will be cited subsequently in the text as *DüD.* German original: "Man muß Vordergrunds-, Mittelgrunds-, und Hintergrunds-Figuren haben und es ist ein Fehler wenn man alles in das volle Licht des Vordergrundes rückt. . . . Die Personen müssen gleich beim ersten Auftreten so gezeichnet sein, daß der Leser es weg hat, ob sie Haupt- oder Nebenpersonen sind. Auf das räumliche Maß der Schilderung kommt es dabei nicht an, sondern auf eine gewisse Intensität, die den Fingerzeig gibt."

³ The significance of secondary figures in Fontane's fiction climaxes with the publication of *Stine* in 1890. His conscious emphasis on the secondary figures in this novella is documented in his letters. See, for example, his letter to Emil Dominik: "Die Hauptperson ist nicht Stine, sondern deren ältere Schwester: Witwe Pittelkow. Ich glaube, sie ist eine mir gelungene und noch nie dagewesene Figur" (January 3, 1888); or his letter to M. Harden: "Es ist richtig, daß meine Nebenfiguren immer die Hauptsache sind, in Stine nun schon ganz gewiß, die Pittelkow ist mir als Figur viel Wichtiger als die ganze Geschichte" (August 20, 1890).

⁴ For further information about "Psychographie und Kritik," see Hans-Heinrich Reuter, *Fontane* (Berlin: Verlag der Nation, 1968) 644ff. German original: "Die beiden Hauptelemente, auf denen Fontane später seine 'ganze Produktion' begründet sah, 'Psychographie und Kritik,' waren an seinem ersten Roman noch nicht in gleicher Weise beteiligt. Psychologi-

sche Durchdringung — dürfen wir hier einmal den Begriff der 'Psychographie' vereinfachend so übersetzen — blieb analytischer Selbstzweck, um nicht zu sagen isoliertes poetisches Spiel, episches Training" (548).

[5] Fontane's use of the term "novel" must be understood within the context of his tendency to shift frequently in his use of the genre terms "novel," "novella," and "narrative" when referring to his works.

[6] "Es ist das Eintreten einer großen Idee, eines großen Moments in an und für sich sehr einfache Lebenskreise" (*DüD*, 189).

[7] See Reuter's discussion: "Die Auseinandersetzung über den Roman hatte bereits begonnen, noch ehe eine Zeile davon gedruckt war. . . . König intervenierte im Namen der Romantik: 'Der Stoff wäre wundervoll, Gesinnung, Tendenz ebenso und die Sorglichkeit der Behandlung evident, aber alles zu breit, nicht gerade aufs Ziel los, Exkurse, Überflüssigkeiten' (es ist genau das Urteil, das über ein Jahrhundert lang immer wieder nachgesprochen werden sollte)" (543).

[8] German original: "Meinst Du nicht auch, daß neben den Romanen, wie beispielsweise Copperfield, in denen wir ein Menschenleben von seinem Anbeginn an betrachten, auch solche berechtigt sind, die statt des Individuums einen vielgestaltigen Zeitabschnitt unter die Loupe nehmen? Das größere dramatische Interesse, soviel räum ich ein, wird freilich immer den Erzählungen 'mit einem Helden' verbleiben, aber auch der Vielheitsroman, mit seinen Porträtmassen und Episoden, wird sich dem Einheitsroman ebenbürtig — nicht an Wirkung, aber an Kunst — an die Seite stellen können, wenn er nur nicht willkürlich verfährt, vielmehr immer nur solche Retardierungen bringt, die, während sie momentan den Gesamtzwerck zu vergessen scheinen, diesem recht eigentlich dienen" (December 9, 1878).

[9] The letter was written only three days after Fontane mentioned his fear of Gutzkow's emphatic negative criticism of *Vor dem Sturm*. Fontane also stresses that his preoccupation with *Grete Minde* made him hesitant to read Gutzkow's criticism: "Ist es sehr schlimm, so les ich es jetzt, wo ich inmitten einer Novelle (Grete Minde) stecke, und zwar an der wichtigsten Stelle, lieber nicht" (Fontane to Hertz, December 6, 1878).

[10] Globig's concerns about the historical authenticity of *Grete Minde* and his own archival research lead him to conclude: "Schon aus dieser freien Kombination historischer Tatsachen läßt sich entnehmen, daß es Fontane nicht auf absolute historische Treue der Darstellung ankam, daß es sich hierbei nicht um eine 'historisierende,' die Geschichte bloß verlebendigende, schriftstellerische Fleißarbeit handelt, sondern daß Fontane das historisch Nachweisbare nur als Rohstoff seinen eigenen Gestaltungswünschen unterordnete, um Eigenes auszudrücken" (*Fontane Blätter* 32:709). Later Globig claims that Fontane intended to criticize his own

society through the conscious distortion of historical fact and attributes *Grete Minde*'s lack of contemporary success to that intent: "Daß dieser Spiegel, gerade wenn es kein Zerrspiegel, sondern ein klarer und verzerrungsfreier Spiegel ist, nicht unbedingt geliebt wird, daß man lieber eine Verschleierung des eigenen Bildes als die unangenehme Realität sehen würde, ist verständlich und läßt auch verstehen, warum Fontane trotz der auch hier bewiesenen formalen Meisterschaft nicht den Erfolg erringen konnte, auf den er Anspruch gehabt hätte. . ." (712). Globig also views the conclusion of *Grete Minde* as symbolizing drastic societal change: "Die Zerstörung der Stadt Tangermünde symbolisiert den gewaltsamen Umsturz der bestehenden Gesellschaft" (710), and states later "In dieser Novelle wird das verwirklicht, was als Anspruch an die künstlerische Gestaltung eines historischen Stoffes zu erheben ist: ohne Verbiegung der historischen Gestalten und Situationen den Zeitgenossen einen Spiegel vorzuhalten, der ihnen die eigenen Handlungen möglicherweise in einem deutlicheren Licht erscheinen läßt, ihnen auch für ihre eigene Zeit gültige Erkenntnisse vermittelt" (712). "Hier wird die generelle Kritik Fontanes an einer auf Gewalt, auf einer Position der Stärke beruhenden Haltung legitimen Ansprüchen anderer gegenüber mit Händen greifbar: eine Kritik, die in der historischen Situation des Jahres 1878 außerordentlich mutig war" (711). It is my contention that although Fontane intended his work to be socially critical in nature, he did not deviate from historical events for political reasons, but for purely novelistic ones. Furthermore, he never claimed historical veracity, but rather spoke of the events he used as "ein durchaus vorzüglicher Stoff. . . ." (See also Paulsen's *Im Banne der Melusine*, 5–6).

[11] In a critical comment, Volker Giel states, however: "Fontane geht es, . . . nicht um eine Auflösung des angegebenen Widerspruchs, sondern mehr um die Verdeutlichung und Problematisierung desselben, da wie Fontane richtig erkennt, in einer sich zunehmend kapitalisierenden Wirklichkeit für die Verwirklichung des menschheitsemanzipatorischen Anspruchs immer weniger Raum bleibt. . . . Nur Einsicht und Erkenntnis der objektiven Gesetze der Gesellschaft kann zu einer im menschlichen Sinne positiven Veränderung dieser Gesellschaft führen, wodurch einzig und allein auch der Anspruch auf menschheitliche Emanzipation erfüllbar werden kann" (Giel, 73). With this statement, Giel not only contradicts Globig's position, he also places the novella in a broader "historical" context.

[12] For all quotations from *Grete Minde* in this article, the second Aufbau edition has been used: *Theodor Fontane: Romane und Erzählungen*. Berlin and Weimar: Aufbau, 1973. The page numbers given in parentheses in

text and footnotes refer to this edition. Translations into English are given in text for the convenience of the non-German-speaking reader.

[13] "Ach Trud, Trud. Trud ist deine Schwieger, und eine Schwieger ist nicht mehr als eine Schwester" (8). "Ich kann sie nicht leiden" (9). "Hubsch ist sie, aber hübsch und bös" (9).

[14] "doch hübsch und klug . . . weiß, was sie will, und paßt ins Haus und hat eine vornehme Art" (26). "Eine schöne, junge Frau, Frau Trud Minde, modisch gekleidet, aber mit strengen Zügen . . . hatte sich hinter einem Weinspalier versteckt" (11). "Das Blut steigt ihr zu Kopf, und Neid und Mißgunst zehrten an ihrem Herze" (12); "die widerstreitendsten Gefühle, nur keine freundlichen, hatten sich in ihrer Brust gekreuzt (12).

[15] "[I]n einem Anfluge von Teilnahme" (22). ". . . als sie aber den Namen Gretens zum dritten Mal aus seinem Munde hörte, wandte sie sich wieder ab und schritt unruhig und übellaunig im Zimmer auf und nieder" (22). War sie tot? Es war oft ihr Wunsch gewesen; aber dieser Anblick erschütterte sie doch. 'Gott, Grete!' rief sie und sank in einen Stuhl" (22).

[16] Trud's personal distance from her baby seems to repeat the relationship Gerdt's mother apparently had to him and indirectly serves to indicate the similarity between the two women: their stiffness, their impersonal manner, and distanced attitude toward others, although their physical appearance is strikingly different. Trud is described as beautiful and Gerdt's mother appears rather masculine — "Wie der Stendhalsche Roland" (Like Stendhal's Roland) (25). Both are also viewed by others as greedy and without love; thus Regina notes of Gerdt's mother: "sie hatte keine Liebe, und wer keine Liebe hat, der findt auch keine. Das ist so der Lauf der Welt, und es war just so, wie's mit der Trud ist" (26).

[17] German original: "Denn seine hämische Natur kannte nichts Liebres als den Ärger andrer Leute, seine Frau nicht ausgenommen" (52).

[18] German original: "es ist und bleibt der Gerdt, und ist ihm wie aus dem Gesicht geschnitten" (44).

[19] Grete's words also serve to reveal a hidden motivation for her later destruction of her nephew. German original: "Denn du mußt wissen, es ist ein häßlich Kind, und alles an ihm hat eine falsche Stell und paßt nicht recht zusamm', und ich seh es in Gedanken schon groß, wie's dann auch so hin und her schlenkert, grad wie der Gerdt, und sitzt immer krumm und eingesunken und streckt die Beine weit, weit von sich. Ach, es hat schon jetzt so lange dünne Beinchen. Wie die Spinn an der Wand" (44).

[20] German original: "Meinst du, daß diese Hexe sich an die Landstraße setzen und dir zuliebe sterben und verderben wird?! Oh, Gerdt, Gerdt, es kann nicht guttun. Ich hätt's gedurft, vielleicht gedurft, denn wir waren uns fremd und feind von Anfang an. Aber du! Du durftest es nicht. Ein

Unheil gibt's! Und du selber hast es heraufbeschworen. Um guten Namens willen, sagst du? Geh; ich kenn dich besser. Aus Geiz und Habsucht und um Besitz und Goldes willen! Nichts weiter" (97).

[21] German original: "So gehab dich wohl, und dein Leben sei wie dein Erbarmen" (96).

[22] German original: "Er sieht einen so durch und durch. Und seine roten Augen, die keine Wimpern haben . . ." (10). "Gigas ist gut. Es muß nur kein Kalvinscher sein oder kein Katholscher. Da wird er gleich bös und Feuer und Flamme" (10).

[23] German original: "Aber ich fürchte mich vor Gigas. . . . mir ist immer, als mein er, ich verstecke was in meinem Herzen und sei noch katholisch von der Mutter her" (26).

[24] German original: "Er sah, daß Grete zitterte und immer auf Trud blickte, aber nicht um Rat und Trostes willen, sondern aus Scham und Scheu. Und Gigas, der nicht nur das menschliche Herz kannte, sondern sich aus erbitterten Glaubenskämpfen her auch einen Schatz echter Liebe gerettet hatte, wandte sich jetzt an Trud und sagte, 'Ich spräche gern allein mit dem Kind'" (28).

[25] German original: "Auf diesem Tisch, zwischen aufgeschlagenen Büchern und zahlreichen Aktenstößen, aber bis an die Kruzifixwand zurückgeschoben, erhob sich ein zierliches, fünfstufiges Ebenholztreppchen, das, in beabsichtigtem oder zufälligem Gegensatz, oben einen Totenkopf und unten um seinen Sockel her einen Kranz von roten und weißen Rosen trug. Eigene Zucht" (27).

[26] German original: "Ich kann Euch nicht folgen, Frau Trud, in dem, was Ihr mir über das Kind gesagt habt,' sagte Gigas. 'Ihr verkennt es. Es ist ein verzagtes Herz und kein trotzig Herz. Ich sah, wie sie zitterte, und der Spruch, den sie sagen sollte, wollt ihr nicht über die Lippen. Nein, es ist ein gutes Kind und ein schönes Kind. Wie die Mutter" (30).

[27] German originals: "Denn ihr beherrschet das Haus"; "Es ist etwas Böses in ihr"; "'In uns allen, Frau Trud. Und zwei Dinge sind, es zu bändigen: der Glaube, den wir uns erbittern, und die Liebe, die wir uns erziehn. Liebt Ihr das Kind?' Und sie senkte den Blick" (31); "wir waren uns fremd und feind von Anfang an" (97).

[28] German originals: "Denn sieh, unsre guten Werke sind nichts und bedeuten nichts, weil all unser Tuen sündig ist vom Anfang an" (29); ". . . Ihr wißt es wohl, aller Samen, der vom Unkraut fällt und wuchert, ist Unheil und schädigt uns das Korn für unsre himmlischen Scheuren" (31).

[29] German original: "Heiden und Türken sind's. Sahst du die Frau? Und wie der lange schwarze Schleier ihr vom Kopfe hing?" (17).

[30] German originals: "Jetzt erst sah man ihre Gestalt. Es war ein halbwach-senes Mädchen, sehr zart gebaut, und ihre feinen Linien, noch mehr das Oval und die Farbe ihres Gesichts, deuteten auf eine Fremde" (8). "Auch die dunkelfarbige Frau, die zwischen den beiden anderen zu Pferde saß, verneigte sich. Sie schien groß und stattlich und trug ein Diadem mit langem schwarzem Schleier, in den zahllose Goldsternchen eingenäht wa-ren" (16).

[31] German originals: "Ihr war, als würde sie selbst vor Gottes Thron geru-fen, und ihr Herz schlug und ihre zarte Gestalt zitterte" (19). "Niemand achtete des Wechsels, der in Besetzung der Rollen stattgefunden hatte. Zenobia spielte den Engel" (107).

[32] German originals: "sie hatte keine Liebe, und wer keine Liebe hat, der findet auch keine" (26); "sie war wie ein Engel."

[33] German original: "'Sieh Gerdt, das ist deine Schwester.' Aber er wollte dich nicht sehen. Und als ich ihm zuredete und sagte: 'Sieh doch nur ihre schwarzen Augen; die hat sie von der Mutter,' da lief er fort und sagte: 'Von ihrer Mutter. Aber das ist nicht meine'" (25).

[34] German original: "Diese Giebelstube teilte sie mit der alten Regine, die von lange her das Mindesche Hauswesen führte. Freilich, seit Trud da war, war es anders geworden, aber zu niemandes rechter Zufriedenheit. Am wenigsten zur Zufriedenheit der alten Regine. Diese setzte sich jetzt an das Bett ihres Lieblings, und Grete sagte: "Weißt du, Regine, Trud ist bö-se mit mir" (24).

[35] German original: "Kind, Kind, das tut nicht gut, das kann sie dir nicht vergessen" (38). "Aber Grete war übermütig geworden und sagte: 'Sie fürchtet sich vor mir. Laß sehen; ich habe nun bessere Tage.'"

[36] German original: "Und wirklich, es war, als ob Grete recht behalten sollte. . . . Aller Groll schien vergessen, und Grete, die, nach Art leiden-schaftlicher Naturen, ebenso rasch zu gewinnen als zu reizen war, ge-wöhnte sich daran, in den Stunden, wo Gerdt außerhalb des Hauses sei-nen Geschäften nachging, in Truds Schlafzimmer zu sitzen und ihr vorzu-plaudern oder vorzulesen, was sie besonders liebte" (38).

[37] German original: "Eine Waise war sie, und sie sollt es nur allzubald empfinden. Anfangs ging es . . . als aber Ostern herankam, wurd es anders im Haus . . . Trud genas eines Knäbleins. Da war nun die Freude groß, und auch Grete freute sich. Doch nicht lange. Bald mußte sie wahr-nehmen, daß das Neugeborene alles war und sie nichts. . . ." (41).

[38] Although Fontane has one protagonist, a maid, claim that "Wir haben keine Nonnen mehr" (84), I refer to the two women as "nuns" following his own labelling of them. The focus is on the Domina because of the de-cisive role she plays in Grete's life. Although her personality is not defined,

Ilse Schulenburg, as friend and "right hand" of the Domina, gains importance as a conversational partner, as commentator and initiator of discussion.

[39] German original: "Ich hab an die Nonnen von Arendsee gedacht, das ist nicht zu nah und nicht zu weit. Und da gehört sie hin. Denn sie hat ein katholisch Herz, trotz Gigas, und immer, wenn sie mit mir spricht, so sucht sie nach dem Kapselchen mit dem Splitter und hält es mit ihren beiden Händen fest. Und schweigt sie dann, so bewegen sich ihre Lippen, und ich wollte schwören, daß sie zur Heiligen Jungfrau betet." (65)

[40] In contrast to the other secondary figures, the Domina receives additional positive characterization from a farmer who describes her in his dialect: "Un so groot se is, so good is se" (And she is as good as she is tall) (91). While the use of dialect and the comparison of the Domina's tall stature with her goodness might reduce the impact of his words, the genuine appreciation expressed in the farmer's simple words and the authenticity and honesty they convey serve to underscore the positive portrayal of the Domina. German original: "[Grete] solle nur Mut haben und nach der Domina fragen oder, wenn die Domina krank sei (denn sie sei sehr alt), nach der Ilse Schulenburg. Die habe das Herz auf dem rechten Fleck und sei der Domina rechte Hand" (83).

[41] German original: "Und sie [Grete] blieb stehen, duckte sich und hob sich wieder, und es war ihr, als ob diese wuchernde Gräberwildnis, diese Pfadlosigkeit unter Blumen, sie mit einem geheimnisvollen Zauber umspinne" (84).

[42] "Engelsgestalten, die schwebend einen Toten trugen" (83); "wie ein Engel" (25).

[43] German original: ". . . stelle dich hier ins Licht, denn mein Ohr ist mir nicht mehr zu Willen, und ich muß dir's von den Lippen lesen" (85).

[44] German original: "Ja, Kind, ich habe viele Zeiten gesehen, und sie waren nicht schlechter, als unsere Zeiten sind (86). "Und nun sage mir, Kind, woher du kommst und wohin du gehst? Ich frag es um deinetwillen. Sage mir, was du mir sagen kannst und sagen willst" (88). "Aber ich sah den Tod auf ihrer Stirn. Und hab acht, Ilse, sie lebt keinen dritten Tag mehr!" (89).

[45] German originals: "Den Tag danach saßen Ilse Schulenburg und die Domina wieder an der Efeuwand ihres Hauses, und alles war wie sonst" (107). "'Armes Kind . . . Ist heute der dritte Tag . . . Ich wußte es'. . . . So ging ihr Gespräch" (107).

[46] "Der Saal war gefüllt und der Beifall groß. Niemand achtete des Wechsels, der in Besetzung der Rollen stattgefunden hatte." "Zenobia spielte den Engel" (107).

Works Cited

Adorno, Theodor W. "Der Essay als Form." In Adorno, T. W., *Noten zur Literatur: Schriften*. 3rd ed. Frankfurt am Main: Suhrkamp Verlag, 3. Auflage 1974; rpt. 1990.

Allenhöfer, Manfred. "Vierter Stand und alte Ordnung bei Fontane." In *Zur Realistik des bürgerlichen Realismus*. Stuttgart: Akademischer Verlag, 1986.

Aschoff, Volker. "Die elektrische Nachrichtentechnik im 19. Jahrhundert." *Technikgeschichte* 33/34, 1984.

Auerbach, Erich. *Mimesis: Dargestellte Wirklichkeit in der europäischen Literatur*. Bern/Munich: Francke, 1946.

Aust, Hugo. *Theodor Fontane: "Verklärung." Eine Untersuchung zum Ideengehalt seiner Werke*. Bonn: Bouvier, 1974.

Bakhtin, Mikhail Mikhailovich. *The Dialogic Imagination: Four Essays*. Austin: U of Texas P, 1981.

Bange, Pierre. *Ironie et dialogisme dans les romans de Theodor Fontane*. Grenoble: Presses Universitaires, 1974.

Barthes, Roland. "The Reality Effect." *The Rustle of Language*. Trans. Richard Howard. New York: Hill and Wang, 1984.

Bell, Susan G., ed. *Women from the Greeks to the Middle Ages*. Stanford: Stanford UP, 1975.

Bense, Max. "Über den Essay und seine Prosa." *Merkur* 3 (1947).

Bensmaïa, Réda. *The Barthes Effect: The Essay as Reflective Text*. Minneapolis: U of Minnesota P, 1987.

Berg-Ehlers, Luise. *Theodor Fontane und die Literaturkritik*. Bochum: Winkler, 1990.

Berger, Peter. *The Sacred Canopy: Elements of a Sociological Theory of Religion*. New York: Doubleday, 1966.

Berger, Peter, and Thomas Luckmann. *The Social Construction of Reality*. New York: Doubleday, 1966.

Berman, Russell. *The Rise of the Modern German Novel: Crisis and Charisma*. Cambridge, MA: Harvard UP, 1986.

Biener, Joachim. "Zur Diskussion." *Fontane Blätter* 5 (1982) 1: 80–82.

Blumenberg, Hans. "Wirklichkeitsbegriff und Möglichkeit des Roman." In *Nachahmung und Illusion: Poetik und Hermeneutik*, vol. 1, ed. H. R. Jauss. Munich: Fink, 1969.

Böckmann, Paul. "Der Zeitroman Fontanes." In *Der Deutschunterricht*, 1959. Repr. in *Theodor Fontane: Wege zur Forschung*. Ed. W. Preisendanz. Darmstadt: Wissenschaftliche Buchgesellschaft, 1977.

Boltzmann, L. *Populäre Schriften*. Braunschweig/Wiesbaden, 1979. Includes "Über statistische Mechanik."

Bos, Jan. "Die kritische Funktion der religiösen Motivik in Fontanes *Grete Minde*." Diss., Utrecht, 1980.

Bosshart, Adelheit. "Theodor Fontanes historische Romane." Diss., Zürich and Winterthur, 1957.

Boydston, Jeanne. *Home and Work: Housework, Wages, and the Ideology of Labor in the Early Republic*. New York: Oxford UP, 1990.

Brinkmann, Richard. *Theodor Fontane: Über die Verbindlichkeit des Unverbindlichen*. Munich: R. Piper, 1967; reprint, Munich: Max Niemeyer, 1977.

——, ed. *Begriffsbestimmung des literarischen Realismus*. Darmstadt: Wiss. Buchgesellschaft, 1974.

Brinkmann, Richard, and Wiethölter, Waltraud, eds. *Dichter über ihre Dichtungen*. Munich: Heimeran, 1973.

Buber, Martin. *Werke I*. Ed. W. Preisendanz. Darmstadt: Wissenschaftliche Buchgesellschaft, 1977.

Büsch, K. "Die Militärisierung von Staat und Gesellschaft im alten Preußen." In *Ausstellung Preußen: Versuch einer Bilanz*, vol. 2, ed. M. Schlenke. Reinbek: Rowohlt, 1981.

Craig, Gordon A. *Germany 1866–1914*. Oxford: Oxford UP, 1978.

Deleuze, Gilles, and Clair Parnet. *Dialogues*. London: Athlone, 1987.

Delp, W. E. "Around Fontane's *Grete Minde*." *Modern Languages* 40 (1959): 18–19.

Demetz, Peter. *Formen des Realismus: Theodor Fontane. Kritische Untersuchungen*. Munich: Hanser, 1964. 91–99.

Derrida, Jacques. "Struktur, Zeichen, Spiel." *Die Schrift und die Differenz.* Frankfurt am Main: Suhrkamp, 1977.

——. *Sporen: Die Stile Nietzsches.* Chicago/London: U of Chicago P, 1978.

——. "My Chances/mes changes." In *Talking Chances: Derrida, Psychoanalysis and Literature.* Ed. Joseph Smith and William Kerrigan. Baltimore: Johns Hopkins UP, 1984.

Doebeling, Marion. *Theodor Fontane im Gegenlicht: Ein Beitrag zur Theorie des Essays und des Romans.* Würzburg: Königshausen & Neumann, 2000. (Author's name appears as Marion Villmar-Doebeling.)

Dutschke, Manfred. "Geselliger Spießrutenlauf." *Text und Kritik. Sonderband Theodor Fontane.* Ed. H. L. Arnold. Munich: Text und Kritik, 1989.

De Lauretis, Teresa. "Technologies of Gender." In *Technologies of Gender: Essays on Film, Theory, and Literature.* Bloomington: Indiana UP, 1987.

Eagleton, Terry. *Literary Criticism: An Introduction.* Minneapolis: U of Minnesota P, 1983.

Eco, Umberto. *Lector in Fabula.* Munich: Carl Hanser Verlag; Deutscher Taschenbuch Verlag, 1987.

Eisele, Ulf. "Empirischer Realismus: Die epistemologische Problematik einer literarischen Konzeption." In *Bürgerlicher Realismus: Grundlagen und Interpretationen,* ed. Klaus-Detlef Müller. Königstein: Athenäum, 1981.

Elshtain, Jean Bethke. "Aristotle, the Public-Private Split and the Case of the Suffragists." In *The Family in Political Thought,* ed. Jean Bethke Elshtain. Amherst: U of Massachusetts P, 1982.

Ester, Hans. *Der selbstverständliche Geistliche: Untersuchungen zur Gestaltung und Funktion des Geistlichen im Erzählwerk Theodor Fontanes.* Leiden: n.p., 1975.

——. "Zur Gesellschaftskritik in Fontanes *Grete Minde.*" *Fontane Blätter* 5 (1982) 1: 73–78.

Fechner, Gustav Theodor. *Vorschule der Ästhetik.* Leipzig: Breitkopf/ Härtl, 1876.

Felman, Shoshana. "Turning the Screw of Interpretation." *Yale French Studies* 55–56 (1977): 94–207.

——. *Writing and Madness: Literature/Philosophy/Psychoanalysis.* Ithaca: Cornell UP, 1985.

Field, G. W. "The Idiosyncrasies of Dubslav von Stechlin: A Fontane 'Original.'" In *Formen realistischer Erzählkunst: Festschrift for Charlotte Jolles*. Ed. Jörg Thunecke and Eda Sagarra. Nottingham: Sherwood, 1979.

Flax, Jane. "The Family in Contemporary Feminist Thought: A Critical Overview." In *The Family in Political Thought*, ed. Jean Bethke Elshtain. Amherst: U of Massachusetts P, 1982.

Fontane, Theodor. *Briefe an Georg Friedländer*. Ed. K. Schreinert. Heidelberg: Quelle & Meyer, 1954.

——. *Delusions, Confusions* and *The Poggenpuhl Family*. The German Library, vol. 47. Ed. Peter Demetz, trans. William L. Zwiebel. New York: Continuum, 1989.

——. *Dichter über ihre Dichtungen: Theodor Fontane*. 2 vols. Ed. R. Brinkmann. Munich: Heimeran, 1973.

——. "Die öffentliche Denkmäler." In *Sämtliche Werke*, vol. 17.

——. *Effi Briest*. Trans. Douglas Parmee. London: Penguin, 1967.

——. "Erinnerungen. Ausgewählte Schriften und Kritiken." In *Sämtliche Werke*. Abteilung 3, vol. 1. Ed. Walter Keitel. Munich: Hanser, 1962.

——. *Fontanes Briefe in zwei Bänden, Ausgewählt und erläutert von Gottherd Erler*. Berlin and Weimar: Aufbau, 1968.

——. "Hermann Grimm. Goethe." In *Sämtliche Werke*, vol. 21/1. Munich: Nymphenburger Verlagshandlung, 1974.

——. "Irrungen, Wirrungen." In *Sämtliche Werke*, Abteilung 1, vol. 2. Ed. Walter Keitel. Munich: Hanser, 1962.

——. "London." In *Sämtliche Werke*, vols. 17, 19.

——. *Romane und Erzählungen*. Berlin and Weimar: Aufbau, 1973.

——. *Sämtliche Werke*. Munich: Nymphenburger Verlagshandlung, 1959–1974.

——. "Schach von Wuthenow." In *Sämtliche Werke*. Abteilung 1, vol. 2. Ed. W. Keitel. Munich: Hanser, 1962.

——. *Theodor Fontane: Short Novels and Other Writings*. The German Library, vol. 48. Ed. Peter Demetz. New York: Continuum, 1982.

——. "The Times." In *Sämtliche Werke*, vol. 19.

——. *Theodor Fontane: Romane und Erzählungen*. Berlin and Weimar: Aufbau, 1973.

———. "Unsere lyrische und epische Poesie seit 1848." In *Sämtliche Werke*, vol. 21/1. Ed. Kurt Schreinert. Munich: Nymphenburger Verlagshandlung, 1963.

Foucault, Michel. "Discipline and Punish." In *The Foucault Reader*. ed. Paul Rabinow. New York: Pantheon, 1984.

———. *The History of Sexuality: An Introduction*. Vol. 1. Trans. Robert Hurley. New York: Vintage Books, 1978.

———. "Prison Talk." In *Power/Knowledge: Selected Interviews and Other Writings 1972–1977*. ed. Colin Gordon. New York: Pantheon Books, 1980.

Fraser, Nancy. *Unruly Practices: Power, Discourse and Gender in Contemporary Social Theory*. Minneapolis: U of Minnesota P, 1989.

Frege, Gottlieb. *Begriffsschrift: Eine arithmetisch nachgebildete Formelsprache des reinen Denkens*. Halle, 1879; repr. Darmstadt, 1974.

Friedrich, Gerhard. "Die Witwe Pittelkow." *Fontane-Blätter* 3: 2 (1974).

Gadamer, Hans-Georg. *Truth and Method*. New York: Crossroads, 1988. English translation of *Wahrheit und Methode*.

Gärtner, K.-H. "Literatur und Politik bei Theodor Fontane." In *Formen realistischer Erzählkunst: Festschrift für Charlotte Jolles*, ed. Jörg Thunecke and Eda Sagarra. Nottingham: Sherwood Press, 1979.

Gasché, Rodolphe. "Das Wilde Denken und die Ökonomie der Repräsentation." In *Orte wilden Denkens*, ed. Lepenies/Ritter. Frankfurt am Main: Suhrkamp, 1970.

Gates, Henry Lewis Jr. "'Talkin' that Talk,' 'Writing "Race" and the Difference It Makes,'" In *"Race," Writing and Difference*. Chicago and London: U of Chicago P, 1986.

Gauger, Martin. "Sprachbewußtsein im *Stechlin*." In *Bild und Gedanke: Festschrift für G. Baumann*, ed. Günter Schnitzler. Munich: Fink, 1980.

Geffcken, Hanna. "Ästhetische Probleme bei Theodor Fontane und im Naturalismus." *Germanisch-Romanische Monatsschrift* 8 (1920).

Giel, Volker. "Zur Anlage des Aufsatzes von Klaus Globig; *Grete Minde*: Versuch einer Interpretation." *Fontane Blätter* 5 (1982) 1: 68–73.

Gilbert, Mary-Enole. *Das Gespräch in Fontanes Gesellschaftsromanen*. Leipzig: Mayer & Müller, 1930.

Globig, Klaus. "Theodor Fontanes *Grete Minde*: Psychologische Studie, Ausdruck des Historismus oder sozialpolitischer Appell?" *Fontane Blätter* 4 (1981) 8: 706–713.

Goldschmidt, Hermann Levin. *Dialogik: Philosophie auf dem Boden der Neuzeit*. Frankfurt am Main: Europäische Verlagsanstalt, 1964.

——. *Freiheit für den Widerspruch*. Schaffhausen: Novalis, 1976.

——. *Haltet Euch an Worte: Betrachtungen zur Sprache*. Schaffhausen: Griffel-Verlag, 1977.

Goodman, Nelson. *Languages of Art: An Approach to a Theory of Symbols*. Brighton/Sussex: Harvester Press, 1981.

Greenberg, Valerie C. "The Resistance of Effi Briest: An (Un)told Tale." *Papers of the Modern Language Association* 106 (1991): 770–782.

Groh, John E. *Nineteenth Century German Protestantism: The Church as Social Model*. Washington, D.C.: UP of America, 1982.

Habermas, Jürgen. *Theorie des kommunikativen Handelns: The Theory of Communicative Action*. Trans. Thomas McCarthy. Boston: Beacon Press, 1987.

——. *The Structural Transformation of the Public Sphere*. Cambridge: MIT Press, 1989.

——. *Der Philosophische Diskurs der Moderne*. Frankfurt am Main: Suhrkamp, 3. Aufl., 1986.

——. *Strukturwandel der Öffentlichkeit*. Darmstadt: Luchterhand, 1986.

Harrison, Thomas. *Essayism: Conrad, Musil, Pirandello*. Baltimore: Johns Hopkins UP, 1992.

Hass, Ulrike. *Theodor Fontane: Bürgerlicher Realismus am Beispiel seiner Berliner Gesellschaftsromane*. Bonn: Bouvier, 1979.

Hegel, G. W. F. *The Philosophy of Right*. Trans. T. M. Knox. London: Oxford UP, 1952.

Heidegger, Martin. *Prolegomena zu einer Geschichte des Zeitbegriffs*. Frankfurt am Main: V. Klostermann, 1988.

Herding, Gertrud. "Theodor Fontane im Urteil der Presse. Ein Beitrag zur Geschichte der literarischen Kritik." Diss., Munich, 1945.

Hertling, Gunter H. "Kleists *Michael Kohlhaas* und Fontanes *Grete Minde*: Freiheit und Fügung." *German Quarterly* 40 (1967): 24–40.

Hertling, G. H. *Theodor Fontanes Stine: Eine entzauberte Zauberflöte? Zum Humanitätsgedanken am Ausklang zweier Jahrhunderte*. Bern: Peter Lang, 1982.

Heyse, Paul, et al., eds. *Deutscher Novellenschatz*. Vol. 1. Munich: Oldenburg, n.d., xiv.

Hildebrandt, Bruno F. O. "Fontanes Altersstil in seinem Roman 'Der Stechlin.'" *German Quarterly* 38 (1965).

Hobsbawm, Eric J. *The Age of Empire 1875–1914.* New York: Random House, 1989.

Hofmiller, Josef. "Stechlin-Probleme." *Ausgewählte Werke.* Rosenheim: Rosenheimer Verlagshaus, 1975.

Hölderlin, Friedrich. *Werke und Briefe.* Ed. F. Beissner and J. Schmidt. Frankfurt am Main: Insel, 1969.

Horkheimer, Max. *Critical Theory.* New York: Herder and Herder, 1972.

Holub, Robert. *Reflections of Realism: Paradox, Norm, and Ideology in Nineteenth-Century German Prose.* Detroit: Wayne State UP, 1991.

Irigaray, Luce. *The Sex Which is Not One.* Trans. Catherine Porter with Carolyn Burke. Ithaca, NY: Cornell UP, 1985.

Johnson, Barbara. *The Critical Difference.* Baltimore: Johns Hopkins UP, 1980/81.

Johnson, Uwe. *Jahrestage* 4. Frankfurt am Main: Suhrkamp, 1970.

Jolles, Charlotte. "Fontane als Essayist und Journalist." *Jahrbuch für internationale Germanistik* 2 (1975).

———. "'Gideon ist besser als Botho.' Zur Struktur des Erzählschlusses bei Fontane." In *Festschrift für Werner Neuse,* ed. H. Lederer and J. Seyppel. Berlin: Die Diagonale, 1967.

———. "'Der Stechlin': Fontanes Zaubersee." In *Fontane aus heutiger Sicht. Analysen und Interpretationen,* ed. Hugo Aust. Munich: Nymphenburger Verlagshandlung, 1980.

———. *Theodor Fontane.* Stuttgart: Metzler, 1983.

Kahrmann, Cordula. *Idylle im Roman: Theodor Fontane.* Munich: Fink, 1973.

Kaiser, Gerhard. *Pietismus und Patriotismus im Literarischen Deutschland: Ein Beitrag zum Problem der Säkularisation.* Wiesbaden: F. Steiner, 1961.

Kant, Immanuel. "Beantwortung der Frage: Was ist Aufklärung?" In *Kants Gesammelte Schriften,* ed. Königlich Preußische Akademie der Wissenschaften. Berlin: de Gruyter, 1923.

Keitel, Walter, and Helmut Nürnberger, eds. *Theodor Fontane. Briefe.* 4 volumes. Frankfurt/Main: Ullstein, 1986.

Kittler, Friedrich A. *Aufschreibesysteme 1800/1900.* Munich: Fink, 1985.

Klaus, Detlef Müller, ed. *Bürgerlicher Realismus: Grundlagen und Interpretationen.* Königstein/Taunus: Athenäum, 1981.

Koltai, Eugen. "Untersuchungen zur Erzähltechnik Theodor Fontanes dargestellt an den Werken 'Vor dem Sturm,' 'Irrungen Wirrungen,' und 'Effi Briest.'" Diss., Univ. of New York, 1969.

Konieczny, Hans-Joachim. "Fontanes Erzählwerke in Presseorganen des ausgehenden 19. Jahrhunderts. Eine Untersuchung zur Funktion des Vorabdruckes ausgewählter Erzählwerke." Diss., Paderborn, 1978.

Koopmann, Helmut, ed. *Handbuch des deutschen Romans.* Düsseldorf: Bagel, 1983.

Krausch, Heinz-Dieter. "Die natürliche Umwelt in Fontanes 'Stechlin.' Dichtungen und Wirklichkeit." *Fontane Blätter* 1 (1968).

Krause, Edith H. *Theodor Fontane: Eine rezeptionsgeschichtliche und übersetzungskritische Untersuchung.* Bern: Peter Lang, 1989.

Kunz, Josef. *Novelle.* Darmstadt: Wissenschaftliche Buchgesellschaft, 1973.

Landes, Joan B. "Hegel's Conception of the Family." In *The Family in Political Thought,* ed. Jean Bethke Elshtain. Amherst: U of Massachusetts P, 1982.

Lacan, Jacques. *Schriften.* Olten: Walter, 1975.

——. *Écrits: A Selection.* Trans. Alan Sheridan. New York: Norton, 1977.

——. *Écrits I.* Paris: Éditions du Seuil, 1966.

Langendorf, Erich. *Zur Entstehung des bürgerlichen Familienglücks: Exemplarische Studien anhand literarischer Texte.* Frankfurt am Main: Peter Lang, 1983.

Lash, Scott. *Sociology of Postmodernism.* London: Routledge, 1990.

Lazarus, Moritz. "Über Gespräche." In *Die Kunst des Gesprächs: Texte zur Geschichte der europäischen Konversationstheorie,* ed. Claudia Schmölders. Munich: Deutscher Taschenbuch Verlag, 1986.

Leitner, Ingrid. *Sprachliche Archaisierung: Historisch-typologische Untersuchung zur deutschen Literatur des 19. Jahrhunderts.* Frankfurt am Main: Peter Lang, 1978.

Liebrand, Claudia. *Das Ich und die Anderen: Fontanes Figuren und ihre Selbstbilder.* Freiburg: Rombach, 1990.

Ludwig, Otto. "Der poetische Realismus." In *Bürgerlicher Realismus,* ed. Andreas Huyssen. Stuttgart: Philipp Reclam, 1974.

Lübbe, Hermann. "Fontane und die Gesellschaft." In *Literatur und Gesellschaft: Festgabe für Benno von Wiese,* ed. H. J. Schrimpf. Bonn: Bouvier, 1963.

Lüdke, W. Martin. "Was Neues vom alten Fontane. Historischer Prozeß und ästhetische Form am Beispiel von Fontanes letztem Roman 'Der Stechlin.'" *Diskussion Deutsch* 9 (1978).

Lugowski, Clemens. *Die Form der Individualität im Roman.* Frankfurt am Main: Suhrkamp, 1976.

Lukács, Georg. "Ästhetik Teil 1. Die Eigenart des Ästhetischen." In *Werke,* vol. 11, part 1. Darmstadt and Neuwied: Luchterhand, n.d.

———. "Der alte Fontane." In *Deutsche Realisten des 19. Jahrhunderts.* Bern: Francke, 1951; Berlin: Aufbau, 1952.

Lyotard, Jean François. *The Postmodern Condition: A Report on Knowledge.* Trans. Geoff Bennington and Brian Massumi. Minneapolis: U of Minnesota P, 1984.

MacKinnon, Catherine. *Toward a Feminist Theory of the State.* Cambridge, MA: Harvard UP, 1989.

Mann, Thomas. "Der alte Fontane." In *Theodor Fontane: Wege der Forschung,* ed. W. Preisendanz. Darmstadt: Wissenschaftliche Buchgesellschaft, 1973.

Manthey, Jürgen. "Die zwei Geschichten in einer. Über eine andere Lesart der Erzählung 'Schach von Wuthenow.'" In *Text und Kritik.* Munich: Weber, 1983.

Martini, Fritz. *Deutsche Literatur im bürgerlichen Realismus 1848–1898.* Stuttgart: Metzler, 1974; 1981.

Matthias, Klaus. "Theodor Fontane — Skepsis und Güte." *Jahrbuch des Freien Deutschen Hochstifts,* 1973.

McCarthy, John. *Crossing Boundaries: A Theory and History of Essay Writing in Germany 1618–1815.* Philadelphia: U of Pennsylvania P, 1989.

Meyer, Hermann. *Das Zitat in der Erzählkunst.* Stuttgart: Metzler, 1961.

Millet, Kate. *Sexual Politics.* New York: Ballantine Books, 1970.

Minder, Robert. "Über eine Randfigur bei Fontane." In *Hölderlin unter den Deutschen und andere Aufsätze zur deutschen Literatur.* Frankfurt am Main: Suhrkamp, 1968.

Minden, Michael. "'Effi Briest' and 'Die Historische Stunde des Takts.'" *Modern Language Review* (76): 1981.

Mittenzwei, Ingrid. *Die Sprache als Thema. Untersuchungen zu Fontanes Gesellschaftsromanen*. Bad Homburg: Gehlen, 1970.

Mockey, Fernande. "War Fontane ein Gesellschaftsmensch?" *Fontane-Blätter* 4 (1979): 509–520.

Mommsen, Katharina. "Vom 'Bamme-Ton' zum 'Bummel-Ton.' Fontanes Kunst der Sprechweisen." In *Formen realistischer Erzählkunst: Festschrift für Charlotte Jolles*, ed. Jörg Thunecke and Eda Sagarra. Nottingham: Sherwood, 1979.

Mommsen, Katharina. *Gesellschaftskritik bei Theodor Fontane und Thomas Mann*. Heidelberg: Stiehm, 1973.

Mommsen, Wolfgang. *Imperial Germany 1867–1918: Politics, Culture, and Society in an Authoritarian State*. Trans. Richard Deveson. London: Arnold, 1995.

Montaigne, Michel de. *Œuvres complètes*. Ed. A. Thibaudet and M. Rat. Bibliothèque de la Pléiade. Paris: Gallimard, 1962.

Müller-Seidel, Walter. *Theodor Fontane: Soziale Romankunst in Deutschland*. Stuttgart: J. B. Metzler, 1975.

Nägele, Rainer, ed. *Benjamin's Ground: New Readings of Walter Benjamin*. Detroit: Wayne State UP, 1988.

Nedelsky, Jennifer. "Laws, Boundaries and the Bounded Self." *Representations* 30 (1990): 162–189.

Neumeister-Taroni, Brigitta. *Theodor Fontane: Poetisches Relativieren — Ausloten einer uneindeutigen Wirklichkeit*. Bonn: Bouvier, 1976.

Nietzsche, Friedrich. *Zur Genealogie der Moral*. In *Werke*, vol. 2. Munich: C. Hanser 1960.

——. "Fünf Vorreden zu fünf ungeschriebenen Büchern." In *Kritische Studienausgabe* (KSA). Berlin: de Gruyter, 1981.

Nochlin, Linda. *Realism*. New York: Penguin, 1971.

Oberliesen, Rolf. *Information, Daten und Signale: Geschichte technischer Informationsverarbeitung*. Reinbek: Rowohlt, 1982.

Ohl, Hubert. *Bild und Wirklichkeit: Studien zur Romankunst Raabes und Fontanes*. Heidelberg: Lothar Stiehm, 1968.

Osborne, John. "Wie lösen sich die Rätsel?" Motivation in Fontane's *Grete Minde*." *Modern Languages* 64 (1983): 245–251.

Pastor, Eckart. "Das Hänflingsnest: Zu Theodor Fontanes *Grete Minde*." *Revue des Langues Vivantes* 44 (1978): 99–110.

Paulsen, Wolfgang. "Zum Stand der heutigen Fontane-Forschung." *Jahrbuch der Deutschen Schillergesellschaft* 1981.

———. "Theodor Fontane. The Philosemitic Antisemite." *Leo Baeck Yearbook* 26 (1981).

———. *Im Banne der Melusine: Theodor Fontane und sein Werk.* Bern: Peter Lang, 1988.

Peirce, Charles Sanders. *Collected Papers.* Cambridge, MA: Belknap Press, 1993.

———. *Semiotische Schriften.* Vol. 1. Frankfurt am Main: Suhrkamp, 1986.

Petersen, Julius. "Fontanes Altersroman." *Euphorion* 29 (1928).

Philip, Mark. "Michel Foucault." In *The Return of Grand Theory in the Human Sciences,* ed. Quentin Skinner. Cambridge: Cambridge UP, 1985.

Pniower, Otto. "Grete Minde." *Dichtungen und Dichter: Essays und Studien.* Berlin, 1912.

Plümer, Monika. "Kontingente Wirklichkeit und allegorischer Stil in Theodor Fontanes *Stechlin.*" Magisterarbeit, Göttingen, 1989.

Poltermann, "'Frau Jenny Treibel' oder die Profanierung der hohen Poesie." *Text und Kritik. Sonderband: Theodor Fontane.* Munich: Weber, 1989.

Preisendanz, Wolfgang. *Wege des Realismus.* Munich: Fink, 1977.

———. *Humor als dichterische Einbildungskraft.* Munich: Eidos, 1963.

Reuter, Hans-Heinrich. *Theodor Fontane.* 2 vols. Munich: Nymphenburger Verlagshandlung, 1968.

Rosenzweig, Franz. *Briefe und Tagebücher.* 2 vols. Haag: Martinus Nijhoff, 1979.

Rosenberg, Rosalind. *Beyond Separate Spheres: The Intellectual Roots of Modern Feminism.* New Haven: Yale UP, 1982.

Rost, Wolfgang E. "Örtlichkeit und Schauplatz in Fontanes Werken." Diss., Berlin 1930.

Rousseau, Jean Jacques. *Emile.* Trans. Barbara Foxley. New York: Dutton, 1974.

Rudolph, Ekkehart. "Über die Darstellung des redenden Menschen in den epischen Prosadichtungen Theodor Fontanes." *Wissenschaftliche Zeitschrift der Friedrich-Schiller-Universität Jena* 7 (1957/58).

Rychner, Max. "Theodor Fontane." In *Welt im Wort: Literarische Aufsätze.* Zurich: Manesse, 1949.

Sagarra, Eda. *Theodor Fontanes "Der Stechlin."* Munich: Fink, 1986.

Said, Edward. *Orientalism.* New York: Random House, 1978.

Saussure, Ferdinand de. *Course in General Linguistics.* Trans. Wade Baskin. New York: Philosophical Library, 1959.

Scherpe, Klaus R. "Die Rettung der Kunst im Widerspruch von bürgerlicher Humanität und bourgeoiser Wirklichkeit: Theodor Fontanes vierfacher Roman 'Der Stechlin.'" In *Poesie der Demokratie: Literarische Widersprüche zur deutschen Wirklichkeit vom 18. zum 20. Jahrhundert.* Cologne: Pahl-Rugenstein, 1980.

Schillemeit, Jost. *Theodor Fontane: Geist und Kunst seines Alterswerk.* Zurich: Atlantis, 1961.

Schlaffer, Heinz. "Das Schicksalsmodell in Fontanes Romanwerk. Konstanz und Auflösung." *Germanisch-Romanische Monatsschrift* n.s. 16 (1966).

Schlegel, August Wilhelm. *Kritische Schriften und Briefe.* Ed. Edgar Lohner. Stuttgart: Kohlhammer, 1965.

Schmalbruch, Ursula. "Zum Melusine-Motiv in Fontanes *Cecile.*" *Text und Kontext* 7–8 (1979/1980).

Schmidt, Siegfried J. "Medien, Kultur, Medienkultur." *Kognition und Gesellschaft: Der Diskurs des radikalen Konstruktivismus.* 2d Ed. Frankfurt am Main: Suhrkamp, 1992.

Schmölders, Claudia, ed. *Die Kunst des Gesprächs: Texte zur Geschichte der europäischen Konversationstheorie.* Munich: Deutscher Taschenbuch Verlag, 1986.

Scholz, Hans. *Theodor Fontane.* Munich: Kindler, 1978.

Scott, Joan. *Gender and the Politics of History.* New York: Columbia UP, 1988.

Sieper, Clara. *Der historische Roman und die historische Novelle bei Raabe und Fontane.* Weimar, 1930.

Silz, Walter. *Realism and Reality: Studies in the German Novelle of Poetic Realism.* Chapel Hill: U of North Carolina P, 1965.

Simmel, Georg. *Der Konflikt der modernen Kultur: Ein Vortrag.* Munich and Leipzig: Duncker & Humblot, 1921.

——. *Grundfragen der Soziologie.* Berlin: Walter de Gruyter, 1970.

———. *Schriften zur Soziologie.* Ed. H.-J. Dahme and O. Rammstedt. Frankfurt am Main: Suhrkamp, 1983.

Simon, Ernst. "Theodor Fontanes jüdische Ambivalenz." *Neue Zürcher Zeitung,* August 16, 1970. Rpt. in Ernst Simon, *Entscheidung zum Judentum.* Frankfurt am Main: Suhrkamp, 1980.

Smith, Joseph, and William Kerrigan, eds. *Talking Chances: Derrida, Psychoanalysis, and Literature.* Baltimore: Johns Hopkins UP, 1984.

Sperber, Jonathan. *Popular Catholicism in Nineteenth-Century Germany.* Princeton, NJ: Princeton UP, 1984.

Stallybrass, Peter, and Allon White. *The Politics and Poetics of Transgression.* Ithaca: Cornell UP, 1986.

Stansell, Christine. *City of Women: Sex and Class in New York, 1787–1869.* New York: Knopf, 1986.

Stephan, Inge. "'Das Natürliche hat es mir seit langem angetan.' Zum Verhältnis von Frau und Natur in Fontanes *Cecile.*" In *Natur und Natürlichkeit.* Ed. Jost Hermand and Hermann Grimm. Frankfurt am Main: Suhrkamp, 1981.

Sterne, P. *Über literarischen Realismus.* Munich: Beck, 1983.

Swales, Erika. "Private Mythologies and Public Unease: On Fontane's *Effi Briest.*" *Modern Language Review* 75 (Part 1): January 1980.

Taub, Elizabeth, and Nadine Schneider. "Women's Subordination and the Role of Law." In *The Politics of Law: A Progressive Critique,* ed. David Kairys. New York: Pantheon Books, 1990.

Teitge, Hans-Erich, and Joachim Schobeß, eds. *Fontanes Realismus: Wissenschaftliche Konferenz zum 150. Geburtstag Theodor Fontanes in Potsdam.* Berlin: Akademie, 1972.

Thanner, Josef. "Symbol and Function of the Symbol in Theodor Fontane's 'Effi Briest.'" *Monatshefte* 57:1 (January 1965).

Thum, Reinhard H. "Symbol, Motif and Leitmotif in Fontane's Effi Briest." *Germanic Review* 54:3 (Summer 1979).

Thunecke, Jörg. "Klosteridyll und Raubmörderidyll." *Fontane Blätter* 5:1 (1982): 78–80.

———, and Eda Sagarra, eds. *Formen realistischer Erzählkunst: Festschrift for Charlotte Jolles.* Nottingham: Sherwood, 1979.

Turk, Horst. "Alienität und Alterität." *Jahrbuch für Internationale Germanistik,* XXII, vol. 1. Bern, New York: Peter Lang, 1990.

——. "'Mimesis Praxeos.' Der Realismus aus der Perspektive einiger neu-erer Theoriensätze." *Jahrbuch der Raabe-Gesellschaft* 1983.

——. "Realismus in Fontanes Gesellschaftsroman. Zur Romantheorie und zur epischen Integration." *Jahrbuch der Wittheit zu Bremen* 9 (1965): 407–456.

——. "Die Schrift als Ordnungsform des Erlebens. Diskursenanalytische Überlegungen zu Adalbert Stifter." *Diskurstheorien und Literatur-wissenschaft.* Ed. J. Fohrmann and H. Müller. Frankfurt am Main: Suhr-kamp 1988.

Ueding, Cornelie. "Utopie auf Umwegen. Zwei Szenen in Fontanes *Cé-cile.*" In *Literatur ist Utopie,* ed. G. v. Ueding. Frankfurt am Main: Suhrkamp, 1978.

Vance, Carol S. "Pleasure and Danger: Toward a Politics of Sexuality." In *Pleasure and Danger: Exploring Female Sexuality,* ed. Carole Vance. Routledge: Boston, 1984.

Vischer, Friedrich Theodor. *Ästhetik.* Reutlingen: Mäcken, 1846–58.

Wandrey, Conrad. *Theodor Fontane.* Munich: C. H. Beck, 1919.

Weber, Werner. *Forderungen: Bemerkungen und Aufsätze zur Literatur.* Zurich: Artemis, 1970.

——. "Theodor Fontane." In *Berliner Geist: Fünf Vorträge der Bayrischen Akademie der schönen Künste.* Berlin: Propyläen, 1963.

Weedon, Chris. *Feminist Practice and Poststructuralist Theory.* Oxford and New York: Basil Blackwell, 1987.

Wessels, Paul. "Schein und Anstand: Zu Fontanes Roman *Stine.*" In *For-men Realistischer Erzählkunst: Festschrift für Charlotte Jolles,* ed. Jörg Thunecke and Eda Sagarra. Nottingham: Sherwood, 1979.

Index